CYBERSPACE AND NATIONAL SECURITY

CONTAINS MULTIPLE ESSAYS

CYBERSPACE AND NATIONAL SECURITY

Threats, Opportunities, and Power in a Virtual World

DEREK S. REVERON

Editor

Georgetown University Press / Washington, DC

Library of Congress Cataloging-in-Publication Data

Cyberspace and national security: threats, opportunities, and power in a virtual world / Derek S. Reveron, editor.
    p.   cm.
Includes bibliographical references and index.
ISBN 978-1-58901-918-8 (pbk. : alk. paper)
1. Cyberterrorism.   2. National security.   3. Conflict management.   I. Reveron, Derek S.
HV6773.15.C97C93   2012
355′.033002854678—dc23
2011051019

⊗ This book is printed on acid-free paper meeting the requirements of the American National Standard for Permanence in Paper for Printed Library Materials.

19 18 17 16 15 14 13 12   9 8 7 6 5 4 3 2   First printing

CONTENTS

List of Illustrations   vii

Acknowledgments   ix

PART I: THINKING ABOUT CYBER

CHAPTER 1
An Introduction to National Security and Cyberspace   3
Derek S. Reveron

CHAPTER 2
Speculative Security   21
Patrick Jagoda

CHAPTER 3
Operational Considerations in Cyber Attack and Cyber Exploitation   37
Herbert Lin

CHAPTER 4
Joining Cybercrime and Cyberterrorism: A Likely Scenario   57
Steven Bucci

PART II: ARMED CONFLICT AND CYBER DEFENSE

CHAPTER 5
***Inter arma silent leges* Redux? The Law of Armed Conflict and Cyber Conflict**   71
David P. Fidler

CHAPTER 6
The Emerging Structure of Strategic Cyber Offense, Cyber Defense, and Cyber Deterrence   89
Richard B. Andres

CHAPTER 7
A New Framework for Cyber Deterrence   105
Jeffrey R. Cooper

CHAPTER 8
Cybered Conflict, Cyber Power, and Security Resilience as Strategy   121
Chris Demchak

PART III: NATIONAL APPROACHES TO
CYBERSECURITY AND CYBERWAR

CHAPTER 9
Persistent Enemies and Cyberwar: Rivalry Relations in an Age of
Information Warfare   139
Brandon Valeriano and Ryan Maness

CHAPTER 10
Competing Transatlantic Visions of Cybersecurity   159
James Joyner

CHAPTER 11
The Bear Goes Digital: Russia and Its Cyber Capabilities   173
Nikolas K. Gvosdev

CHAPTER 12
China in Cyberspace   191
Nigel Inkster

CHAPTER 13
Toward a Theory of Cyber Power: Strategic Purpose in Peace and
War   207
John B. Sheldon

CHAPTER 14
Conclusion   225
Derek S. Reveron

Contributors   231

Index   237

ILLUSTRATIONS

Figure

4.1   The Cyber Threat Environment   58

Tables

1.1   World Internet Users   6

1.2   Cyber Threats Defined   8

1.3   Sources of Cyber Insecurity   12

1.4   Malicious Activity by Country, July–September 2010   14

3.1   A Comparison of Key Characteristics of Cyber Attack vs.
      Kinetic Attack   38

3.2   Possible Ends and Ways of Cyber Exploitation   52

7.1   Understanding Cooperation, Competition, and Conflict   111

9.1   Overall Cyberwar Strength among Key Countries   147

9.2   Cyber Attacks between Russia and Georgia   149

9.3   Cyber Attacks between Israel and Iran   151

ACKNOWLEDGMENTS

CREATING AN EDITED VOLUME has many challenges. Authors have different writing styles and schedules, editors struggle to ensure coherence, and publishers need timeliness and relevance. On these points, any flaws are my own, and I am grateful to the patience and guidance that Don Jacobs and the rest of the staff of Georgetown University Press provided.

As a professor at the US Naval War College, I benefit greatly from my colleagues and my students who continuously challenge contemporary ideas about national security. When it comes to cyber, there is no shortage of thoughts, and Newport, Rhode Island, is extremely rich with faculty dedicated to thinking about national security. In particular, I would like to thank Vice Adm. Phil Wisecup, Amb. Maryann Peters, Rear Adm. Roger Nolan, and Dean John Garofano for encouraging my research on national security and cyberspace. I am grateful for the trust they placed in me as the EMC informationist chair to stimulate research, writing, and teaching about cyber issues in Newport.

My NWC "cyber colleagues" Roy Petty, Dick Crowell, Stephanie Helm, and Chris Demchak continue to be very supportive and helpful as we sort through the implications of cyberspace on how the Defense Department trains, equips, and organizes in cyberspace. I look forward to future collaborations as we consider national security challenges in the virtual world.

As always, I thank my family, who continue to create a rich environment for me to think, research, and write.

PART I

Thinking about Cyber

CHAPTER 1

An Introduction to National Security and Cyberspace

Derek S. Reveron

IN ITS SHORT HISTORY, individuals and companies have harnessed cyberspace to create new industries, a vibrant social space, and a new economic sphere that are intertwined with our everyday lives. At the same time, individuals, subnational groups, and governments are using cyberspace to advance interests through malicious activity. Terrorist groups recruit, train, and target through the Internet, organized criminal enterprises exploit financial data with profits that exceed drug trafficking, and intelligence services steal secrets.

Today individuals tend to pose the greatest danger in cyberspace, but nonstate actors, intelligence services, and militaries increasingly penetrate information technology networks for espionage and influence. This is likely to continue in the future as governments seek new ways and means to defend their interests in cyberspace and to develop their own offensive capabilities to compete in cyberspace. As an early example, the Obama administration released *International Strategy for Cyberspace* in May 2011, which defines four key characteristics of cyberspace: open to innovation, secure enough to earn people's trust, globally interoperable, and reliable.[1] Ensuring reliability against threats seems to dominate national security discussions today and raises concerns when thinking about future warfare.

Since the early 1990s analysts have forecast that cyberwar in the twenty-first century would be a salient feature of warfare. Yet, nearly twenty years later, individual hackers, intelligence services, and criminal groups pose the greatest danger in cyberspace, not militaries. But the concept of using cyber capabilities in war is slowly emerging. An example of this was the cyber attack that accompanied Russia's invasion of Georgia in 2008. As Russian tanks and aircraft were entering Georgian territory, cyberwarriors attacked the Georgian Ministry of Defense. Though it had a minimal effect, the attack was a harbinger; future conflicts will have both a physical dimension and a virtual dimension. While not destructive, the attacks were disruptive. In the future, malicious code infiltrated through worms will disrupt communication systems, denial of service attacks will undermine governments' strategic messages, and logic bombs could turn out the lights in national capitals. This approach was discussed during the 2011 NATO campaign in Libya, but was left largely in the conceptual phases.[2]

As a preview of what is to come, the 2010 Stuxnet worm was the first worm specifically designed to attack industrial control systems.[3] Had the worm not been detected, hackers could have obtained control of power plants, communication systems, and factories by hijacking the infected systems. Theoretically, this outside actor could manipulate a control system in a power plant to produce a catastrophic failure. The source of the worm is purely speculative, but some experts saw this as the first true cyber attack against Iran's nuclear infrastructure and credit it for slowing down Iran's program.[4]

The 2010 Quadrennial Defense Review foreshadowed the dangers of Stuxnet and highlighted that, although it is a man-made domain, cyberspace is now as relevant a domain for Defense Department activities as the naturally occurring domains of land, sea, air, and space. The United States and many other countries, including China, Russia, Israel, and France, are preparing for conflict in the virtual dimension. In the United States, a joint cyber command was launched in 2010. With a modest two thousand personnel at its headquarters, the command derives support from fifty-four thousand sailors, eighteen thousand airmen, twenty-one thousand soldiers, and eight hundred marines who have been designated by their services to support the emerging cyber mission. The head of US Cyber Forces, Gen. Keith Alexander, sees future militaries using "cyberspace (by operating within or through it) to attack personnel, facilities, or equipment with the intent of degrading, neutralizing, or destroying enemy combat capability, while protecting our own."[5] The 2011 National Military Strategy directed joint forces to "secure the '.mil' domain, requiring a resilient DoD cyberspace architecture that employs a combination of detection, deterrence, denial, and multi-layered defense."[6] The Defense Department strategic initiatives for operating in cyberspace include the following:

◇ Treat cyberspace as an operational domain to organize, train, and equip so that the Defense Department can take full advantage of cyberspace's potential.
◇ Employ new defense operating concepts to protect Department of Defense networks and systems.
◇ Partner with other US government departments and agencies and the private sector to enable a whole-of-government cybersecurity strategy.
◇ Build robust relationships with US allies and international partners to strengthen collective cybersecurity.
◇ Leverage the nation's ingenuity through an exceptional cyberworkforce and rapid technological innovation.[7]

With this in mind, this book considers the current and future threats in cyberspace, discusses various approaches to advance and defend national interests in cyberspace, contrasts the US approach with European and Chinese views, and posits a way of using cyber capabilities in war. To be sure, the nature of and the role for cyberwar is still under debate.[8] But this book establishes a coherent framework to understand how cyberspace fits within national security.

Cyberspace Defined

Writer William Gibson coined the term "cyberspace" in a short story published in 1982. Once confined to the cyberpunk literature and science fiction such as the movie *The Matrix*, cyberspace entered the real world in the 1990s with the advent of the World Wide Web. In 2003 the Bush administration defined cyberspace as "the nervous system of these [critical national] infrastructures—the control system of our country. Cyberspace comprises hundreds of thousands of interconnected computers, servers, routers, switches, and fiber optic cables that make our critical infrastructures work."[9] Today, the US Defense Department defines it as "a global domain within the information environment consisting of the interdependent network of information technology infrastructures, including the Internet, telecommunications network, computer systems, and embedded processors and controllers."[10]

Like the physical environment, the cyber environment is all-encompassing. It includes physical hardware, such as networks and machines; information, such as data and media; the cognitive, such as the mental processes people use to comprehend their experiences; and the virtual, where people connect socially. When aggregated, what we think of as cyberspace serves as a fifth dimension where people can exist through alternate persona on blogs, social networking sites, and virtual reality games. Larry Johnson, chief executive officer of the New Media Consortium, predicts that over the next fifteen years we will experience the virtual world as an extension of the real one. Johnson believes that "virtual worlds are already bridging borders across the globe to bring people of many cultures and languages together in ways very nearly as rich as face-to-face interactions; they are already allowing the visualization of ideas and concepts in three dimensions that is leading to new insights and deeper learning; and they are already allowing people to work, learn, conduct business, shop, and interact in ways that promise to redefine how we think about these activities—and even what we regard as possible."[11]

Gone are the stereotypes of young male gamers that dominate cyberspace; those that inhabit virtual worlds are increasingly middle-aged, employed, and female. For example, the median age in the virtual world "Second Life" is thirty-six years old, and 45 percent are women. Among Facebook users, about half are women.[12] There are more Facebook users aged twenty-six to thirty-four than there are aged eighteen to twenty-five. The Internet has been the primary means of this interconnectivity, which is both physical and virtual. Due to the highly developed economies and its important role in the information technology sector, the highest Internet penetration rate is in North America. Yet, given its population size and rapid development, Asia has the most users (see table 1.1).

TABLE 1.1
World Internet Users

World Regions	Internet Users 2011	Penetration (% population)	Growth 2000–2011 (%)
Africa	139,875,242	13.5	2,988.4
Asia	1,016,799,076	26.2	789.6
Europe	500,723,686	61.3	376.4
Middle East	77,020,995	35.6	2,244.8
North America	273,067,546	78.6	152.6
Latin America/Caribbean	235,819,740	39.5	1,205.1
Oceania / Australia	23,927,457	67.5	214.0
WORLD TOTAL	2,267,233,742	32.7	528.1

Source: Internet World Stats, www.internetworldstats.com/stats.htm.

Cyberspace and National Security

The link between national security and the Internet has been developing since the Clinton administration in the 1990s. Yet there are significant differences between traditional domains such as airspace that make protecting cyberspace difficult. To begin with, no single entity owns the Internet; individuals, companies, and governments own it and use it. It is also arguable that there is not just one Internet but many. Governments also do not have a monopoly on operating in cyberspace. In contrast to heavily regulated airspace, anyone with a good computer or phone and an Internet connection can operate there. And, making it more challenging for governments, most of the cyber expertise resides in information technology companies. Yet, all are affected equally by disruptions in cyberspace; a computer virus disruption that occurs through a commercial website can slow down the Internet for government and military users as well as for private citizens.

As it relates to war, the Internet is both a means and a target for militaries. Former US deputy defense secretary William J. Lynn underscored how important the information infrastructure is to national defense. "Just like our national dependence [on the Internet], there is simply no exaggerating our military dependence on our information networks: the command and control of our forces, the intelligence and logistics on which they depend, the weapons technologies we develop and field—they all depend on our computer systems and networks. Indeed, our 21st century military simply cannot function without them."[13] Additionally, governments use the Internet to shape their messages through media outlets hosted throughout the Web. US military commanders use public blogs and operational units post videos to YouTube. This gives both the military and citizens unprecedented insight from pilots after they bomb a target, or from marines as they conduct humanitarian assistance. The transparency is intended to reduce suspicion, counter deceptive claims made by adversaries, and improve the image of the military. Yet there are limits to these potential advantages; the Pentagon is concerned that its personnel can also share too much data through Facebook or project a poor image that runs counter to its efforts through YouTube videos. Or, in illegal cases, military personnel can steal classified data and post hundreds of thousands of classified documents to sites like Wikileaks, which can undermine national security.

In contrast to traditional warfighting domains such as land, air, or sea, governments are not the only powers in cyberspace. Rather, individuals can readily harness technology to compete on a global scale. And it is worth noting that virtualization will continue this trend of democratizing the Internet, giving individuals tremendous power that was unthinkable even ten years ago. Satellite imagery used to be highly classified and limited by the US intelligence community, but now anyone can access imagery from an iPhone using Google Earth. Likewise, the complexity and cost of building a nuclear weapon limits their production to governments, but the same cannot be said for the virtual weapon of mass destruction that can destroy data and networks, undermine international credibility, and disrupt commerce. Malicious activity through worms, viruses, and zombies regularly disrupts Internet activity (see table 1.2). And there are already many examples of virtual activities impacting the physical world such as terrorists being recruited, radicalized, and trained on the Internet; communications being severed; or power production being disrupted. Illegal groups use cyberspace to move money, conceal identities, and plan operations, which makes it extremely difficult for the governments to compete. Consequently, governments are increasingly concerned with the cyber domain as a new feature within the national security landscape.

In some sense, there has always been an implicit national security purpose for the Internet. After all, the Internet was originally conceived of and funded by one of the Defense Department's research organizations, then known as Advanced Research Projects Agency (ARPA). Given the state of telecommunications and stand-alone computer systems that existed in the 1960s, researchers wanted to create a reliable network where a user's system or location was unimportant to his or her ability to participate on the network. Charles Herzfeld, ARPA director from 1965 to 1967, explains the genesis of the network:

> The ARPANET was not started to create a Command and Control System that would survive a nuclear attack, as many now claim. To build such a system was clearly a major military need, but it was not ARPA's mission to do this; in fact, we would have been severely criticized had we tried. Rather, the ARPANET came out of our frustration that there were only a limited number of large, powerful research computers in the country, and that many research investigators who should have access to them were geographically separated from them."[14]

This vision of a network became a reality in 1969 when a computer link was established between the University of California–Los Angeles and Stanford University. At the time, the connection was called "internetworking," which later was shortened to the Internet. For thirty years, the Internet was largely the domain of

TABLE 1.2
Cyber Threats Defined

Term	Definition
Botnet	A network of zombie machines used by hackers for massive coordinated system attacks. Employing a botnet to send massive simultaneous requests to servers prevents legitimate use of the servers and produces a denial-of-service attack.
Logic bomb	Camouflaged segments of programs that destroy data when certain conditions are met.
Trojan horse	Stealthy code that executes under the guise of a useful program but performs malicious acts such as the destruction of files, the transmission of private data, and the opening of a back door to allow third-party control of a machine.
Virus	Malicious code that can self-replicate and cause damage to the systems it infects. The code can delete information, infect programs, change the directory structure to run undesirable programs, and infect the vital part of the operating system that ties together how files are stored.
Worm	Similar to a virus, a worm is distinctive for its ability to self-replicate without infecting other files in order to reproduce.
Zombie	A computer that has been covertly compromised and is controlled by a third party.

universities, colleges, and research institutes. But when Tim Berners-Lee and his colleagues created the World Wide Web in 1990, commercial and social applications exploded. Within a few short years, companies such as Amazon (1995), Ebay (1995), Wikipedia (2001), Facebook (2004), and Khan Academy (2009) founded a new industry and changed the way we live and work. Ongoing trends in web development tools suggest that the gap between the virtual and physical worlds is indeed narrowing.

Academic and commercial companies were pioneers in harnessing the Internet, and the government was a relative latecomer. Cyberspace first emerged as a distinct national security policy area in 1998 when President Clinton signed Presidential Decision Directive 63, which established a White House structure to coordinate government and private action to "eliminate any significant vulnerability to both physical and cyber attacks on our critical infrastructures, including especially our cyber systems."[15] The March 2005 National Defense Strategy identified cyberspace as a new theater of operations and assessed cyberspace operations as a potentially disruptive challenge, concluding that in "rare instances, revolutionary technology and associated military innovation can fundamentally alter long-established concepts of warfare." The 2008 National Defense Strategy explored the implications of this further, assessing that small groups or individuals "can attack vulnerable points in cyberspace and disrupt commerce and daily life in the United States, causing economic damage, compromising sensitive information and materials, and interrupting critical services such as power and information networks."[16] And the 2011 National Military Strategy assessed that the cyber threat is expanded and exacerbated by lack of international norms, difficulties of attribution, low barriers to entry, and the relative ease of developing potent capabilities."[17] The 2012 strategic defense guidance identified one of the primary missions of the US armed forces as operating effectively in cyberspace.[18]

In spite of recognizing vulnerabilities and threats to cyberspace, there are clear gaps in both policy and law. There are no clear answers on important issues such as how to respond to cyber intrusions, whether computer network attacks constitute a form of warfare, and whether the United Nations conception of self-defense applies in cyberspace. Yet the threat remains ongoing. Former deputy defense secretary William Lynn said the Defense Department's culture regarding cybersecurity issues must change because "we're seeing assaults come at an astonishing speed—not hours, minutes or even seconds—but in milliseconds at network speed."[19] While the Pentagon has a plan to stop an air attack against the United States, there is no corresponding plan to reduce malicious activity on the Internet. Given privacy and legal concerns, it is also unclear what role the Defense Department can and should play in defending networks.

In an effort to understand the challenges and raise awareness of cyberspace, the Center for Strategic and International Studies bluntly warned in 2008, "America's failure to protect cyberspace is one of the most urgent national security problems facing the new administration."[20] In recognition of this, President Barack Obama declared October 2009 to be national cybersecurity awareness month due to "our Nation's growing dependence on cyber and information-related technologies, coupled with an increasing threat of malicious cyber attacks and loss of privacy."[21] A month later, a former NATO commander declared, "The cybersecurity threat is real. Adversaries target networks, application software, operating systems, and even the ubiquitous silicon chips inside computers, which are the bedrock of the United States' public and private infrastructure."[22] Retired army general Wesley Clark and Peter Levin argued that "all evidence indicates that the country's defenses are already being pounded, and the need to extend protection from computer networks and software to computer hardware is urgent. The US government can no longer afford to ignore the threat from computer-savvy rivals or technologically advanced terrorist groups, because the consequences of a major breach would be catastrophic."[23] Finally, the Department of Defense Strategy for Operating in Cyberspace highlighted "low barriers to entry for malicious cyber activity, including the widespread availability of hacking tools, mean that an individual or small group of determined cyber actors can potentially cause significant damage to both DoD and US national and economic security. Small-scale technologies can have an impact disproportionate to their size; potential adversaries do not have to build expensive weapons systems to pose a significant threat to US national security."[24]

The global security implications of this are profound. Whereas the Atlantic and Pacific Oceans and borders with Canada and Mexico can provide barriers to international threats, the United States lacks comparable barriers in cyberspace. Strategic thinking equates national security with global security in a world inhabited by threats without borders. US strategic thinking is not alone. Hamadoun Touré, secretary general of the United Nations Telecommunications Union has warned:

> The next world war could take place in the cyberspace and this needs to be avoided. The conventional wars have shown us that first of all, there is no winner in any war and second, the best way to win a war is to avoid it in the first place. So we need to plant the seeds for a safer cyberspace together. And it can only be done at the global level because the criminal needs no longer to be on the crime scene and you can attack many places at the same time in the cyberspace.[25]

With these concerns in mind, the United Nations is working on a no-first-strike policy for its members, which is reminiscent of nuclear-weapons-use policy. This approach certainly makes sense given that the United Nations is organized around the nation-state concept, but it can have little effect on contemporary vulnerabilities to the Internet, where many threats emanate from small groups and nonstate actors. Security challenges in cyberspace are another indication that traditional nation-state approaches to national security cannot address contemporary challenges like those in cyberspace. Furthermore, there is an inherent deniability of Internet-based attacks, which makes any agreement extremely difficult to monitor or enforce.

Threats to the Cyber Domain

When attempting to examine cyber threats, the point of origin is very difficult to determine. Unlike a missile launch that has a discrete signature and geographic location, those that employ cyber tactics can easily hide their origin, which makes attribution extremely difficult. James Lewis has argued, "Uncertainty is the most prominent aspect of cyber conflict—in attribution of the attackers['] identity, the scope of collateral damage, and the potential effect on the intended target from cyber attack."[26] Without the ability to attribute to or assign blame for an attack, relying on threat of retaliation to prevent attacks is difficult. Thus, when trying to analyze the threats to the cyber domain, it is best to take a comprehensive approach. Accordingly, we can classify by actor, such as individual and government; by target, such as financial sector or defense department; or by means, such as virus, worm, or denial of service.

In terms of the actor, those that use cyber tactics for nefarious purposes range from individual hackers and organized criminal groups to intelligence services and governments. Table 1.3 captures these sources of cyber insecurity, but it is important to be careful. As Peter Singer notes, when

> it comes to talking about cyber attacks, senior defense leaders have lumped together teen-agers defacing public DoD websites, disgruntled soldiers leaking documents, hackers stealing industry secrets, terrorists using YouTube and foreign military agents accessing classified networks to plant worms, as if they were all one and the same, simply because their activities all involved a digital series of 0s and 1s. This is akin to treating the threat posed by a teenager with a bottle rocket, a robber with a revolver, an insurgent with a bomb or a state with a cruise missile as the same simply because they all involve gunpowder.[27]

As the diversity of actors illustrates, the barriers to entry for cyberspace are low. One only needs a good Internet connection, a decent computer, and the technical know-how to conduct attacks. Unfortunately, all three are cheap, which helps explain why cyber intrusions have become commonplace. The head of the United Nations International Telecommunications Union noted, "there is no such thing anymore as a superpower in the cyberspace because every individual is one superpower in itself because it's a human brain that makes a difference in this field. And this is one natural resource that is equally distributed everywhere in the globe."[28] Likewise, once malicious code is in the "wild" of cyberspace, it can be modified for other purposes and be redirected against other targets. For example, those wishing to launch a "son of Stuxnet" attack have the original Stuxnet as a starting point. In general reaction to this phenomenon, Deputy Secretary of Defense Lynn summed up the challenge. "Once the province of nations, the ability to destroy via cyber means now also rests in the hands of small groups and individuals."[29] Thus, in cyberspace, human and national security are inextricably linked. In spite of this, there is genuine disagree-ment on whether cyber should be treated as a warfighting domain equivalent to air, space, land, and sea. This is based as much on the newness of cyberspace as on the security landscape that does not lend itself to easy divisions between acts of war and criminal acts. It seems that the debate remains on the nature of conflict begun after the Cold War and continued through the global war on terrorism; national security challenges cannot be neatly defined between those that rise to the level of military activity and those that can be addressed through law enforcement.

So far criminals constitute the majority of bad actors as they take advantage of the Internet for nefarious purposes. Web-based attacks are the common source of malicious activity, which often happens by exploiting a vulnerable web application or exploiting some vulnerability present in the underlying host operating system. For example, the 2010 Stuxnet worm exploited four vulnerabilities in Microsoft Win-dows. In general, attackers concentrate their attacks for financial gain by stealing

TABLE 1.3
Sources of Cyber Insecurity

Threat Source	Motivation
Intelligence services	Foreign intelligence services use cyber tools as part of their information gathering and espionage activities. These include exploitation and potential disruption or destruction of information infrastructure.
Criminal groups	Criminal groups use cyber intrusions for monetary gain.
Hackers	Hackers sometimes crack into networks for the thrill of the challenge or for bragging rights in the hacker community. While remote cracking once required a fair amount of skill or computer knowledge, hackers can now download attack scripts and protocols from the Internet and launch them against victim sites. Thus, attack tools have become more sophisticated and easier to use.
Hacktivists	These groups and individuals conduct politically motivated attacks, overload e-mail servers, and hack into websites to send a political message.
Disgruntled insiders	The disgruntled insider, working from within an organization, is a principal source of computer crimes. Insiders may not need a great deal of knowledge about computer intrusions because their knowledge of a victim system often allows them to gain unrestricted access to cause damage to the system or to steal system data.
Terrorists	Terrorists seek to destroy, incapacitate, or exploit critical infrastructures to threaten national security, cause mass casualties, weaken the US economy, and damage public morale and confidence. The CIA believes terrorists will stay focused on traditional attack methods, but it anticipates growing cyber threats as a more technically competent generation enters the ranks.

Source: Government Accountability Office, *Statement for the Record to the Subcommittee on Terrorism and Homeland Security, Committee on the Judiciary, US Senate; Cybersecurity: Continued Efforts are Needed to Protect Information Systems from Evolving Threats,* November 17, 2009.

online banking credentials and credit card information. Phishing has become a common way to steal financial information by soliciting confidential information from an individual, group, or organization by mimicking (or spoofing) a specific brand. To counter this, cybersecurity specialists can lure hackers to spoofed computer systems to provide disinformation to attackers and study the attack style.

The United States and China are the top two countries of attack origin, accounting for 23 percent and 4 percent, respectively, of worldwide activity (see table 1.4).[30] Given the large number of computers in the United States and China, it is not surprising that these two countries top the list of malicious activity. When broken down by region, there are some differences by type of infection.[31] For example, 35 percent of trojans were reported from North America; 34 percent from Europe, Middle East, or Africa; 24 percent from Asia-Pacific; and just 6 percent from Latin America. The Asia-Pacific region dominated worm infections with 40 percent, whereas North America was just 13 percent. The increased proportion of virus infections was linked to the greater proportion of worms reported from the region because viral infection is a common component of worms. It seems that antivirus programs are more prevalent in North America and that pirated operating systems ubiquitous elsewhere are more prone to infection.

The biggest threat to civilian infrastructure is through cyber attacks of supervisory control and data acquisition (SCADA) systems. A SCADA system collects data from remote systems and relays it to a central computer in what is usually a closed loop requiring little in the way of human intervention. SCADA is widely used in industries that manage remote systems, such as electric power, traffic signals, mass transit systems, water management systems, and manufacturing systems. Due to their heavily automated nature, SCADA systems are especially susceptible to computer attack. Control systems, signal hardware, controllers, networks, communications equipment and software are all vulnerable to determined adversaries.

Cyber and War

Cyber and war have been considered long before the current fascination with cyberwar began. Cyberwar was first discussed at the Pentagon in 1977; offensive planning began in 1981, and the 1991 war against Iraq saw the first attempt to use malicious code in war. In 1993 John Arquilla and David Ronfeldt forecast that cyberwar in the twenty-first century would be the equivalent of Nazi Germany's highly successful blitzkrieg operations in the twentieth century. In war, militaries would use "cyberspace (by operating within or through it) to attack personnel, facilities, or equipment with the intent of degrading, neutralizing, or destroying enemy combat capability, while protecting our own."[32] To date there has not been a cyberwar that meets this definition by producing significant damage or political coercion. Instead, cyber attacks have accompanied traditional warfare with limited impact. Defacement of government websites, denial-of-service attacks, and data stealing have been conducted over the Internet, but these do not constitute warfare. The doctrine and capabilities for cyberwar are still developing.[33] But this may not be true for long, and

TABLE 1.4

Malicious Activity by Country, July–September 2010

Rank	Location	Overall Percentage	Malicious Code Rank	Spam Zombies Rank	Phishing Websites Host Rank	Bots Rank	Virus Source Rank
1	United States	23	1	3	1	2	1
2	Brazil	6	6	2	4	3	–
3	India	6	2	1	–	20	3
4	Germany	5	11	5	2	4	–
5	China	4	3	28	7	6	–
6	United Kingdom	4	4	7	3	9	2
7	Taiwan	4	23	12	–	1	–
8	Italy	4	21	11	–	5	–
9	Russia	3	15	9	6	16	–
10	Canada	3	8	41	5	17	10

Sources: Symantec Intelligence Quarterly, July–September 2010; and Symantec Intelligence Report, January 2012.

senior military leaders worry about US vulnerabilities created by an information technology-based military and the potential irrelevance of current capabilities to cyber threats.

In contrast to the defense establishment, other government civilian leaders are offering an alternative vision. Jane Holl Lute, the deputy secretary of Homeland Security, and Bruce McConnell, senior counselor at the Department of Homeland Security wrote: "Conflict and exploitation are present there [on the Internet], to be sure, but cyberspace is fundamentally a civilian space—a neighborhood, a library, a marketplace, a school yard, a workshop—and a new, exciting age in human experience, exploration and development. Portions of it are part of America's defense infrastructure, and these are properly protected by soldiers. But the vast majority of cyberspace is civilian space."[34] In other words, government must be careful about militarizing cyberspace. Just as Americans would object to having a M1 tank at every shopping mall, Americans do not relish US Cyber Command "patrolling" Amazon .com or Facebook.

While cyberwar has not yet occurred and civilians clearly dominate cyberspace, the military services have recognized the importance of cyberspace both in peace and in war. For example, the air force has claimed cyberspace as one of its three operating domains (air and space are the others).[35] The navy created the Fleet Cyber Command (10th Fleet) and the director of national intelligence created a joint interagency cyber task force. At the same time, service capabilities are aggregated under the joint strategic command, which is responsible for developing and implementing integrated operations for defense and attack in the cyber domain. In thinking about the future, the United States military sees itself uncomfortably vulnerable in the cyber domain and expects other countries to exploit it. Wesley Clark and Peter Levin argue: "There is no form of military combat more irregular than an electronic attack; it is extremely cheap, is very fast, can be carried out anonymously, and can disrupt or deny critical services precisely at the moment of maximum peril. Everything about the subtlety, complexity, and effectiveness of the assaults already inflicted on the United States' electronic defense indicates that other nations have thought carefully about this form of combat."[36]

For a number of reasons that include its economic growth and defense expenditures, China is often identified as a likely cyberwar opponent. When speaking about China, Robert K. Knake noted that the Chinese military "plan[s] to thwart US supremacy in any potential conflict we get into with them. They believe they can deter us through cyber warfare."[37] The Chinese military *PLA Daily* stated that "Internet warfare is of equal significance to land, sea, and air power and requires its own military branch," and that "it is essential to have an all-conquering offensive technology and to develop software and technology for net offensives . . . able to launch attacks and countermeasures."[38] The Chinese seem impressed and inspired by US cyber capabilities and are closely following events. Ming Zhou, a China specialist, noted that "information warfare is not just a theology, they can integrate it into nation-state interests."[39] Beyond China, a number of countries have sophisticated cyber–national security capabilities, including Russia, Israel, India, and France.

Because of this, the US military is wrestling over the meaning of this as it relates to warfare and sees cyberspace as critical to its operations, which requires defense.

Volume Overview

The next chapter by Patrick Jagoda reminds us that our vocabulary and thinking about cyberwar are rooted in fiction. The scenarios depicted in science fiction might expand the parameters of our thinking and help us plan for previously unanticipated cyber attacks. The chapter by Herbert Lin bounds imagination by explaining the technical and operational considerations for conducting cyber attacks and cyber exploitation. To bring practical insight, Steve Bucci considers the confluence of cyber-crime and terrorism in chapter 4. This former army ranger and deputy assistant secretary of defense thinks that cyber threats can be grouped into seven categories that form a spectrum beginning with hackers and ending with nation-states.

As cyber tools become institutionalized into traditional defense establishments, understanding the legal implications of this are important. In chapter 5 legal scholar David P. Fidler sees the emergence of cyberspace as a new dimension for national security, military strategy and tactics, and conflict. This new dimension raises questions about how the international law regulating armed conflict operates in this new realm of realpolitik.

In chapter 6 Richard B. Andres explores cyber deterrence and the emergence of cyber militias. With this foundation in deterrence, Jeffrey R. Cooper in chapter 7 considers the mechanisms to implement networked deterrence. This chapter builds on the financial services concept of networked deterrence that rests on four elements: penalty, futility, dependency, and counterproductivity. These elements provide a useful starting place for effective cyber deterrence. To augment and enhance these, this chapter adds two other components: intolerance and security cooperation.

Chapter 8 by Chris Demchak considers how cyberwar differs from "cybered" conflict. She writes, "The new normalcy of cybered conflict is its enduring potential for cascading unexpected outcomes anywhere across the deeply interconnected and complex critical systems of a modern society." In chapter 9, Brandon Valeriano and Ryan Maness place cyberwarfare in the context of international relations theory that increasingly hinges on cyber technologies for diplomacy, business, social relations, and commerce. In chapter 10 James Joyner offers an exposition on European security and cyberspace. While cybersecurity has moved to the forefront of national security thinking in the United States as evidenced by the creation of several cyber–military commands, the same cannot be said among the advanced countries in Europe. Cyber-security is an immature issue in the European security community; furthermore, Europe differs greatly from the United States on interpreting the significance of cyber attacks. What is a military issue in the United States is viewed almost as an exclusively civil matter in Europe.

In chapter 11 Nikolas K. Gvosdev explains the implications of when the Russian "bear goes digital." Although Russia was not one of the leaders in the digital revolution and compared to other industrialized countries still lags behind in the adoption and integration of the new technologies, it is trying to catch up. The Kremlin has begun to take much more seriously nonmilitary applications of power and force, including a growing interest in cyberwar capabilities, and it is becoming aware of Russia's own vulnerabilities in these areas.

Nigel Inkster, writing in chapter 12, sees China as both exploitative and exploited in cyberspace. His view is important since China is often recognized as posing the greatest cyber challenge to the United States. This has as much to do with realist predictions about the inevitable conflict of great powers as it does with Chinese cyber behavior. To make sense of this behavior, John B. Sheldon presents a theory of cyber power in chapter 13. This is important because noted strategist Colin Gray sees that "we lack adequate strategic theory to help guide practice [in cyberspace]," which is now on par with air, land, sea, and space.[40]

Notes

1. White House, "International Strategy for Cyberspace: Prosperity, Security, and Openness in a Networked World," May 2011. www.whitehouse.gov/sites/default/files/rss_viewer/in ternationalstrategy_cyberspace.pdf?bcsi_scan_24DE46460B4E2EF0 = 0&bcsi_scan_filename = internationalstrategy_cyberspace.pdf.

2. Eric Schmitt and Thom Shanker, "US Debated Cyberwarfare in Attack Plan on Libya," *New York Times*, October 17, 2011. www.nytimes.com/2011/10/18/world/africa/cyber-warfare-against-libya-was-debate d-by-us.html.

3. According to Symantec, "Stuxnet represents a malicious code milestone in the breadth of its attack vectors: it is the first identified worm that exploits four zero-day vulnerabilities; in addition, it compromises two separate digital certificates, as well as injecting malicious code into industrial control systems while hiding that code from the ICS operator. It remains to be seen whether or not Stuxnet is the vanguard of a new generation of malicious code that targets real-world infrastructure—as opposed to the majority of current attacks that target more virtual or individual assets—or if it is just an isolated anomaly. Stuxnet is of such great complexity that it requires significant resources to develop. As a result, few attackers will be capable of easily producing a similar threat to such an extent that Symantec does not expect an explosion of similar, copycat threats to suddenly appear. That said, Stuxnet highlights how direct-attack attempts on critical infrastructure are possible and not just a plotline in an action film." See Marc Fossi, *Symantec Intelligence Quarterly*, July–September 2010, www.symantec.com/business/theme.jsp?themeid = threatreport.

4. The worm's origin has largely remained in the speculative realm. Given that the primary target was Iran's nuclear infrastructure, the governments of Israel and the United States have been identified as the likely sources. As of this writing, neither government would confirm this. In chapter 9, the motive suggests that Israel was the likely source.

5. Keith B. Alexander, "Warfighting in Cyberspace," *Joint Force Quarterly*, no. 46 (July 31, 2007), 60. www.military.com/forums/0,15240,143898,00.html.

6. Chairman of the Joint Chiefs of Staff, "National Military Strategy of the United States," Washington, DC: Joint Staff, February 8, 2011.

7. Department of Defense, "Strategy for Operating in Cyberspace," July 2011, www .defense.gov/news/d20110714cyber.pdf?bcsi_scan_24DE46460B4E2EF0 = 0&bcsi_scan_file name = d20110714cyber.pdf.

8. Thomas Rid and Peter McBurney, "Cyber-Weapons," *Rusi Journal* 157, no. 1 (February 2012): 6–13, doi:10.1080/03071847.2012.664354.

9. White House, "The National Strategy to Secure Cyberspace," February 2003, 1. www.us-cert.gov/reading_room/cyberspace_strategy.pdf.

10. Christopher J. Castelli, "Defense Department Adopts New Definition of 'Cyberspace'," *Inside the Air Force*, May 23, 2008. http://integrator.hanscom.af.mil/2008/May/05292008/05292008-24.htm.

11. Larry Johnson, "Thru the Looking Glass: Why Virtual Worlds Matter, Where They Are Heading, and Why We Are All Here," Keynote address to the Federal Consortium on Virtual Worlds, April 24, 2008.

12. Ken Burbary, "Facebook Demographics Revisited—2011 Statistics," *Web Business by Ken Burbary*, March 7, 2011, www.kenburbary.com/2011/03/facebook-demographics-revisited-2011-statistics-2/.

13. Quoted in Donna Miles, "Gates Establishes New Cyber Subcommand," *American Forces Press Service*, June 24, 2009. www.defense.gov/news/newsarticle.aspx?id=54890.

14. "Inventors," *About.com*, http://inventors.about.com/library/inventors/bl_Charles_Herz feld.htm.

15. Presidential Decision Directive 63, "Critical Infrastructure Protection," May 22, 1998, section II. www.fas.org/irp/offdocs/pdd/pdd-63.htm.

16. Secretary of Defense, "National Defense Strategy of the United States" (Washington, DC: Pentagon, 2008), 7.

17. Chairman of the Joint Chiefs of Staff, "National Military Strategy of the United States" (Washington, DC: Pentagon, 2011), 3.

18. "Sustaining US Global Leadership Priorities for 21st Century Defense," January 3, 2012, graphics8.nytimes.com/packages/pdf/us/20120106-PENTAGON.PDF.

19. Quoted in Jim Garamone, "Lynn Calls for Collaboration in Establishing Cyber Security," *American Forces Press Service*, October 1, 2009. www.defense.gov/news/newsarticle .aspx?id=56063.

20. CSIS Commission on Cybersecurity for the 44th Presidency, *Securing Cyberspace for the 44th Presidency*, December 2008, 11. http://csis.org/files/media/csis/pubs/081208_securing cyberspace_44.pdf.

21. White House, "Press Release: National Cybersecurity Awareness Month," October 1, 2009. www.whitehouse.gov/the_press_office/Presidential-Proclamation-National-Cybersecur ity-Awareness-Month/.

22. Wesley K. Clark and Peter L. Levin, "Securing the Information Highway: How to Enhance the United States' Electronic Defenses," *Foreign Affairs* (November/December 2009), 10.

23. Ibid.

24. Department of Defense, "Strategy for Operating in Cyberspace," July 2011, 3. www .defense.gov/home/features/2011/0411_cyberstrategy/docs/DoD_Strategy_for_Operating_in _Cyberspace_July_2011.pdf.

25. Quoted in "ITU Chief Stresses Need for Cooperation to Protect Cyberspace," United Nations Radio, October 6, 2009. www.unmultimedia.org/radio/english/2009/10/itu-chief-calls-stresses-need-for-cooperation-to-protect-cyberspace/.

26. James Andrew Lewis, "The 'Korean' Cyber Attacks and Their Implications for Cyber Conflict," CSIS, October 23, 2009. http://csis.org/publication/korean-cyber-attacks-and-their-implications-cyber-conflict.

27. P. W. Singer, "A Defense Policy Vision," *Armed Forces Journal*, June 2011. www.armedforces journal.com/2011/06/6462790.

28. Quoted in "ITU Chief Stresses Need for Cooperation to Protect Cyberspace."

29. Quoted in John J. Kruzel, "Cybersecurity Poses Unprecedented Challenge to National Security, Lynn Says," *American Forces Press Service*, June 15, 2009. www.defense.gov/news/newsarticle.aspx?id = 54787.

30. For current data, see "Threat Activity Trends," *Symantec*, www.symantec.com/business/threatreport/topic.jsp?id = threat_activity_trends&aid = malicious_activity_by_source.

31. "Symantec Global Internet Security Report, Trends for 2008, April 2009," *Symantec*, www.symantec.com/connect/downloads/symantec-global-internet-security-threat-report-trends-2008.

32. Alexander, "Warfighting in Cyberspace," 60.

33. Head of the National Security Agency, Gen. Keith Alexander claimed, "We have yet to translate these strategies into operational art through development of joint doctrine for cyberspace." Ibid., 59.

34. Jane Holl Lute and Bruce McConnell, "A Civil Perspective on Cybersecurity," *Wired Danger Room*, February 14, 2011. www.wired.com/threatlevel/2011/02/dhs-op-ed/.

35. Air force officials converted more than forty-three thousand total force enlisted airmen from former communications career fields to cyberspace support on November 1, 2009. The new air force specialty is made up of three former career fields: communications-electronics, knowledge operations management, and communications-computer systems. The new cyberspace support career field is broken into eleven new air force specialties: knowledge operations management, cyber systems operations, cyber surety, computer systems programming, client systems, cyber transport systems, radio frequency transmission systems, spectrum operations, ground radar systems, airfield systems, and cable and antenna systems. The navy did something similar on October 1, 2009, when it created the Fleet Cyber Command (10th Fleet) and consolidated several career fields into information dominance.

36. Clark and Levin, "Securing the Information Highway," 2.

37. Quoted in Ellen Nakashima and John Pomfret, "China Proves to Be an Aggressive Foe in Cyberspace," *Washington Post*, November 11, 2009. www.washingtonpost.com/wp-dyn/content/article/2009/11/10/AR2009111017588_pf.html.

38. Quoted in Alexander, "Warfighting in Cyberspace,"59.

39. Quoted in Nakashima and Pomfret, "China Proves to Be an Aggressive Foe in Cyberspace."

40. Colin S. Gray, "The 21st Century Security Environment and the Future of War," *Parameters*, Winter 2008–9, 23. www.carlisle.army.mil/usawc/parameters/Articles/08winter/gray.pdf.

Vocabulary + Thinking on Cyberware Are Rooted in Fiction.

CHAPTER 2

Speculative Security

Patrick Jagoda

Cyber

ON MAY 22, 2010, the Pentagon launched a new core operation: the US Cyber Command (USCYBERCOM). This command is responsible for protecting American military computer networks from a host of digital threats, including "foreign actors, terrorists, criminal groups and individual hackers."[1] The operation, which achieved full readiness later that year, has announced that it seeks to "direct the operations and defense of specified Department of Defense information networks," to "conduct full-spectrum military cyberspace operations in order to enable actions in all domains," and to "ensure US/Allied freedom of action in cyberspace and deny the same to our adversaries."[2] Overall, the organization takes on the difficult task of securing fifteen thousand military computer networks, which are probed and attacked thousands of times each day.

My areas of research—digital media studies, contemporary literature, and the history of computing—differ from the primary fields that inform this volume, particularly security studies and international relations. Nevertheless, I find myself intrigued by the formation of the USCYBERCOM, its cultural context, and the growing digital infrastructure that makes such an operation possible, even necessary. In descriptions of USCYBERCOM and similar recent initiatives, two ubiquitous terms require more careful analytical unpacking than they generally receive: "cyber" and "networks." As we begin the second decade of the twenty-first century, the prefix "cyber" has been attached to countless roots. Writers and journalists frequently invoke concepts such as "cyberculture," "cybersex," and "cyberwar," all of which are linked to the realm of digital media, virtual reality, and the Internet. In popular culture, the prefix similarly imbues various words with a vaguely futuristic sense, as is the case with the literary movement of "cyberpunk." Similarly, since the advent of the Internet, the word "network" has become a prominent metaphor and has taken center stage in practically every contemporary discipline and major institution.

Omnipresent by the 1980s, "cyber" finds its origin several decades earlier in Norbert Wiener's coinage of the term "cybernetics" in 1948.[3] In his popular book *The Human Use of Human Beings* (1950), Wiener describes cybernetics as "the study of

21

messages as a means of controlling machinery and society." Fundamentally, the purpose of cybernetics is "to develop a language and techniques that will enable us indeed to attack the problem of control and communication in general."[4] Wiener's selection of this root for the emerging interdisciplinary study of cybernetics, which served as the basis for computing following World War II, makes good sense. Etymologically, "cybernetics" derives from the Greek word "kybernetes," which means "steersman" and metaphorically describes a "guide" or "governor."[5] As the name suggests, cybernetics was not only a theory of communication but also one of control.

Given this etymology and Wiener's application, the establishment of a "cyber command" suggests an imperative to control information networks. In fact, the US Department of Defense announced its explicit intent to secure "command and control systems."[6] Admittedly, the pursuit of control, broadly speaking, is far from unique to the rise of cyberwarfare in the twentieth century. It can be traced through a much longer history of information warfare and military strategy.[7] Nevertheless, control has taken on new meaning in an era governed by computer software and network protocols. Through an analysis of Internet culture, which turns to both network architecture and technological science fiction, this essay contends that the "cyber" frame that privileges control as a definitive security goal might not be the best way to approach the network era and its emerging threats. To explain this claim I turn more extensively to a second key term of cybersecurity that complicates any straightforward language of control: networks.

Networks

As with all things cyber, "network" has been, since the middle of the twentieth century, a ubiquitous term that carries rarely interrogated meanings. In an era of globalization in which people around the world are increasingly interconnected via transportation and communication infrastructures, the network is both a material and a metaphorical reality. The language of links and nodes is frequently invoked to describe terrorist organizations, economic systems, disease ecologies, social structures, and of course computer webs. As I have argued elsewhere, understanding networks is not just a matter of studying their physical architecture. To make sense of these complex systems that seem to exceed our capacity to comprehend them, it is also critical to think about the rhetorical and aesthetic techniques that fiction writers, journalists, and politicians use to describe them.[8]

Discussions about computer networks in particular tend to depict these structures in two drastically different ways. Since the development of the Internet in the 1970s and 1980s and the introduction of the World Wide Web in the 1990s, the primary approaches to discussing the future of the Internet have been those of utopian cheerleading and dystopian terror. The Internet has been, simultaneously, celebrated as a technological instantiation of participatory democracy and as a precarious infrastructure that opens its users to unimaginably dangerous conse-quences. These extremes are not as far removed from one another as they may at first appear. Both positions misuse metaphorical network language and misunder-stand the physical dimension of computer networks.

In the realm of cybersecurity, political, military, and corporate actors often repre-sent computer networks as threatening structures that can be infiltrated by malevolent actors or destroyed by systemic collapse. This approach is not entirely unwarranted and has much to do with the history of both the personal computer and the Internet. In the 1960s International Business Machines (IBM), the first commercial computer company, introduced a different business model than the one that hard-ware developers follow today. IBM leased its mainframe computers on a monthly basis to interested parties. At the same time, it sold appliances such as the Friden Flexowriter typewriter, which were hardwired to perform only a predetermined series of tasks. Such electronic appliances served very specific purposes and could not be reprogrammed by users. It was not until 1969 that the threat of an antitrust suit led IBM to unbundle its hardware from its software, which produced more flexible machines that allowed third-party software development. In this way IBM moved from vendor-controlled computers to a less centrally regulated model. It was not until the release of the Apple II microcomputer in 1977, however, that personal computing became a commercially successful technology. With hardware already unbundled from software, amateurs and hobbyists began to experiment with the machine's affordances. Jonathan Zittrain contends that the personal computer departed so drastically from previous devices as a result of its "generativity." As he explains, "Generativity is a system's capacity to produce unanticipated change through unfiltered contributions from broad and varied audiences." A generative system, such as the personal computer, is founded on leverage, adaptability, ease of mastery, accessibility, and transferability.[9]

The worldwide system of interconnected computer networks—the Internet—operates according to similar principles of generativity as the personal computer. Early in the twentieth century, AT&T regulated both telephone networks and the devices attached to them. A 1955 legal decision, however, changed network regulation dra-matically, allowing for third-party innovations to the phone system, which eventually gave rise to inventions such as the fax machine. This change also enabled the develop-ment of dial-up modems, including the commercially viable Smartmodem in 1981, which allowed communication among personal computers.[10] In the 1980s and early 1990s proprietary networks run by AOL, CompuServe, and Prodigy dominated the fledgling market. Thus, even as uses of physical network cables were no longer under sole control of telephone companies, the computer networks accessed by most users were owned and regulated by corporations. These companies ran a tight ship, allowing the exchange of data (via email or instant messaging) but not of programs that could radically reconfigure the network.

Parallel to these proprietary networks, the system known as the Internet already enjoyed popularity. In the end, it supplanted networks such as CompuServe. The major advantage of the Internet was that it was designed to circumvent centralized governance. The Internet Protocol was designed to package and move data, leaving the majority of its features to be adjusted and reconfigured by users.[11] The architecture of the Internet—unlike that of top-down proprietary networks—was designed by academics and government researchers to have separate conceptual levels, including a physical layer, protocol layer, application layer, content layer, and social layer. Zittrain demonstrates the benefit of this model when he observes, "Tinkerers can work on one layer without having to understand much about the others, and there need not be any coordination or relationship between those working at one layer and those at another. For example, someone can write a new application like an instant messenger without having to know anything about whether its users will be connected to the network by modem or broadband."[12] As with the personal computer, the Internet was thus a truly generative system.

Unfortunately, the greatest advantages of generative systems—their openness and flexibility—are also their greatest drawbacks. A flexible system spurs innovation and participation, but such freedom also opens the door to viruses, worms, and spam engineered by users seeking to wreak havoc or simply to make a profit. Since 1988—the year that Robert Morris developed and released the first worm—computer networks have suffered from a rapidly increasing string of threats, including distributed denial-of-service attacks and automated botnets made up of thousands of zombie computers. Costly hacks have been engineered by crafty hackers, technologically savvy entrepreneurs, and even governments. An already prominent cultural fear of networks—structures that are large, complex, distributed, and susceptible to infiltration—became even more palpable as personal computers grew more vulnerable. Computer viruses have developed from anomalous inconveniences to conventional features of the computer network landscape. They have become widespread over the last twenty years because of "faster networks, more powerful processors, and less-skilled users."[13] A string of malicious programs, from the Lovebug worm (2000) to the Sasser worm (2004) to the Conficker worm (2009), have already compromised personal data, incapacitated computers, and caused billions of dollars in damage. These incidents have spurred security industry talk of an imminent "digital Pearl Harbor" that could suddenly debilitate major American networks.[14]

Without denying the reality of disruptive network-transmitted computer viruses or the high probability of growing risks, I believe that we need to be careful about mobilizing both the language of network fear and system control in ongoing efforts to strengthen cybersecurity. Like the architecture of the Internet itself, the efforts to defend this system are made up of numerous interconnected layers, including the linguistic, the cultural, the technical, and the physical. In order to suggest how these layers inform each other and why computer culture is an integral dimension of the cybersecurity puzzle, I turn to a genre that has offered some of the most clear-eyed and imaginative reflections on cyberwar—namely, science fiction.

Speculative Security

In 1984 writer William Gibson coined the term "cyberspace" in his breakthrough science fiction novel *Neuromancer*. This novel influenced many of the computer scientists who created the web and designers who later constructed online worlds such as *Ultima Online* (1997) and *Second Life* (2003). Gibson's vision of a digital space of communication and control continues to shape discussions about cybersecurity. In a famous passage in the novel, Gibson describes cyberspace metaphorically, as "a consensual hallucination experienced daily by billions of legitimate operators, in every nation. . . . A graphic representation of data abstracted from the banks of every computer in the human system. Unthinkable complexity. Lines of light ranged in the nonspace of the mind, clusters and constellations of data. Like city lights, receding."[15] This image of a transcendent space of "unthinkable complexity" is evocative and sublime, but it takes too abstract and romantic a view of present-day networks. In the early years of the twenty-first century, we must approach cyberspace and the networks on which it depends as something very different—as immanent spaces of *thinkable* complexity.

In order for the problem of cybersecurity to be thinkable, we must take into account not only network protocols and security systems but also the cultural, aesthetic, and social dimensions of cyberspace. Science fiction literature, films, television shows, and digital games are especially helpful in working through these aspects of the problem. Writer Gardner Dozois observes that we live in "an interlocking and interdependent gestalt made up of thousands of factors and combinations thereof: cultural, technological, biological, psychological, historical, environmental." Science fiction, he continues, is a genre uniquely able to explore these factors and the underlying *"interdependence* of things."[16] At a surface level, science fiction certainly generates possible scenarios that may help cybersecurity planners prepare for previously unanticipated exploits. There are also, however, noninstrumental benefits to analyzing this strand of literature and popular culture. Through its system-savvy aesthetics, science fiction can help us understand the psychology of hackers, the social effects of computer attacks, and alternative paradigms for our rapidly changing world. Science fiction is most useful not as a model for tactical thought but as a creative framework for thinking about and through networks. Creativity, when approached with an open mind, can be much more than an algorithmic tool for generating possible future situations that fall within our current network paradigm. It can itself serve as a generative system that helps us see the world from radically different perspectives.

A generalized anxiety about computer networks and their vulnerabilities has been a prominent aspect of science fiction for several decades. Movies such as *Wargames* (1983) and computer games such as *Uplink: Hacker Elite* (2003) deal with threats posed by individual hackers. Films such as *Terminator 2* (1991) and *The Matrix* trilogy (1999–2003) imagine networked machines that slip out of human control and wreak havoc on the world. Popular novels, such as Neal Stephenson's *Snow Crash* (1992) and Michael Crichton's *Prey* (2002), have explored fears associated with evolutionary algorithms, emergent computing, and network science. The vulnerability of networks even fueled the premise of the recent television show *Battlestar Galactica* (2004–9). In the pilot episode of that series, artificially constructed "Cylons" achieve sentience and escape from their human creators. After developing their own military force, the Cylons launch a massive attack against human civilization. In this devastating assault, the only human-operated military "battlestar" to survive a near-total nuclear genocide does so precisely by *not* being linked into the computerized defense network that is incapacitated by a powerful virus. Instead of serving humanity, interconnectivity in this series enables dangerous hacks that compromise every node in the network.

The problem of network security saturates the history of science fiction. In the 1980s this issue even gave rise to a short-lived yet influential genre known as cyberpunk, which focuses on hackers who are engaged in cyberwarfare with corporations, governments, and military organizations. The technological visions of William Gibson, as well as writers such as Bruce Sterling, Pat Cadigan, John Shirley, and Neal Stephenson, have spilled over to other media and come to shape the popular imagination of cyberwar.[17] I would like to offer a brief reading of two contemporary writers who were inspired by the cyberpunk tradition but who approach the problems of network security in a more direct manner. These authors—Daniel Suarez and Cory Doctorow—treat computer networks as both material and metaphorical constructs. Their fictions examine the contemporary uses and abuses of network systems in order to promote a serious response to security problems that relies not on a paralyzing politics of fear but on the generative affordances of distributed Internet communities.

Daemon

Beginning in the late twentieth century, the Western world became increasingly dependent on information networks. As Jussi Parikka argues, such dependence exposed the world to "new kinds of dangers, accidents that have to do with information disorders—viruses, worms, bugs, malicious hackers etc."[18] Daniel Suarez's exemplary techno-thriller *Daemon* (2009) carefully exposes this vulnerability of present-day computer networks. The novel suggests that the primary technological threats of our era may not be individual hackers, uncontrollable sentient computer singularities, or global systems that eliminate individual agency. Instead, Suarez demonstrates that we need to be careful lest the generalized fear of distributed computer networks legitimates increased regulation, promotes greater dependence on automation, and contributes to a loss of the Internet's community-driven generativity.

In *Daemon*, Matthew Sobol, a software designer and founder of CyberStorm Entertainment, creates the most sophisticated massively multiplayer games on the market. After dying from brain cancer, Sobol leaves behind a menacing "Daemon"—"a computer program that runs continuously in the background and performs specified operations at predefined times or in response to certain events." The Daemon triggers the deaths of several CyberStorm personnel and automatically initiates a chain reaction that gives the program significant control over computer networks and financial markets. Along with such technological hacks, the program recruits an extensive distributed network of human hackers and gamers to contribute to its plans. The Daemon is thus "comprised of distributed networked systems with a companion human network."[19] After discovering the existence of the Daemon, government, military, and industry players struggle to destroy it, a process that is complicated by its inextricable integration with major Internet systems. Even as this narrative includes several subtle innovations, it also reproduces a number of plot points common to technological science fiction.

Daemon makes computer webs thinkable by staging technical processes, but more importantly, the novel makes them affectively accessible. Specifically, the novel analyzes three levels of network fear that derive from different cultural ideas about contemporary technologies of interconnection. The first fear is that of hackers and the viruses they produce. Before authorities thoroughly understand the nature of the Daemon, they suspect that a criminal, presumably a still-living Matthew Sobol, is using network capabilities to commit murder. As police investigator Pete Sebeck puts it, "At least one of the victims appears to have been murdered through the Internet."[20] In this formulation, Sebeck figures the Internet as a tool, a weapon, or a medium *through* which an individual breaks the law.[21] The Internet, in this conception, is not a true network but a reified object put to malevolent use by a cybercriminal or cyberterrorist. This focus on the hacker, rather than the exploit or the underlying system that enables the exploit, reflects a broader cultural attitude toward hacking. Alexander Galloway demonstrates that the metaphor of a digital virus originated in the AIDs culture of the 1980s.[22] By the 1990s, however, when fears began to shift from the computer virus itself to the virus's programmer-author, this disruptive entity was framed increasingly as a criminal, even terrorist, tool.[23] In Suarez's novel, hacker Brian Gragg recognizes this fear. He "knew the government wasn't afraid of guns, but it *was* afraid of laptops—and what the government feared, it punished."[24] This fear of hackers assumes linear causality. According to this view, eliminating the human source of a virus neutralizes the threat and achieves justice. The terror associated with hackers still rests on a comforting worldview in which individuals can be "punished" for cybercrimes.

The second type of network fear that *Daemon* explores is the terror of the Internet as a single system that exceeds any individual. After some investigation, a number of governmental agencies realize that the Daemon is not actually a program being controlled by a malevolent mastermind. Matthew Sobol may have created the Daemon but it has since become largely automated and decentralized. A number of characters describe the program as a monstrous entity. For example, a CEO named Vanowen encounters a manifestation of the Daemon: "As he sat there, still shaking, he suddenly realized the enormity of the monster that had just brushed past him. It was colossally huge. And as powerful as he had always felt, he felt insignificant before it."[25] At the interface level, the Daemon, which communicates via VoIP-enabled logic trees, takes the form of a powerful demon. In designing the program, Sobol recognizes that most people will only be able to interact with it in personified form. To capture the enormity of a system that exceeds individual understanding, Suarez himself personifies the Daemon, drawing heavily on gothic aesthetics. In particular, he uses the "cyber gothic"—a style that is prevalent in a wide range of science fiction, including Gibson's *Neuromancer*—to make sense of a global haunting entity.[26] This second fear of networks that surpass the individual is often expressed in science fiction plots through technological singularities and sentient networks that turn against their human creators in computer games such as Valve's *Portal* series and film series such as *The Matrix* and *The Terminator*. While this fear engages with networks at a systemic level, it still anthropomorphizes the Internet and information networks.

The third fear that *Daemon* explores is a cultural anxiety about the paradigm shift from a hierarchal society to one organized through distributed networks. As Suarez shows, the generative Internet suggests an infrastructure that transforms individual identity, social organization, and the operation of the public sphere. It is only after the Daemon has produced considerable damage that government authorities begin to recognize a more unsettling feature of global networks. In a meeting of key US agencies, including the FBI and the CIA, the director of DARPA explains, "Our best guess is that [the Daemon] consists of hundreds or even thousands of individual components spread over compromised workstations linked to the Net. Once a component is used, it's probably no longer needed." The Daemon, in other words, is not simply frightening because it is a systemic entity that threatens individual actors but because it is spread across a *distributed* network. When the FBI director suggests that they "shut down the Internet" temporarily in order to wipe out the Daemon, the DARPA director points out that even this radical proposal would fail. "The Internet is not a single system," he explains. "It consists of hundreds of millions of individual computer systems linked with a common protocol. No one controls it entirely. It can't be 'shut down.' And even if you could shut it down, the Daemon would just come back when you turned it back on."[27]

The reason that distributed networks inspire such acute fear in *Daemon* is not simply related to the way in which they exacerbate threats to technological systems. The greater threat is arguably the challenge that global networks pose to the existing sociopolitical order. From the start, the Daemon challenges the already unstable Cold War paradigm of competing yet discrete nation-states. Shortly after discovering Sobol's exploit, computer systems expert Jon Ross explains that "the Daemon probably spread to the four corners of the world in minutes. It's too late for containment." Enemies are no longer bounded states that respond to a range of diplomatic and military maneuvers. Even so, Suarez demonstrates that the Cold War "culture of secrecy" still permeates the National Security Agency and other government organizations. "However," he adds, "with the explosion of technology throughout the nineties, even the NSA was no longer able to keep up with the worldwide flow of digital information, and they were forced to let the rumors of their omniscience hide a brutal reality: no one knew where the next threat was coming from. Nation states were no longer the enemy. The enemy had become a catchall phrase: *bad actors*." Such "bad actors" may be causes for concern. Nevertheless, the architecture of distributed networks marks a deeper status quo vulnerability.[28]

As *Daemon* gradually demonstrates, Sobol's Daemon is not merely a disruptive virus. Before his death Sobol records a message for Sergeant Sebeck that explains: "I'll tell you what the Daemon is: the Daemon is a remorseless system for building a distributed civilization. A civilization that perpetually regenerates. One with no central authority." Sobol contends that in our current global order, "decreasing freedom" and increasing regulation are used to conceal that "the assumptions upon which our civilization is based are no longer valid." In another posthumous monologue directed to major American security agencies and corporations, Sobol explains, "the Great Diffusion has begun—an era when the nation state dissolves. Technology will cause this. As countries compete for markets in the global economy, diffusion of high technology will accelerate. It will result in a diffusion of power. And diffusion of power will make countries an ineffective organizing principle." Over time, "Threats to centralized authority will multiply. Centralized power will be defenseless against these distributed threats."[29] Since global networks are a foundational reality of our world, distributed daemons, viruses, and worms are also inevitable. In the early twenty-first century, total cybersecurity is not a viable goal.

In *Daemon* (as well as its sequel *Freedom*™), the Daemon serves to exacerbate an already ongoing paradigm shift. It organizes a social network of users who pursue a sustainable existence with the aid of digital technologies. Suarez suggests that the greatest peril to global order in coming years will not be generative computer networks and their accompanying viruses. Instead, it will be the growth of multinational corporations and the network regulation that they promote. In a fascinating twist, the novel's Daemon largely ignores government agencies and instead begins to disrupt corporate entities such as the Leland Equity Group. This investment group already taps into social, political, economic, and technological global networks. Its decisions "ruled the daily lives of two hundred million Third World people. . . . They had since formed private equity partnerships with local leaders for strip mining in Papua New Guinea, water privatization in Ecuador, marble quarrying in China, oil drilling in Nigeria, and pipeline construction in Myanmar." It is precisely through a network that Leland controls and exploits foreign labor. "Leland's equity offerings used tedious statistical analysis to mask the fact that their business centered on enslaving foreign people and ravaging their lands. They didn't do this directly, of course, but they hired the people who hired the people who did."[30] Network organization, in other words, provides corporations—not only governments or malevolent hackers—with increased power.[31]

While Suarez builds on the broader anticorporate critiques of writers such as Naomi Klein and David C. Korten through his fiction, his work offers a more targeted warning about how far we should be willing to go in pursuit of cybersecurity. The fear of insecure networks may spur innovative defenses, but it also risks the wrong types of regulation. As Zittrain explains this point, "If security problems worsen and fear spreads, rank-and-file users will not be far behind [corporations] in preferring some form of lockdown—and regulators will speed the process along. In turn, that lockdown opens the door to new forms of regulatory surveillance and control."[32] Devices such as the generative PC are already giving way to networked video game consoles, mobile phones, and digital video recorders, which are centrally controlled. The fear of insecure networks is giving rise to networks that are largely safer but heavily regulated. One does not have to subscribe to particularly radical pro-privacy politics in order to wonder about the effects that this trend might have on online communities, amateur innovation, and network security in coming years.

To consider the future possibilities that overly aggressive cybersecurity might foreclose upon, I turn briefly to the science fiction of Cory Doctorow.

Little Brother

Cory Doctorow's science fiction focuses on early-twenty-first-century hackers. In an introduction to his short story "Anda's Game," Doctorow points out, "The easiest way to write futuristic (or futurismic) science fiction is to predict, with rigor and absolute accuracy, the present day."[33] Some of the most successful speculative literature lures in readers through fantasy and futuristic landscapes but actually seeks to offer a description of what is happening at our current historical moment. Indeed, one of the reasons that technological science fiction can appear futuristic has to do with a lack of knowledge, among the majority of computer users, about the machines and the networks on which they depend daily. This lack of digital literacy—the ability to read, write, and understand computer processes—represents a greater threat to cybersecurity than any single computer virus.

While some of Doctorow's fiction, such as the 2007 story "When Systemadmins Ruled the Earth," explores cultural fears that accompany network threats, much of his work concerns threats to creativity and privacy that are mobilized in response to the perception of such threats. Doctorow's 2008 novel Little Brother demonstrates how science fiction can offer insights into the cyberwar without simply providing potential scenarios or fictionalized case studies. The seventeen-year-old protagonist of Little Brother, Marcus Yallow, engages in numerous security hacks throughout the novel. He penetrates firewalls at his school, spoofs gait-recognition software, disrupts data-mining-based surveillance, uses indie network connections set up through onion routers to bypass visible networks, hacks into an Xbox game system, and jams "arphid" (radio frequency identification tag) signals. At one point he uses what has become an all-too-common hacking technique, deploying a botnet composed of hundreds of zombie computers to crash an antagonist's phone by sending thousands of messages to it simultaneously.

Unlike earlier cyberpunk novels, Little Brother replaces abstract network aesthetics with technical histories and suggestions about how to keep information technologies generative. Marcus offers practical advice about cheap antisurveillance hacks, teaching readers to detect pinhead video cameras and to avoid detection in cyberspace. In other cases he offers overview explanations that encourage additional online research. At the heart of the novel Doctorow imagines an operating system called ParanoidLinux, adapted by white hat hackers from a system used by Chinese and Syrian dissidents in order to shake government surveillance. This operating system keeps documents secret while producing "chaff" communications that disguise covert actions. As Marcus explains, "while you're receiving a political message one character at a time, ParanoidLinux is pretending to surf the Web and fill in questionnaires and flirt in chat rooms."[34] The real messages being sent are hidden within a sea of information—converted to needles in a haystack.[35] In another passage the novel offers an extensive guide to the way cryptography works, leading the reader through the nuances of terms such as "cleartext," "ciphertext," "ciphers," "keys," "public-key cryptography," and other key concepts.[36] This description of Paranoid-Linux and cryptographic primer are not merely embedded glossaries necessary for understanding the nuances of the plot. They are the core of Doctorow's style, which seeks to make sense of our culture's technological substratum rather than emphasizing its terrifying or romantic qualities.

Instead of settling for the type of operational secrecy practiced by the government agencies in Suarez's *Daemon*, *Little Brother* contends that an open-source and antiregulation approach better fits our present-day network paradigm. The novel synthesizes information about cryptography and hacking, and includes two brief essays by security technologist Bruce Schneier and Xbox hacker Andrew Huang. Instead of defending privacy for the sake of privacy, the novel and the accompanying essays contend that a minimally regulated cyberspace can actually produce a stronger cybersecurity culture. While secrecy reduces the collective resources available for identifying and stopping a malignant worm, privacy encourages innovation. As Schneier points out, "Only bad security relies on secrecy; good security works even if all the details of it are public."[37] Similarly, Doctorow's protagonist Marcus notes, "You have to publish a cipher to know that it works. You have to tell *as many people as possible* how it works, so that they can thwack on it with everything they have, testing its security." He later adds, "The important thing about security systems isn't how they work, it's how they fail."[38]

In his writing on cyberwarfare, Martin C. Libicki similarly extends Sun Tzu's and Plato's philosophical imperative to self-knowledge to the realm of cyber defense. "There is no substitute," he writes, "for understanding how a military system is likely to fail, if it is to be prevented from failing under a cyberattack."[39] Libicki's logic of productive failure as a route to better understanding should be extended beyond military experts to the broader public sphere. In an era when nation-state control is ceding increasingly to a distributed form of network power, anachronistic hierarchies can no longer keep us safe. Knowledge and creativity must also transition from individual to community oriented attributes.

Safety in Networks

For both Suarez and Doctorow, the experimentation practiced by amateur hacker communities can contribute to the efforts of security experts. The public imagination may better be served by an education in computer security and digital media than by top-down regulation. Science fiction, which I view as a powerful critical genre, can play a significant part in an education that encourages technological knowledge, ethical engagement, and creative imagination in the use of networked computers. Indeed science fiction as a mode of thought is not restricted to media such as novels, films, and television shows. Digital gaming is an important interactive medium that draws heavily on science fiction and has a history of application by both the computer community and the military. Games model global systems instead of simply representing them. In recent years science fiction has influenced a great deal of digital media design and inspired some very serious interactive multi-player games. For example, the 2007 alternate reality game *World without Oil*, pro-duced by Ken Eklund and Jane McGonigal, was a serious online game that used Internet-based storytelling methods to imagine the first thirty-two weeks of a global oil crisis. Anyone could play the game and participate in the story by contributing fictional personal narratives in the form of emails, phone calls, blog posts, photos, videos, twitter, and more. This game took the form of collectively narrated science fiction that envisioned life during a terminal oil crisis. Together players followed a futuristic story and brainstormed some very inventive solutions to problems created by a lack of oil. When the brief game finished in June 2007, it included more than fifteen hundred active players and sixty-eight thousand participating viewers.[40]

Similar models of collective net-based science fiction could be used to work through the near-future of cybersecurity and to encourage the massive imaginative capacities of thousands of people. Through role-playing, players could explore very serious computer threats, hacker motivations, and aspects of an unfolding cyberwar. There are already countless examples of complex political and technological prob-lems being solved by emergent communities of users that came about as a result of minimal organizational efforts.[41] Serious cybersecurity-themed games would invite imaginative thinking and citizen participation in addressing national cybersecurity problems. As Andrew Huang explains, "It's in a hacker's nature to question conven-tions and be tempted by intricate problems. Any complex system is sport for a hacker; a side effect of this is the hacker's natural affinity for problems involving security."[42] If this is true, why not tap into the desire—the temptation to crack secur-ity problems—and channel it toward ethically responsible ends? Instead of training games that use a first-person shooter format, such as *America's Army*, a more genera-tive (and less expensive) design challenge would be to create games that are narrative-based and encourage the active generation user content. Such a game is only one idea. The larger point is that science fiction—in its various transmedia forms—encourages us to think about the social, political, and ethical consequences of the way we use emerging technologies. In an era of new media and social networking, science fiction could be used in the service of understanding network security that must be both collective and public in nature.

The cyber frame has been inherited from an older moment that lasted from the nineteenth century through much of the Cold War. In an era of distributed net-works, control and order become more elusive values, especially when they are sought through a filter of secrecy. There is no denying that malevolent programs will continue to affect military, political, economic, and social activities in our world of always-on computing. Even Zittrain, who fears an excess of regulation, admits that in the face of cyber threats, "We need a latter-day Manhattan project, not to build a bomb but to design the tools and conventions by which to continually defuse one."[43] However, given the nature of computer networks, such an endeavor cannot have a purely military or corporate basis. To succeed, it must be more Wikipedia than Manhattan Project, drawing from the knowledge of distributed Internet communities to respond to problems as they arise. It takes networks to understand, manage, and build networks. In the early-twenty-first century, total control—however well intentioned—is a dangerous fantasy that misapprehends the social, cultural, and technological nature of distributed networks.

Building on this cultural understanding of cyberspace, succeeding chapters consider the intersections between cyberspace and national security. Since cyberspace is governed by principles of physics and engineering, the next chapter by Herb Lin explores what it means to conduct cyber attacks and cyber exploitations. While similar in a number of ways, "attack" and "exploitation" have unique legal, policy, and technical properties, which Lin explores in his operational analysis.

Notes

1. William H. McMichael, "DoD Cyber Command Is Officially Online," *Navy Times*, May 21, 2010, www.navytimes.com/news/2010/05/military_cyber_command_052110/.

2. US Department of Defense, "US Cyber Command Fact Sheet," May 25, 2010, www.defense.gov/home/features/2010/0410_cybersec/docs/cyberfactsheet%20updated%20replaces%20may%2021%20fact%20sheet.pdf.

3. Norbert Wiener, *Cybernetics: Or Control and Communication in the Animal and the Machine*, 2nd rev. ed. (Paris: MIT Press, 1961).

4. Norbert Wiener, *The Human Use of Human Beings: Cybernetics and Society* (Garden City, New York: Doubleday, 1954), 15 and 17.

5. "Cybernetics, *n.*" *Oxford English Dictionary. OED Online*, 3rd ed. (Oxford University Press, August 2010); online version, November 2010.

6. US Department of Defense, "US Cyber Command Fact Sheet."

7. In *War in the Age of Intelligent Machines*, Manuel De Landa traces information warfare all the way back to Sun Tzu who, in *The Art of War*, "locates the essence of combat not in the exercise of violence, but in foreknowledge and deception" (New York: Zone Books, 1991), 179.

8. Patrick Jagoda, "Terror Networks and the Aesthetics of Interconnection." *Social Text* 28, no. 4 (105): 65–89. doi:10.1215/01642472-2010-011.

9. Jonathan Zittrain, *The Future of the Internet and How to Stop It* (New Haven, CT: Yale University Press, 2008), 12, 70, and 71–73.

10. Ibid., 21–22. The 1955 Hush-A-Phone and the 1968 Carterphone decisions encouraged innovation and loosened AT&T's control over telephone networks.

11. Ibid., 69.

12. Ibid., 68. This layer of Internet structure is known as an "hourglass architecture."

13. Ibid., 38.

14. The phrase "digital Pearl Harbor" was coined by D. James Bidzos in 1991 and popularized in the policy realm by Richard Clarke in the early twenty-first century.

15. William Gibson, *Neuromancer* (New York: Ace Books, 1984), 51.

16. Gardner R. Dozois, *Living the Future: You Are What You Eat*, Writer's chapbook series, #31 (Eugene, OR: Writer's Notebook Press, Pulphouse Pub, 1991).

17. Films that have come to be associated with cyberpunk include *Blade Runner, Johnny Mnemonic, Strange Days,* and *The Matrix.*

18. Jussi Parikka, "Viral Noise and the (Dis)Order of the Digital Culture," *M/C Journal* 7 no. 6 (January 2005), http://journal.media-culture.org.au/0501/05-parikka.php, 1.

19. Daniel Suarez, *Daemon* (New York: Signet, 2010), front matter and 468.

20. Ibid., 30.

21. This fear of the Internet as a material threat appears in a number of science fiction texts, including Frederic Brown's 1954 short story "Answer," Neal Stephenson's 1992 novel *Snow Crash,* and Graham Watkins's 1995 novel *Virus.*

22. For a history of viral metaphors and the role of the virus as a threat to the circulation of information, see, Priscilla Wald, *Contagious: Cultures, Carriers, and the Outbreak Narrative* (Durham, NC: Duke University Press, 2008). For a more specific history of the computer virus, see Jussi Parikka, *Digital Contagions: A Media Archaeology of Computer Viruses* (New York: Peter Lang, 2007).

23. Alexander Galloway, *Protocol: How Control Exists after Decentralization* (Cambridge, MA: MIT Press, 2004), 178–84.

24. Suarez, *Daemon,* 171.

25. Ibid., 453.

26. For a discussion of "cyber gothic" fiction see Alan Lloyd-Smith, *American Gothic Fiction: An Introduction* (New York: Continuum International Publishing, 2004), 29.

27. Suarez, *Daemon,* 150 and 152.

28. Ibid., 140 and 150.

29. Ibid., 612, 610, and 466.

30. Ibid., 414.

31. *Daemon*'s critique of networked corporatism finds precursors in second-generation cyberpunk novels, including Pat Cadigan's *Synners* and Marge Piercy's *He, She, and It,* as well as in science fiction collections such as Walter Mosley's *Futureland.*

32. Zittrain, *Future of the Internet,* 4.

33. Cory Doctorow, "Anda's Game," in *Overclocked,* 57–100 (Philadelphia: Running Press, 2007).

34. Cory Doctorow, *Little Brother* (New York: Tom Doherty Associates, 2008), 87.

35. This fictional system inspired a number of real-world programmers to create an actual version of ParanoidLinux. Though the final system never proved nearly as effective as its fictional counterpart, it is significant that a novel could inspire this form of real-world hacking.

36. Doctorow, *Little Brother,* 97–100.

37. Bruce Schneier, "Afterword," in Doctorow, *Little Brother,* 369.

38. Doctorow, *Little Brother,* 100 and 127. Emphasis in original.

39. Martin C. Libicki, *Cyberdeterrence and Cyberwar* (Santa Monica, CA: RAND, 2009), 164.

40. For more information about *World without Oil,* see www.worldwithoutoil.org/.

41. Large-scale amateur contributions to a serious computing problem were made possible, for example, through the *ESP Game* created by Luis von Ahn. This game addresses the difficult problem of creating metadata. Upon beginning the game, a new player is automatically paired with a random partner. The two partners, who are not allowed to communicate during the game play, are presented with fifteen images to which they have to assign descriptive labels. To win, the players have to come up with matching labels. One of the most innovative aspects of the ESP game is that it compiles the data generated during its numerous sessions to create

image searches that are more accurate than anything generated by a computer alone. By creating a fun game Ahn was able to interest a large enough group of players to gather useful data and improve online image searches.

42. Andrew Huang, "Afterword," in Doctorow, *Little Brother*, 371.

43. Zittrain, *Future of the Internet*, 173.

CYBERATTACK → ONE-WAY (w/ POTENTIAL FOR REVERSE INFECTION)

CHAPTER 3 *CYBER EXPLOITATION → TWO-WAY · ATTACK or EXPLOIT + SEND BACK INFO (STEALING)*

Operational Considerations in Cyber Attack and Cyber Exploitation

Herbert Lin

IN THE PREVIOUS CHAPTER, Dr. Jagoda reminds us that much of our thinking and vocabulary to describe cyberspace has its roots in fiction. Yet it is science that governs what is possible. This chapter focuses on the technical and operational dimensions of cyber attack and cyber exploitation. This includes various operational considerations associated with "weaponizing" the basic technologies of cyber attack, and these considerations are relevant both to the attacker, who uses various cyber attack methodologies of one's own choosing, and to the defender, who must cope with and respond to incoming cyber attacks launched by an attacker. In some cases, the attacked must launch counterattacks in order to defend itself. Next, the chapter addresses cyber exploitation and examines how its technical and operational dimensions differ from cyber attack. The chapter concludes with some lessons that can be learned from examining criminal use of cyber attack and cyber exploitation to inform national security thinking.

The Effects of Cyber Attack

Although the ultimate objective of using any kind of weapon is to deny the adversary the use of some capability, it is helpful to separate the effects of using a weapon into its direct and its indirect effects (if any). The direct effects of using a weapon are experienced by its immediate target. For example, the user of a kinetic weapon seeks to harm, damage, destroy, or disable a physical entity. The indirect effects of using that weapon are associated with the follow-on consequences, which may include harming, destroying, or disabling other physical entities—a runway may be damaged (the direct effect) so that aircraft cannot land or take off (the indirect effect). This distinction between direct and indirect effects (table 3.1) is particularly important in a cyber attack context.

TABLE 3.1

A Comparison of Key Characteristics of Cyber Attack vs. Kinetic Attack

Characteristics	Kinetic Attack	Cyber Attack
Effects of significance	Direct effects usually more important than indirect effects	Indirect effects usually more important than direct effects
Reversibility of direct effects	Low, entails reconstruction or rebuilding that may be time consuming	Often highly reversible on a short time scale
Acquisition cost for weapons	Largely in procurement	Largely in research and development
Availability of base technologies	Restricted in many cases	Widespread in most cases
Intelligence requirements for successful use	Usually smaller than those required for cyber attack	Usually high compared to kinetic weapons
Uncertainties in planning	Usually smaller than those involved in cyber attack	Usually high compared to kinetic weapons

By definition, cyber attacks are directed against computers or networks. The range of possible direct targets for a cyber attack is quite broad. Attackers can target computer chips embedded in other devices, such as weapons systems, communications devices, generators, medical equipment, automobiles, elevators, and so on. In general, these microprocessors provide some kind of real-time capability (e.g., a supervisory control and data acquisition system to control the operation of a generator or a floodgate, a chip in an automobile to control the flow of fuel, a chip in an automatic teller machine to control how cash is dispensed). Another target can be the computing systems controlling elements of the nation's critical infrastructure. For example, the electric power grid, the air traffic control system, the transportation infrastructure, the financial system, water purification and delivery and telephony rely on controllers. A cyber attack against the systems and networks that control and manage elements of a nation's transportation infrastructure could introduce chaos and disruption on a large scale that could drastically reduce the capability for transporting people or freight (including food and fuel). Finally, attackers can target dedicated computing devices such as desktop or mainframe computers in particular sensitive offices, or in critical operational software used in corporate or government computer centers. Dedicated computer systems might also include the routers that control and direct traffic on the Internet or on any other network.

Cyber attacks generally target one of several attributes of these components or devices—they seek to cause a loss of integrity, a loss of authenticity, or a loss of availability. An attack on integrity seeks to alter information (a computer program, data, or both) so that under some circumstances of operation, the computer system does not provide the accurate results or information that one would normally expect even though the system may continue to operate. A computer whose integrity has been compromised might be directed to destroy itself, which it could do if it were instructed to turn off its cooling fan. A loss of integrity also includes suborning a computer for use in a botnet. An attack on authenticity is one in which the source of a given piece of information is obscured or forged. A message whose authenticity has been compromised will fool a recipient into thinking it was properly sent by the asserted originator. An attack on availability may mean that e-mail sent by the targeted user does not go through, or the target user's computer simply freezes, or the response time for that computer becomes intolerably long (possibly leading to catastrophe if a physical process is being controlled by the system). Some analysts also discuss theft of services—an adversary may assume control of a computer to do his bidding. In such situations, the availability of the system has been increased, but for the wrong party (namely, the adversary).

These attributes may be targeted separately or together. For example, a given cyber attack may support the compromise of both integrity and availability, though not necessarily at the same time. In addition, the victim may not even be aware of compromises when they happen—a victim may not know that an attacker has altered a crucial database, or that he or she does not have access to a particular seldom-used emergency system. In some situations, integrity is the key target, as it might well be for a tactical network. A commander that doubts the trustworthiness of the network used to transmit and receive information will have many opportunities for second-guessing himself, and the network may become unreliable for tactical purposes. In other situations, authenticity is the key target—a cyber attack may take the form of a forged message purportedly from a unit's commanders to move from one location to another. And in still other situations, availability is the target—a cyber attack may be intended to turn off the sensors of a key observation asset for the few minutes that it takes for kinetic assets (e.g., airplanes) to fly past it.

The direct effects of some cyber attacks may be easily reversible. (Reversibility means that the target of the attack is restored to the operating condition that existed prior to the attack.) For example, turning off a denial-of-service attack provides instant reversibility with no effort on the part of the attacked computer or its operators. If backups are available, an attack on the integrity of the operating system may take just a few minutes of reloading the operating system. Many effects of kinetic attacks are not as easy to reverse.[1] Virtual disruption is not necessarily physical destruction.

A corollary to this point is that achieving enduring effects from a cyber attack may require repeated cyber strikes, much as repeated bombing of an airstrip might be necessary to keep it inactive. If so, keeping a targeted system down is likely to be much more difficult than bringing it down in the first place, not least because the administrators of the victimized system will be guided by the nature of the first attack to close off possible attack paths. Thus, the attacker may have to find different ways to attack if the goal is to create continued effects. That is, depending on the nature of the goals, the attacker must have operational plans that anticipate possible defense actions and identify appropriate responses should those defense actions occur.

As for the scope of an attack, one cyber attack might seek to affect a very narrow range of targets (such as the computer belonging to a specific important individual or a specific industrial control system made by a particular vendor and used in nuclear plants[2]) and another cyber attack may affect a very broad range of targets.[3] In the latter case, it is helpful to the attacker if the same tactics used to compromise one host can be extended to compromise one thousand hosts—as is usually the case when the attacked systems are part of the same system monoculture all running the same targeted software (such as the same operating system). The best case (from an attacker's standpoint) is when the same vulnerability exists at all levels within large interconnected systems.[4]

Cyber attacks can also proceed in multiple phases that last over a relatively long period of time (months or years). For example, in a distributed denial-of-service (DDOS) attack, an attacker must first take control of thousands of computers by installing their malicious software on them and causing the resulting bots to respond in a coordinated way to the attacker's command and control system. The same bots that are used for DDOS are also used for recruiting new bots through direct attack, sending copies of the malware to addressees in the victimized computer's address book, and so on. The less visible or "noisy" the activity, the longer the multiphase attack can last before being detected and mitigated.

In other cases, attack staging can be used to discover and take advantage of implicit business trust relationships between sites. An attacker can start with the most basic information that can be obtained about a company through open sources (e.g., press releases, organizational descriptions, phone directories, and other data made public through websites and news stories.) Then the attacker uses this information to perform social engineering attacks, a form of pretexting designed to trick users into giving out their passwords so she can gain access to computers inside an organization's network. Once in control of internal hosts, the attacker effectively has insider access and can leverage that access to do more sensitive intelligence gathering on the target. The attacker can learn business relationships, details about active projects and schedules, and anything necessary to fool anyone in the company into opening email attachments or performing other acts that result in compromise of computer systems. (This is basic intelligence collection and analysis.) Control of internal hosts can also be used to direct attacks against other internal hosts.

Indirect Effects

Although the direct effects of a cyber attack relate to computers, networks, or the information processed or transmitted therein, cyber attacks are often launched to obtain some other indirect effect that can be equally or more important. For example, to the US commander in the field, an adversary's air defense radar is more important than the computer that controls it. Similarly, an adversary's computer-controlled generator is probably of greater interest to the commander than the computer itself.[5] Further, indirect effects—which are often the primary goal of a cyber attack—are generally not reversible. For example, an attack on the generator's controller can cause the generator to overheat and destroy itself.

Computers are also integral parts of command-and-control networks. In this case, the indirect effect sought by compromising such a computer is to prevent or delay the transmission of important messages, or to alter the contents of such messages. Cyber attacks are particularly well suited for attacks on the psychology of adversary decision makers who rely on the affected computers, and in this case such effects can be regarded as indirect effects. For example, a single database that is found to be deliberately corrupted, even when controls are in place to prevent such corruption, may call into question the integrity of all of the databases in a system. It is true that all production databases have some errors in them, and savvy users ought to adjust for the possibility that their data may be incorrect. But in practice, they often do not. Being made conscious of the fact that a database may have been compromised has definite psychological effects on a user. Thus, the victim may face a choice of working with data that may—or may not—have been corrupted and suffering all of the confidence-eroding consequences of working in such an environment, or expending enormous amounts of effort to ensure that other databases have not been corrupted or compromised.[6] A second example might be the clandestine alteration of critical data that causes decision makers to make poor decisions.

Lastly, computers are often connected in and share resources on a network. Thus, under many circumstances, an indirect attack can be as successful as a direct attack, given the resources necessary to work through the entire set of log-in relationships between systems. For example, one can attempt to get access to another person's account by attacking that target's laptop or desktop system. This may fail, because the target may secure their personal computers very well. But the target may depend on someone else for system administration of their mail spool and home directory on a shared server. The attacker can thus go after a colleague's, a fellow employee's, or their service provider's computer and compromise it, then use that access to go after an administrator's password on the file server holding the target's account.

Possible Objectives of Cyber Attack

A cyber attack can have a variety of different objectives. An attacker may seek to destroy a network or a system connected to it. Destruction of a network or of connected systems may be difficult if "destruction" means the physical destruction of the relevant hardware, but is much easier if "destruction" simply means destroying the data stored within or eliminating the application or operating systems programs that run on that hardware. For example, an attacker might seek to delete and erase permanently all data files or to reformat and wipe clean all hard disks that it can find. Moreover, destruction of a network also has negative consequences for anything connected to it—power-generation facilities controlled by a network are likely to be adversely affected by a disabled network.

Deception is another important objective, which can sometimes be accomplished by generating bogus traffic. For example, an attacker might wish to masquerade as the adversary's national command authority or as another senior official (or agency) and issue phony orders or pass faked intelligence information. Such impersonation (even under a made-up identity) might well be successful in a large organization in which people routinely communicate with others that they do not know personally. Alternatively, the attacker might pretend to be a nonexistent agency within the adversary's government and generate traffic to the outside world that looks authentic. An impersonation objective can be achieved by an attacker taking over the operation of a trusted machine belonging to the agency or entity of interest (e.g., the national command authority) or by obtaining the relevant keys that underlie their authentication and encryption mechanisms and setting up a new node on the network that appears to be legitimate because it exhibits knowledge of those keys.

An attacker can also clandestinely alter data stored on the network to impact future planning. For example, the logistics deployment plan for an adversary's armed forces may be driven by a set of database entries that describe the appropriate arrival sequence of various items (food, fuel, vehicles, and so on). A planner relying on a corrupted database may well find that deployed forces have too much of certain items and not enough of others. The planner's confidence in the integrity of the database may also be affected.

An attacker might try to degrade the quality of service available to network users by flooding communications channels with large amounts of bogus traffic such as spam attacks, which can render e-mail ineffective. Denial-of-service attacks might be directed at key financial institutions, for example, and greatly degrade their ability to handle consumer financial transactions. A denial-of-service attack on the wireless network (e.g., a jamming attack) used to control a factory's operations might well shut it down. Taking over a telecommunications exchange might give an attacker the ability to overwhelm an adversary's ministry of defense with bogus phone calls and make it impossible for its employees to use its telephones to do any work. A denial-of-service attack might be used to prevent an adversary from using a communications system, and thereby force him to use a less secure method for communications.

Finally, cyber attacks can be carried out in conjunction with kinetic attacks; indeed, the effect of a cyber attack may be maximized if used in such a manner. Nikolas Gvosdev discusses this in chapter 11 of this volume in the context of Russia's 2008 invasion of Georgia. But the ability to cause confusion in the midst of a kinetic attack might well have greater operational significance for the attacker.

Target Identification

As with any other weapon, a cyber attack must be directed at specific computers and networks. Even if a nation-state has been identified as being subject to cyber attack, how can the specific computers or networks of interest be identified in a useful manner? In some instances, the target identification process is a manual, intelligence-based effort. From a high-level description of the targets of interest (e.g., the vice president's laptop, the supervisory control and data acquisition [SCADA] systems controlling the electrical generation facility that powers the air defense radar complex, or the transaction processing systems of a bank), a route to those specific targets must be found. For example, a target system with an Internet presence likely has an Internet Protocol (IP) address. Knowledge of the system's IP address provides an initial starting point for attempting to gain entry to the appropriate component of the target system.

The process of target identification may be more complicated in some ways if the targets of interest are "in the cloud." Cloud computing refers to a style of computing in which shareable computing resources (e.g., processing power, data storage) are placed in some physical location and made accessible to a wide variety of users who access those resources remotely. Any given user of cloud computing may not even know the physical location of his data, for example—a fact that may make it more difficult for an attacker to launch certain kinds of close-access attacks against it.

Sometimes a computer is connected to the Internet indirectly. For example, although it is common for SCADA systems to be putatively "air-gapped" from the Internet, utility companies often connect SCADA systems to networks intended for administrative use so that their business units can have direct real-time access to the data provided by SCADA systems to improve efficiency.[7] Compromising a user of the administrative network may enable an attacker to gain access to these SCADA systems, and intelligence collection efforts might thus focus on such users.

Target identification information can come from a mix of sources, including open source collection, automated probes that yield network topology, and manual exploration of possible targets. Manual target identification is slow but is arguably more accurate than automated target identification. Automated target selection is based on various methods of mapping and filtering IP addresses and domain name system (DNS) names, for example through programmed pattern matching, network mapping, or querying databases (either public ones, or ones accessible though close-access attacks.) The scope of automated attack identification can be limited by the use of network address filtering.

Automated target selection within an internal network is more complicated. An internal network may have one gateway to the Internet, but within the perimeter of the internal network may be any arrangement of internal addresses. Once an attacker gains access to a host inside the network, the internal DNS zone tables can be accessed and decoded to identify appropriate targets. This will not always be possible, but in many cases even internal network ranges can be determined with minimal effort by the attacker. It is also possible to perform simple tests, such as attempting to access controlled websites to test the ability to make outbound (i.e., through the firewall) connections and thus to determine network membership through the resulting internal/external address mappings.[8] If the attacker has sufficient lead time, a "low and slow" network probe can—without arousing suspicion—generally yield connectivity information that is adequate for many attack purposes.

Intelligence Requirements and Preparation

Attacks on the confidentiality, integrity, authenticity, and availability attributes require taking advantage of some vulnerability in the targeted system. However, an attacker seeking to exploit a given vulnerability must know—in advance of the attack—whether the targeted system is in fact vulnerable to any particular attack method of choice. Indeed, the success of a cyber attack (to include both achieving the intended goal and minimizing collateral damage) often depends on many details about the actual configuration of the targeted computers and networks.

Generally, a scarcity of intelligence regarding possible targets means that any cyber attack launched against them can only be "broad-spectrum" and relatively indiscriminate or blunt. (Such an attack might be analogous to the Allied strategic bombing attacks of World War II that targeted national infrastructure on the grounds that the infrastructure supported the war effort of the Axis.) Substantial amounts of intelligence information about targets (and paths to those targets) are required if the attack is intended as a very precise one directed at a particular system or if the attack is to be a close-access attack.[9] Conversely, a lack of such information will result in large uncertainties about the direct and indirect effects of a cyber attack and will make it difficult for commanders to make good estimates of likely collateral damage.

Information collection for cyber-attack planning differs from traditional collection for kinetic operations in that it may require greater lead time and may have expanded collection, production, and dissemination requirements because specific sources and methods may need to be positioned and employed over time to collect the necessary information and conduct necessary analyses.[10] A partial list of intelligence items that may be required to conduct targeted cyber attacks includes:

◊ The target's platform, such as the specific processor model.
◊ The platform's operating system, down to the level of the specific version and even the history of security patches applied to the operating system.
◊ The IP addresses of Internet-connected computers.
◊ The specific versions of systems administrator tools used.
◊ The security configuration of the operating system, e.g., whether certain services are turned on or off, or what antivirus programs are running.
◊ The physical configuration of the hardware involved, e.g., what peripherals or computers are physically attached.
◊ The specific operators of the systems in question, and others who may have physical access to the rooms in which the systems are kept.
◊ The name of the shipping company that delivers computer components to the facility.
◊ The telephone numbers of the help desk for the system in question.

In some cases, such information may be available from public sources, and these sources often have a wealth of useful information. In other cases the required information may not be classified but may be available only through nonofficial sources, such as in the nonshredded office trash. In still other cases, the relevant information may be available through the traditional techniques of human agents infiltrating an organization or interviewing people familiar with the organization. Finally, automated means may be used to obtain necessary intelligence information—an example is the use of automated probes that seek to determine if a system has ports that are open, accessible, and available for use.

A cyber attacker will benefit from knowledge about the adversary's ability to respond in a coordinated manner to a widespread attack. At the low end of this continuum, the adversary is only minimally capable of responding to attacks even on isolated or single systems, and has no capability at all to take coordinated action against attacks on multiple systems. At the high end of this continuum, the adversary can integrate information relating to attacks on all of the systems under its jurisdiction, develop a relatively high degree of situational awareness, and respond in an active and coordinated manner.[11]

Ultimately, the operational commander must make an assessment about whether the information available is adequate to support the execution of a cyber attack. Such assessments are necessarily informed by judgments about risk, which decreases as more information is available. Unfortunately, there is no objective, quantitative way to measure the adequacy of the information available, and no way to quantitatively ascertain the increase in risk as the result of less information being available. In practice, the best way to adapt to a lack of detailed information may be to ensure the availability of skilled personnel who can modify an attack as it unfolds in response to unanticipated conditions.

Effects Prediction and Damage Assessment

In the kinetic world, weapons (or, more precisely, munitions) are aimed against targets. Predicting the effect of a weapon on a given target is obviously important to operational planners, who must decide the most appropriate weapons-to-target matching. In general, characteristics of the weapon such as explosive yield, fusing, and likely miss distances are matched against characteristics of the target (such as target hardness, size, and shape), and its surrounding environment (e.g., terrain and weather).

Damage assessment for physical targets is conceptually straightforward—one can generally know the results of a strike by visual reconnaissance, although a task that is straightforward in principle may be complicated by on-the-ground details or adversary deception. For example, the weather may make it impossible to obtain visual imagery of the target site, or the adversary may be able to take advantage of the delay between weapons impact and damage assessment to create a false impression of the damage caused.

There are similar needs for understanding the effect of cyber weapons and assessing damage caused by cyber weapons. But munitions effects and damage assessment are complex and difficult challenges because the effectiveness of cyber weapons is a strong function of the intelligence available.

In the kinetic world, munitions effects can often be calculated based on computational models that are based on physics-based algorithms. That is, the fundamental physics of explosives technology and of most targets is well known, so kinetic effects on a given target can be calculated with acceptable confidence. Thus, many of the uncertainties in kinetic targeting can be theoretically calculated and empirically validated (e.g., at weapons-effects test ranges), and the remaining uncertainties relate to matters such as target selection and collocation of other entities with the intended target.

But there is no comparable formalism for understanding the effects of cyber weapons. The smallest change in the configuration or interconnections of a computer system or network can result in completely different system behavior, and the direct effects of a cyber attack on a given system may be driven by the behavior and actions of the human system operator and the specific nature of that system as well as the intrinsic characteristics of the cyber weapon involved. Furthermore, these relatively small, obscure, or hidden characteristics are often important in cyber targeting, and information about these things is difficult to obtain through remote intelligence collection methods such as photoreconnaissance, which means that substantial amounts of relevant information may not be available to the attacker.

An example of an error causing unexpected behavior in a cyber attack is the Sapphire/Slammer worm of January 2003. Although the Sapphire worm was the fastest computer worm in history (infecting more than 90 percent of vulnerable hosts within ten minutes), a defective random-number generator significantly reduced its rate of spread.[12] (The worm targeted IP addresses chosen at random, and the random number generator produced numbers that were improperly restricted in range.) In a military attack context, a cyber attack that manifested its effects more slowly than anticipated might be problematic.

An additional complication to the prediction problem is the possibility of cascading effects that go further than expected. For example, in analyzing the possible effects of a cyber attack, there may be no good analog to the notion of a lethal radius within which any target will be destroyed. When computer systems are interconnected, damage to a computer at the NATO Defense College in Italy can propagate to a computer at the US Air Force Rome Laboratory in New York—and whether such a propagation occurs depends on a detail as small as the setting on a single switch, or the precise properties of every device connected at each end of the link, or the software characteristics of the link itself.

Engineers often turn to test ranges to better understand weapons effects, especially in those instances in which a good theoretical understanding is not available. A weapons test range provides a venue for testing weapons empirically—sending them against real or simulated targets and observing and measuring their effects. Such information, suitably refined, is then made available to users to assist them in the weapons selection process.

A certain kind of cyber weapon may need to be tested against different versions of operating systems (and even against different builds of the same operating system), different configurations of the same operating system, and even against different operators of that system. To test for cascading effects, multiple computers must be interconnected. Thus, realistic test ranges for cyber weapons are inevitably complex. It is also quite difficult to configure a cyber test range so that a simulation will provide high confidence that a given cyber attack will be successful.

Some analysts take from these comments that the effects of a cyber attack are impossible to predict. As a blanket statement, this claim is far overstated. It is true that the launch of a worm or virus may go on to infect millions of susceptible computers, and some of the infected machines might happen to control an electric power grid or a hospital information system. The media often report such events as if they were a surprise—and it may well have been a surprise that these particular machines were infected. Nevertheless, after-the-fact analysis of such cyber attacks sometimes leads to the conclusion that the party launching the attack could have predicted the number of susceptible machines fairly accurately.[13]

More customized cyber attacks are quite possible, depending on the goal of the attacker. A software agent introduced into a target machine could, in principle, search its environment and remain resident only if that search found certain characteristics (e.g., if the machine had more than ten files containing the phrases "nuclear weapon" and "Washington DC" and had an IP address in a particular range, which might translate into the nation in which the machine was located). Nevertheless, high degrees of customization may require large amounts of information on machine-identifiable characteristics of appropriate targets. Such information may be obtained through traditional intelligence collection methods.

An issue for uncustomized cyber attacks is "blowback," which refers to a bad consequence returning to the instigator of a particular action. In the cyber attack context, blowback may refer to direct damage caused to one's own computers and networks as the result of a cyber attack that one has launched. For example, if the United States launched a cyber attack against an adversary using a rapidly multiplying but uncustomized worm over the Internet, the worm might return to affect US computers and networks. It might also refer to indirect damage—a large-scale US cyber attack against a major trading partner's economic infrastructure might have effects that could harm the US economy as well.

Another class of weapons effects might be termed "strategic." Tactical effects of using a weapon manifest themselves immediately and generally involve destruction, disabling, or damage of a target—tactical attacks seek an immediate effect on an adversary and its military forces. By contrast, strategic effects may be less tangible and may emerge over longer periods of time—strategic attacks are directed at adversary targets with the intent or purpose of reducing an adversary's war-making capacity or will to make war against the United States or its allies, and are intended to have a long-range rather than an immediate effect on an adversary. Strategic targets include but are not limited to key manufacturing systems, sources of raw material, critical material, stockpiles, power systems, transportation systems, communication facilities, and other such systems.[14]

As for assessing damage caused by a cyber attack, note first that the damage due to a cyber attack is usually invisible to the human eye. To ascertain the effects of a computer network attack over the Internet, an attacker might be able to use Internet tools such as ping and traceroute. These tools are commonly available, and they test the routing from the sending machine to the target machine.[15] More generally, a cyber attack is by definition intended to impair the operation of a targeted computer or network. But from a distance, it can be very difficult to distinguish between the successful outcome of a cyber attack and a faked outcome. For example, an attack may be intended to disrupt the operation of a specific computer. But the attacker is faced with distinguishing between two very different scenarios. The first is that the attack was successful and thus that the targeted computer was disabled; the second is that the attack was unsuccessful and also was discovered, and that the adversary has turned off the computer deliberately—and can turn it on again at a moment's notice.

How might this problem be avoided? Where ping and traceroute as tools for damage assessment depend on the association of a damaged machine with a successful cyber attack, an alternative approach might call for the use of in-place sensors that can report on the effects of a cyber attack. Prior to a cyber attack intended to damage a target machine, the attacker plants sensors of its own on the target machine. These sensors respond to inquiries from the attacker and are programmed to report to the attacker periodically. These sensors could also be implanted at the same time that attack capabilities are installed on the target machine. Such sensors could report on the outcomes of certain kinds of cyber attacks and could in some situations reduce the uncertainty of damage assessment.

It may also be possible to use noncyber means for damage assessment of a cyber attack. For example, if a cyber attack is intended to cause a large-scale power outage in a city, its success or failure may be observable by an individual in that city reporting back to the attackers via satellite phone or by an indigenous news network. But if the intent of the cyber attack is to turn off the power to a specific radar installation in the nation's air defense network at a specific time, it will be difficult to distinguish between a successful attack and a smart and wily defender who has detected the attack and shut the power down himself to deceive the attacker and can turn it on when needed.

The bottom line on damage assessment is that the state of the art in damage assessment techniques for cyber attacks is still primitive in comparison to similar techniques for kinetic attacks. Cyber attackers must therefore account for larger amounts of uncertainty in their operational planning than their physical-world counterparts—and thus may be inhibited from relying solely or primarily on cyber attack for important missions.

Complexity, Information Requirements, and Uncertainty

Planning for cyber attack often involves a much larger range of choices and options than planning for most traditional military operations. For example, cyber-attack planners must account for a wide range of time and space dimensions. The relevant time scales can range from tenths of a second (a cyber attack may interfere with the timing of a real-time process control system) to years (a cyber attack may seek to implant "sleeper" capabilities in an adversary network that might be activated years later.) And the systems targeted may be dispersed around the globe or concentrated in a facility next door. All of these factors increase the complexity of planning a cyber attack.

One of the most difficult-to-handle aspects of a cyber attack is that in contrast to a kinetic attack that is almost always intended to destroy a physical target, the desired effects of a cyber attack are almost always indirect, which means that what are normally secondary effects are in fact of central importance. In general, the planner must develop chains of causality—do x, and y happens, which causes z to happen, which in turn causes a to happen. Also, many of the intervening events between initial cause and ultimate effect are human reactions (e.g., in response to an attack that does x, the network administrator will likely respond in way y, which means that z—which may be preplanned—must take response y into account). Moreover, the links in the causal chain may not all be of similar character; they may involve computer actions and results, or human perceptions and decisions, all of which combine into some outcome.

The result is often a complex execution plan, and complex execution plans have many ways to go wrong—the longer a causal chain, the more uncertain its ultimate outcomes and conclusions. This is not simply a matter of unintended consequences of a cyber attack, though that is certainly a concern. The point also relates to the implications of incomplete or overlooked intelligence. For example, it may be that a cyber attack is entirely successful in disabling the computer controlling an air-defense radar, but also that, as it turns out, there is a backup computer in place that was not mentioned in the intelligence reports used to plan the attack. Or a connection between two systems that is usually in place is disconnected on the day of the attack because of a maintenance schedule that was changed last week, and thus was unknown to the attack planners—resulting in the inability of the attacker to destroy the backup computer.

One way of coping with uncertainty in this context is to obtain feedback on intermediate results achieved through monitoring the execution of the initial plan and then applying "midcourse corrections" if and when necessary. The need to apply midcourse corrections means that contingency plans must be developed, often in advance if midcourse corrections need to be applied rapidly. The need to develop contingency plans in advance adds to the complexity of the planning process.

In practice, execution monitoring may be difficult to undertake. The attacker needs to know outcomes of various intermediate steps in the causal chain as well as what responses the victim has made at various stages of the attack so that he may take appropriate compensating action. The difficulties of collecting such information are at least as hard as those of undertaking damage assessment for the ultimate outcome.

Coordination of Cyber-Attack Activities with
Other Institutional Entities

Within the US government, decision makers have essentially two options in contemplating what to do about an adversary computer or network—render it unavailable for serving adversary purposes or exploit it to gather useful information. In many cases these two options are mutually exclusive—destroying it makes it impossible to exploit it. In some cases, destroying it may also reveal to the adversary some vulnerability or access path previously unknown to him, and thus compromise friendly sources and methods for intelligence gathering. Thus, it is easy to imagine that a lack of interagency coordination might lead to conflicts between those wanting to exploit an adversary network and those wanting to shut it down.

Policy conflicts over such matters are not new with the advent of cyber attack, but in some ways the trade-offs may be easier to manage. For example, because a given instrument for cyber exploitation can be designed with cyber-attack capabilities, the transition between exploitation and attack may be operationally simpler. Also, a cyber attack may be designed to corrupt or degrade a system slowly—and exploitation is possible as long as the adversary does not notice the corruption.

Coordination issues also arise with technical deconfliction as well—different agencies might conduct cyber operations (either cyber attack or cyber exploitation) that might interfere with each other). It may be necessary under some circumstances to consult with the congressional leadership or the relevant congressional committees.

As for the private sector, some degree of coordination with the private sector would not be surprising in the planning and execution of certain kinds of cyber attack because so much IT is designed, built, deployed, and operated privately. For example, a cyber attack may travel over the Internet to an adversary computer, and spillover effects (such as reductions in available bandwidth) may occur that affect systems in the private sector. Or a US cyber attack may prompt an adversary counterattack against US systems and networks in the private sector. Or a US cyber attack against an adversary transmitted through a commercial Internet service provider might be detected (and perhaps suppressed) by that provider, believing it to be the cyber attack of a criminal or acting on the protest of the targeted network. Such possibilities might suggest that the defensive posture of US private-sector systems and networks should be strengthened in anticipation of a US cyber attack (or at least that relevant commercial parties such as Internet service providers be notified), but this notion raises difficult questions about maintaining operational security for the US attack.

Issues of agency coordination and coordination with the private sector also arise with allied nations as well, since allied nations may also have government agencies with interests in cyber-attack activities and private-sector entities whose defensive postures might be strengthened. Another issue is the fact that a cyber attack by the United States might have to be transmitted over facilities controlled by third countries, and just as some nations would deny the United States military overflight rights, they may also seek to deny the United States the rights to transmit attack traffic through their facilities. Routing traffic to avoid certain countries is sometimes possible but may require a significant amount of preplanning and prepositioning of assets depending on the nature of the attack to be launched.

Technical and Operational Considerations for Cyber Exploitation

The cyber exploitation mission is different from the cyber attack mission in its objectives and in the legal constructs surrounding it. Nevertheless, much of the technology underlying cyber exploitation is similar to that of a cyber attack. A successful cyber attack requires a vulnerability, access to that vulnerability, and an executable payload. A cyber exploitation requires the same three things—and the only difference is in the payload to be executed. Payload is what distinguishes a cyber exploitation from a cyber attack. Whereas the attacker might destroy the papers inside a locked file cabinet once he gains access to it, the exploiter might copy them and take them away with him. In the cyber context, the cyber exploiter will seek to compromise the confidentiality of protected information afforded by a computer system or network. Table 3.2 summarizes possible objectives of cyber exploitation.

The ends and ways in table 3.2 suggest certain technical desiderata for cyber exploitations. For instance, it is highly desirable for a cyber exploitation to have a signature that is difficult for its target to detect since the cyber exploitation operation may involve many separate actions spread out over a long period of time in which only small things happen with each action. One reason is that if the targeted party does not know that its secret information has been revealed, it is less likely to take countermeasures to negate the compromise. A second reason is that the exploiter would like to use one penetration of an adversary's computer or network to result in multiple exfiltrations of intelligence information over the course of the entire operation. That is, the intelligence collectors need to be able to maintain a clandestine presence on the adversary computer or network despite the fact that information exfiltrations provide the adversary with opportunities to discover that presence.

Also, an individual payload can have multiple functions simultaneously—one for cyber attack and one for cyber exploitation—and which function is activated at any given time will depend on the necessary command and control arrangements. For example, a payload delivered to an adversary command-and-control network may be designed to exfiltrate information during the initial stages of a conflict and then to degrade service on the network when it receives a command to do so.

In addition, the relationship between technologies for cyber exploitation and cyber attack is strong enough that the cost of equipping a tool for the former with the capability for the latter is likely to be low—so low that in many cases acquisition managers could find it sensible as a matter of routine practice to equip a cyber

TABLE 3.2
Possible Ends and Ways of Cyber Exploitation

Ends	Ways
Exploit information available on a network	Conduct traditional espionage by searching files and passing traffic for keywords such as "nuclear" or "plutonium," and copy and forward to the attacker's intelligence services any messages containing such words for further analysis
Observe a network's topology and traffic	Identify active hosts, to determine the operating system or service versions, to map the network and make inferences about important and less important nodes on it by performing traffic analysis
Obtain technical information from a company's network	Collect economic intelligence to benefit a domestic competitor of that company
Steal authentication credentials for later use	Gain access to compromised accounts, followed by escalation of privileges to locate and exfiltrate files, or to gain more complete control over the host

exploitation tool with attack capabilities (or provide it with the ability to be modified on the fly in actual use to have such capabilities).[16]

Approaches for Cyber Exploitation

As is true for cyber attack, cyber exploitation can be accomplished through both remote-access and close-access methodologies. A hypothetical example of cyber exploitation based on remote access might involve pharming against an unprotected DNS server, such as the one resident in wireless routers.[17] Because wireless routers at home tend to be less well protected than institutional routers, they are easier to compromise. Successful pharming would mean that web traffic originating at the home of the targeted individual (who might be a senior official in an adversary's political leadership) could be redirected to websites controlled by the exploiter. With access to the target's home computer thus provided, vulnerabilities in that computer could be used to insert a payload that would exfiltrate the contents of the individual's hard disk, possibly providing the exploiter with information useful for blackmailing the target.

A hypothetical example of cyber exploitation based on close access might involve intercepting desktop computers in their original shipping cartons while they are awaiting delivery to the victim and substituting for the original video card a modified one that performs all of the original functions and also monitors the data being displayed for subsequent transmission to the exploiter. There is historical precedent for such approaches. One episode is the 1984 US discovery of Soviet listening devices in the Moscow embassy's typewriters—these devices captured all keystrokes and transmitted them to a nearby listening post.[18] A second reported episode involves the installation of cameras installed inside Xerox copiers in Soviet embassies in the 1960s.[19] A third episode, still not fully understood, is the 2004–5 phone-tapping affair in Greece.[20]

Some Operational Considerations for Cyber Exploitation

Because the cyber offensive actions needed to carry out a cyber exploitation are so similar to those needed for cyber attack, they may be difficult to distinguish in an operational context. This fundamental ambiguity—absent with kinetic, nuclear, biological, and chemical weapons—has two consequences. First, the targeted party may not be able to distinguish between a cyber exploitation and a cyber attack. Second, the attacker must have a clear understanding of the different legal authorities.[21] The reason is that cyber exploitation and cyber attack make use of the same kinds of access paths to their targets, and take advantage of the same vulnerabilities to deliver their payloads. In the event that the adversary detects intelligence-gathering attempts, there is no way at all to determine its ultimate intent.

Rules of engagement for cyber exploitation specify what adversary systems or networks may be probed or penetrated to obtain information. A particularly interesting question arises when a possible target of opportunity becomes known in the course of an ongoing cyber exploitation. For example, in the course of exploring one adversary's network (Network A), the exploiter may come across a gateway to another, previously unknown network (Network B). Depending on the nature of Network B, the rules of engagement specified for Network A may be entirely inadequate (as might be the case if Network A were a military command-and-control network and Network B were a network of the adversary's national command authority). Rules of engagement for cyber exploitation must provide guidance in such situations.

In at least one way, command and control for cyber exploitation is more complex than for cyber attack because of the mandatory requirement of report-back—a cyber exploitation that does not return information to its controller is useless. By contrast, it may be desirable for a cyber-attack agent or weapon to report to its controller on the outcome of any given attack event, but its primary mission can still be accomplished even if it is unable to do so. Report-back also introduces another opportunity for the adversary to discover the presence of an exploiting payload, and thus the exploiter must be very careful in how report-back is arranged.

Conclusion: Assessing Cyber Exploitation and Cyber Attacks

The cyber exploitation analog to damage assessment for cyber attack might be termed "effectiveness assessment." If a cyber exploitation does not report back to its controller, it has failed. But even if it does report back, it may not have succeeded. For cyber exploitation, the danger is that it has been discovered, and somehow the adversary has provided false or misleading information that is then reported back. Alternatively, the adversary may have compromised the report-back channel itself and inserted its own message that is mistaken for an authentic report-back message. (In a worst-case scenario, the adversary may use the report-back channel as a vehicle for conducting its own cyber attack or cyber exploitation against the controller.) These scenarios for misdirection are not unique to cyber exploitation, of course—they are possible in ordinary espionage attempts as well. But because it is likely to be difficult for an automated agent to distinguish between being present on a "real" target versus being present on a "decoy" target, concerns about misdirection in a cyber exploitation context are all too real.

Notes

Much of the discussion in this section is based on chapter 2 of the National Research Council's *Technology, Policy, Law, and Ethics Regarding US Acquisition and Use of Cyberattack Capabilities* (Washington, DC: National Academies Press, 2009).

1. For example, the time scales involved may be very different. Restoring the capability of an attacked computer that controls a power distribution system is likely to be less costly or time-consuming compared to rebuilding a power plant damaged by kinetic weapons. (A cyber attack on a computer controlling a power distribution system may even be intended to give the attacker physical control over the system but not to damage it, enabling him to control production and distribution as though he were authorized to do so.)

2. For an example of the latter, see Paul Kerr, John Rollins, and Catherine A. Theohary, "The Stuxnet Computer Worm: Harbinger of an Emerging Warfare Capability" (Washington, DC: Congressional Research Service), December 9, 2010, www.fas.org/sgp/crs/natsec/R41524.pdf.

3. For example, the initial release of the Conficker worm spread rapidly over the Internet to machines running Windows 2000 and Windows XP, infecting more than a million machines in a month. The effect of the Conficker worm on an individual system is to make the system available for use by an unauthorized botnet. See Phillip Porras, Hassan Saidi, and Vinod Swaran, "An Analysis of Conficker's Logic and Rendezvous Points," SRI International Technical Report, March 19, 2009, http://mtc.sri.com/Conficker.

4. See, for example, Daniel E. Geer, "Measuring Security," 2006, 170–78, http://geer.tinho.net/measuringsecurity.tutorialv2.pdf.

5. For example, a test staged by researchers at the Department of Energy's Idaho National Laboratories used a cyber attack to cause a generator to self-destruct. Known as Aurora, the cyber attack was used to change the operating cycle of the generator, sending it out of control.

See Jeanne Meserve, "Staged Cyber Attack Reveals Vulnerability in Power Grid," CNN, September 26, 2007, www.cnn.com/2007/US/09/26/power.at.risk/index.html.

6. For example, in 1982 the United States was allegedly able to "spike" technology that was subsequently stolen by the Soviet Union. Above and beyond the immediate effects of its catastrophic failure in a Soviet pipeline, Thomas Reed writes that "in time the Soviets came to understand that they had been stealing bogus technology, but now what were they to do? By implication, every cell of the Soviet leviathan might be infected. They had no way of knowing which equipment was sound, which was bogus. All was suspect, which was the intended endgame for the entire operation." See Thomas C. Reed, *At the Abyss: An Insider's History of the Cold War* (New York: Ballantine Books, 2004).

7. For example, in January 2003 the Slammer worm downed one utility's critical SCADA network after moving from a corporate network through a remote computer to a virtual private network connection to the control center local area network. See North American Electric Reliability Council, "SQL Slammer Worm Lessons Learned for Consideration by the Electricity Sector," June 20, 2003, www.esisac.com/publicdocs/SQL_Slammer_2003.pdf.

8. An illustration is the use of a query to the DNS as a covert channel.

9. To some extent similar considerations apply to the intelligence required to support precise kinetic weaponry. If a kinetic weapon is intended to be used, and is capable of being used, in a precise manner, more information about the target and its environment will be necessary than if the weapon is blunt and imprecise in its effects.

10. Joint Chiefs of Staff, *Information Operations*, Joint Publication 3-13, US Department of Defense, Washington, DC, February 2006, www.fas.org/irp/doddir/dod/jp3_13.pdf.

11. Even when the capacity and resources exist to be able to operate at a high response level, there are many reasons why system owners may not respond in a cooperative manner to a widespread computer attack. They may not be capable of immediately responding, may lack adequate resources, may be unable to physically attend to the compromised host, or may even speak a different language than the person reporting the incident. There may be active complicity within the organization or a willful disregard of reports that allow the attacker to continue unabated.

12. David Moore, Vern Paxson, Stefan Savage, Colleen Shannon, Stuart Staniford, and Nicholas Weaver, "The Spread of the Sapphire/Slammer Worm," undated publication, www.caida.org/publications/papers/2003/sapphire/sapphire.html.

13. These comments presume that the attack software is written correctly as the attacker intended—mistakes in the worm or virus may indeed lead to unintended effects. A classic example of a worm written with unintended consequences is the Morris worm. See Brendan P. Kehoe, "Zen and the Art of the Internet," www.cs.indiana.edu/docproject/zen/zen-1.0_10.html#SEC91.

14. See DOD definitions for "strategic operations" and "strategic air warfare," in Joint Chiefs of Staff, *Dictionary of Military and Associated Terms*, Joint Publication 1-02, Department of Defense, Washington DC, April 12, 2001 (as amended through October 17, 2008), http://ra.defense.gov/documents/rtm/jp1_02.pdf.

15. Ping is intended to measure the round-trip time for a packet to travel between the sending machine and the target machine—and if the target machine is down, ping will return an error message saying it could not reach the target machine. Traceroute reports on the specific path that a given packet took from the sending machine to the target machine—and if the target machine is down, traceroute returns a similar error message. Thus, the receipt of

such an error message by the attacker may indicate that an attack on the target has been successful. But it also may mean that the operators of the target machine have turned off the features that respond to ping and traceroute to lower their vulnerability to criminal hackers or to mislead the damage assessor about the effectiveness of an attack.

16. If these cyber exploitation tools were to be used against US citizens (more precisely, US persons as defined in EO 12333 [Section 7.3.5]), legal or policy implications might arise if these tools were to have attack capabilities as well. Thus, the observation is most likely to be true for tools that are not intended for such use.

17. "Pharming" is the term given to an attack that seeks to redirect the traffic to a particular website to another bogus website.

18. Jay Peterzell, "The Moscow Bug Hunt," *Time*, July 10, 1989, www.time.com/time/maga zine/article/0,9171,958127-4,00.html.

19. Ron Laytner, "Xerox Helped Win the Cold War," *Edit International*, 2006, www.editinter national.com/read.php?id=47ddf19823b89.

20. In this incident, a number of mobile phones belonging mostly to members of the Greek government and top-ranking civil servants were found to have been tapped for an extended period. These individuals were subscribers to Vodafone Greece, the country's largest cellular service provider. The taps were implemented through a feature built into the company's switching infrastructure originally designed to allow law enforcement agencies to tap telephone calls carried on that infrastructure. However, those responsible for the taps assumed control of this feature to serve their own purposes and were able to conceal their activities for a long time. The sophistication of the programming required to undertake this compromise is considerable and has led to speculation that the affair was the result of an inside job. Vassilis Prevelakis and Diomidis Spinellis, "The Athens Affair," *IEEE Spectrum*, July 2007, www.spectrum .ieee.org/print/5280.

21. For example, Air Force Doctrine Document 2-5 (issued by the secretary of the air force, January 11, 2005) explicitly notes that "military forces under a combatant commander derive authority to conduct NetA [i.e., network attack] from the laws contained in Title 10 of the US Code (USC). However, the skills and target knowledge for effective NetA are best developed and honed during peacetime intelligence or network warfare support (NS) operations. Intelligence forces in the national intelligence community derive authority to conduct network exploitation and many NS [i.e., national security] operations from laws contained in USC Title 50. For this reason, "dual-purpose" military forces are funded and controlled by organizations that derive authority under laws contained in both Title 10 and Title 50. The greatest benefit of these "dual-purpose" forces is their authority to operate under laws contained in Title 50, and so produce actionable intelligence products, while exercising the skills needed for NetA. These forces are the preferred means by which the air force can organize, train, and equip mission-ready NetA forces." www.herbb.hanscom.af.mil/tbbs/R1528/AF_Doctrine_Doc_2_5_ Jan_11__2005.pdf.

CHAPTER 4

Joining Cybercrime and Cyberterrorism

A Likely Scenario

Steven Bucci

Introduction

I N THE PREVIOUS CHAPTER, Herb Lin explained the technical dimensions of conducting cyber attacks and cyber exploitation. In this chapter I describe how these tools can be used by cybercriminals and cyberterrorists. As discussed in chapter 1, the world faces a wide array of cyber threats. The majority of these threats are aimed at the Western democracies and advanced economies of other regions. The reason for this is simple—they are ripe targets. These countries are either highly dependent or almost completely dependent on cyber means for nearly every significant societal interaction, or are racing toward that goal. They seek the speed, accuracy, efficiency, and ease that a "wired" system of systems brings, as well as all the benefits that accrue to such a situation. The danger facing countries such as the United States is the many individuals, groups, and states that desire to exploit those same systems for their own purposes. In spite of this, there is a new threat on the horizon that must be recognized and addressed. We must accept that continual cyber threats are the "new normal." Most are not the concern of national security authorities, but they must still be addressed. Figure 4.1 illustrates the extent of this situation. Ignoring it will not make it go away; national security professionals must adjust this perspective to deal appropriately with it.

The sources of cyber threats of today can be grouped into several categories that can be arrayed along a spectrum from individual hackers to petty criminals and organized criminal groups to foreign intelligence services. Any of these threat groups can attack an individual or a nation-state, and anything in between. These groups will exploit a lazy home computer user, an inefficient corporate IT system, or a weak national defense infrastructure. We are all in danger from these threats, which can be grouped as low, medium, and high. Any construct of this nature is recognized as

FIGURE 4.1
The Cyber Threat Environment

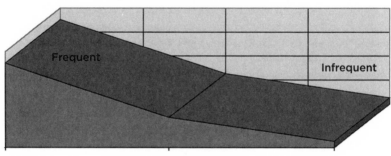

Day-to-Day Threats   Threats to Military Assets   Systemic Threats

LEVEL OF RESPONSIBILITY:

Individual ——————————————————→ **National Security**

a simplification, but having numerous possible actions defined into manageable groups does aid in discussions. There are probably as many ways to group and visualize the threats as there are "experts" to opine upon them. However, this approach allows careful analysis of the threats to ensure that national security professionals address them in a manageable fashion.

The lowest level of cyber threats comes from individual hackers. The hacker operates for his or her own personal benefit—for pride, self-satisfaction, or individual financial gain. The hacker constitutes an annoyance. The hacker category also includes small groups who write malware to prove that they can defeat security systems, or who attack small organizations due to personal or political issues. Along with the hacker at the low end of the spectrum are small criminal enterprises and most disgruntled insiders. These too are low-level annoyances, except to the unfortunate individuals they exploit as their primary targets. These types of groups and individuals operate Internet scams, bilking people out of personal information, and they may even perpetrate extortion through threats. Both of these groups are far more capable today than ever before due to increased access to coding tools and assets that better enable their efforts. Again, it must be noted that if you are the target or victim of a hacker or hacker group, this threat does not seem insignificant at all. That said, they do not present a significant systemic threat. The damage they can do is limited in nature, and thus gets them the place at the bottom of the scale. The mythological evil-genius hack who single-handedly takes down giant entities is frankly just that—a myth. They can steal and they can deface, but the scale of damage has never been huge.

Continuing along a spectrum, the medium-level threats are harder to order by rank. Each threat grouping targets different entities. These targets would consider their attackers very dangerous and a critical threat. These medium-level threats include terrorist use of the Internet, which will be discussed in detail later; cyber espionage (which is also helped by insiders at times) of both corporate and national security types, including probes for vulnerabilities and implementation of back-doors; and high-level organized crime, which will also receive a separate treatment below. All three of these groupings can have extremely detrimental effects on a person, a business, a government, or a region. They occur regularly and define the bulk of the ongoing significant cyber threats of today. The incredible dependence our society now has on digital infrastructure cannot be overstated. Nearly every aspect of our lives depends on data, and many entities are trying to get it, corrupt it, or destroy it for their own benefit.

The high-level systemic threats involve the full power of nation-states. Some non-state entities are moving in the direction of achieving a level of cyber power that could eventually emulate a nation-state, but they have not yet achieved this goal. Subsequent sections will address the terrorist/organized crime nexus that comprises that growing possibility. Today these high-level systemic threats come in two major groups. The first is a full-scale nation-state cyber attack. The closest example of this was the assault made on Estonia in 2007. There, the highly developed network of a small country was temporarily brought to its knees. Although portrayed by some as a simple display of public outrage over the moving of a Soviet-era statue valued by ethnic Russians, most experts felt there was more to the assault. Simply, the level of sophistication suggested that a government hand was at play. This dispute over the responsibility makes this an imperfect example, but it is a highly troubling harbinger of the future. A former senior Department of Defense (DoD) leader stated that more than one million computers were used in this event, coming from more than seventy countries. The seriousness of the attack was epitomized by NATO's consideration of invoking Article V (collective defense) at Estonia's request, but NATO was unable to reach consensus. Today, NATO is very close to having a declaratory policy that cyber attacks will be met with a consolidated response, which means a cyber attack on one NATO country will be considered and treated as a cyber attack on the other twenty-seven NATO countries as well.

In the fall 2010 Strategic Concept, the Alliance committed to "develop[ing] further our ability to prevent, detect, defend against and recover from cyber-attacks, including by using the NATO planning process to enhance and coordinate national cyber-defence capabilities, bringing all NATO bodies under centralized cyber protection, and better integrating NATO cyber awareness, warning and response with member nations."[1] This is not the equivalent of Article V, but NATO increasingly recognizes the role cyber plays in national and collective defense. "Cyber attacks are becoming more frequent, more organised and more costly in the damage that they inflict on government administrations, businesses, economies and potentially also transportation and supply networks and other critical infrastructure; they can reach a threshold that threatens national and Euro-Atlantic prosperity, security and stability. Foreign militaries and intelligence services, organised criminals, terrorist and/or extremist groups can each be the source of such attacks."[2]

The other possibility is the cyber support of a kinetic or a physical attack. So far we can only look to the 2008 assault on Georgia to study this category. Georgia was not as dependent on the cyber realm as was Estonia, but the cyber assault that preceded the Russian military's ground attack into Ossetia severally hindered Georgia's response. This will be further discussed in the chapter by Nikolas Gvosdev, but it may be an imperfect example that has given us much to consider. Former chairman of the Joint Chiefs of Staff Gen. Peter Pace told a group of my IBM colleagues that Russia's "cyber special operations forces isolated the [Georgian] president by disabling all his cyber connectivity, then their cyber air force carpet bombed the entire national network, and finally their cyber Delta Force infiltrated and re-wrote code that kept their network from working correctly even after it was brought back up."[3] It was a highly sophisticated attack. These two potential threats constitute the high-end of the cyber-threat spectrum.

A Construct for Planning

During the Cold War and beyond, the military and security communities used a paradigm for planning that allowed them to determine among a large number of possible threats they should plan. They would determine both the most dangerous threat and the most likely threat. These were seldom the same. During that period, there was near universal agreement that full-scale thermonuclear exchange between the United States and NATO, on one side, and the Soviet Union and the Warsaw Pact, on the other, was the most dangerous threat. Fortunately, this most dangerous scenario was not the most likely. Mutually assured destruction kept the fingers off the triggers. Planners therefore had to ascertain what scenario was the most likely. For NATO, this was a large-scale conventional war on the plains of Northern Europe, which all hoped would remain nonnuclear. The United States added to this smaller scale proxy wars outside the European context such as supporting armed groups in Angola, Nicaragua, and Afghanistan. Today US policymakers can use a similar process to thoughtfully address cyber threats. Too often cyber specialists focus on the most catastrophic scenarios and ignore the most likely. Fortunately, during the Cold War they resisted this tendency and prepared for both the most likely as well as the most dangerous. The differences in the two categories make it essential that we can do both, and that we are fully cognizant that both could occur.

I show in this chapter that although we face a scenario emerging from the cyber-threat spectrum that fully fits the part of the most dangerous threat, we must also face and prepare for the most likely scenario that is unique and, frankly, is not yet on the cyber-threat spectrum. This threat will involve the joining of the growing cybercrime capability that we see today with a terrorist revelation that the cyber realm is ripe for exploitation. Therefore, the most likely threat is terrorists joining or employing cybercriminals. To do this, the most dangerous scenario will be outlined more fully, and it will be shown why, despite its horrific potential, it is not likely to occur on a large scale or to produce physical destruction comparable to car bombs or suicide attacks. Instead, terrorist use of the Internet as it presently occurs will be discussed to set the contemporary context. Next, I look at cybercrime in general terms and show which criminal capabilities will be desired and sought by terrorists in the very near future. Finally, I present a new threat that sits at the confluence of cybercrime and cyberterrorism. The type of collaboration and possible results of this unholy alliance are discussed. My goal is to raise awareness of this emergent threat to ensure that national leaders address this overlooked area.

The Most Dangerous Cyber Threat: Nation-State Attacks

Clearly, as one looks at the spectrum of threats presented in figure 4.1, the far end delineates the possibilities we fear most. Developed nation-states, acting as peer competitors, are the most dangerous potential threat. Nation-states possess hard power, including kinetically capable militaries, economic strength, industrial bases, and scale of assets (both in number and in sophistication). In cyber today, to really cause widespread damage (permanent or for a specific time), many high-end assets are needed. Nation-states can marshal the intellectual capital of their countries to develop cyber armies composed of large numbers of operators with the best equipment, skilled at developing and using new forms of attack. These will accomplish the twin tasks of both leveraging and enabling conventional intelligence, signals, and mobility assets. Nation-states can also use their considerable coercive powers to harness civilian assets that technically fall outside the public sector. This can be done by requiring active or passive collusion with the government, or by manipulating public sentiment to stir up patriotic fervor while providing guidance (i.e., targeting) and tools to the faithful.

All these factors allow nation-states with foresight to develop and use enormous capabilities in the cyber realm. What is today merely cyber espionage or probing of defenses can, in the blink of an eye, be turned to a massive attack on the infrastructure of an adversary. It is important to remember that cyber forces do not need to deploy by ship, plane, or truck, so there are no logistical delays or the usual indicators and warnings. Cyber attacks could be used to disable defenses and blind intelligence capabilities in preparation for a devastating kinetic strike. These methods can slow the reactions of defenders by clouding their operational picture or fouling their communications means. Cyber attacks could also bring down key command-and-control nodes altogether, paralyzing any response to the attack.

If the attacker has used weapons of mass destruction (chemical, biological, radiological, nuclear, or high-yield explosives) in the kinetic part of the attack, the cyber component can also hinder the ability to rally consequence management assets. The victim will have suffered a catastrophic attack and will be unable to effectively respond to the results. The continued cyber intrusions will not only keep them from striking back with any real effect, but they may also be ineffectual in mobilizing their first responder forces. This kind of large-scale attack can only come from a nation-state and obviously constitutes the most dangerous scenario. There is a fair amount of agreement on this aspect, both inside government and from outside experts.

Fortunately, the most dangerous scenario is not very likely. Good relations among great powers capable of conducting simultaneous cyber and conventional attacks are reinforced by old-fashioned nuclear deterrence. In the same way the cyber and physical infrastructures make us vulnerable to this scenario, any attacking nation-state must have its own infrastructure capabilities to be able to execute a major cyber effort. Those cyber capabilities and kinetic forces used in the attack are also potential targets, as are the remainder of the attacker's critical infrastructure. Basically, it is unlikely that a nation-state would do this because they also have much at stake. Deterrence, in the same way we have understood it for more than fifty years, still applies to nation-states in all the ways it does not apply to terrorists, criminals, and other nonstate actors. A large-scale cyber attack or cyber-enabled kinetic attack by a peer competitor on another country runs the risk of a large-scale response from the target, or the target's allies and friends. While this will not dissuade every nation-state-backed cyber threat (the thousands of probes, minor attacks, and espionage actions prove that), it has and will continue to keep this type of large-scale nightmare scenario from moving into the "likely category." Prudence suggests that the United States must prepare for the most dangerous scenario, but it must not crowd out the most likely scenarios. Otherwise, the national security bureaucracy will have failed the country.

Terrorist Use of the Cyber Realm: From Small Beginnings

It is fortunate that, so far, major terrorist organizations such as al-Qaeda and its franchises have yet to learn to fully exploit the "opportunities" in the cyber realm. We would be foolish to assume this state of affairs will persist. Presently, terrorists appear to be limited in their understanding of the potential for this medium. They do use it extensively, but not for offensive actions. Most intelligence and law enforcement agencies agree that they are limited to such areas as communications, propaganda, financial dealings (fund-raising and fund transfers), recruitment, and intelligence. There seems to be some potential use for operational planning and reconnaissance, but this is unconfirmed.

Communications security on the Internet is very attractive to terrorists. The anonymity and difficulty of tracing interactions in restricted, password-protected chat rooms and the use of encrypted e-mail give terrorists a much greater degree of operational security than other means of communications. Terrorists can also share e-mail boxes to serve as "dead drops," which reduces the chances that their communications will be intercepted. This will continue to be a major activity for terrorists over cyber channels.

Clearly, terrorists are very good and getting better at using the Internet for propaganda and fund-raising purposes. Every few months, a high-level al-Qaeda member shares his thoughts with the world through video, audio, and print press releases. The increasing sophistication of their messaging shows an understanding of the potential of the cyber medium in this area. They are reaching ever-increasing audiences. YouTube-like videos of terror attacks feed the fervor of the faithful around the world and make them feel a part of the struggle. Messaging over the Internet from the leadership keeps them prominent in the minds of the mass audience and makes the most isolated spokesperson seem relevant. These same channels are superb for fund-raising among the dispersed peoples around the world. The reach and timeliness cannot be matched by other communications means, and greatly aids in their fund-raising efforts. These same characteristics apply to their recruitment programs, and the process of radicalizing individuals no longer has to take place in person but can be greatly enhanced by cyber communication and teaching. This is of great concern to US law enforcement agencies, as US citizens are being radicalized by handlers who remain abroad, thus making them much harder to catch.

In addition to recruitment, terrorists take advantage of many very effective applications available that aid in basic intelligence gathering. Google Earth and similar programs that provide terrorists street-view photos of potential targets as well as excellent route and obstacle information can be obtained for free. There is also free encryption and steganography software that enables terrorists to conceal communications from Western intelligence agencies. The tendency of most Western countries to post nearly everything there is to know about critical infrastructures on unsecured websites is a great boon to the terrorists and requires no more expertise than an ability to use rudimentary search engines that small children have mastered. All of this "research capability" assists the terrorists in making their standard operation procedures much easier and safer to polish to a high degree.

A new wrinkle that is developing is the use of virtual worlds such as Second Life. There is hard evidence of money transfers having been made within these worlds. This is done by using real cash to buy virtual currency, conducting various transactions within the virtual environment, and then converting it back into real cash again in a completely different temporal location. It is all safe, clean, legal, and nearly impossible to trace. These virtual worlds also allow for meetings to occur in cyberspace that are even more deeply covered and protected than secure chat rooms. The avatars used in virtual worlds are very difficult to identify, and rules for interaction online allow for secret activities that further shield those with much to hide. An advanced application that has been discussed by intelligence and law enforcement agencies is the use of virtual worlds to train and rehearse for operations in the real world. This is clearly possible, but no hard evidence is yet available to prove that terrorists are now using the virtual worlds in this way.

For terrorists to exploit cyberspace more effectively, terrorist groups are likely to seek assistance from other groups. From where might that help come? It is unlikely that they will develop their own cyber plans and abilities beyond a few experts to ensure they are not being cheated or to do operational cyber planning correctly. To do more than that would take a great deal of time, and they may be unwilling to wait. Unfortunately, they do not need to wait because they will probably do it by reaching out to the world of cybercrime. There they will find willing partners.

Cybercrime: Follow the Money

Cybercrime continues to be a booming business, starting as an offshoot of individual hackers doing it for fun and pride and growing into a huge (and still expanding) industry that steals, cheats, and extorts the equivalent of many billions of dollars every year. They steal from individuals, corporations, and countries. Cybercrime is big money, whether it is simple scams to get gullible people to give up money and access to their accounts, or whether it is highly sophisticated technical methods of harvesting mass amounts of personal data that can be exploited directly or sold to others. The more sophisticated it gets, the more organized it becomes; and it has matured to a frightening level. Presently, the FBI estimates that organized crime makes far more money through cybercrime methods than it does through the illegal drug trade.

A lucrative target is data well beyond personal identity and financial information. Infiltrating businesses and stealing industrial secrets, pharmaceutical formulas, and similar data can reap huge profits for criminals. There are several reports of utility facilities having their industrial control or supervisory control and data acquisition (SCADA) systems hacked and seized by criminals. The attackers have threatened to shut down the facility or worse if they were not paid enormous ransoms. No one knows if the malefactors could have actually followed through on the shut-down threats because the money was paid in each case. The owners deemed it a credible threat and could not afford to have their enterprise closed or destroyed. In some sense this behavior mirrors Somali piracy that seizes commercial ships until ransoms are paid.

An interesting additive to this issue set is the illegal or quasi-legal franchising of cybercrime. Criminals now market and sell the tools of cybercrime: root kits, hacking lessons, guides to designing malware—it is all available on the Internet. These range from rudimentary "starter kits" to highly sophisticated programs that are potentially very destructive. Law enforcement officials at a recent New York State cyber conference stated that these tools are cheap and easy to find online. Additionally, short amounts of "botnet time" can be purchased for very low costs, and some criminals are now purchasing legitimate cloud services to use when they want to ramp up their operations (cracking passwords or sending high volumes of traffic) instead of bothering with bots at all.

The last, and in my mind, most interesting and insidious threat is the rise of the botnets. Criminals cannot command entire nations of computers, as one would expect that coercive governments could if they need to. Criminal syndicates have, however, developed huge botnets with members all over the world—members that they control without the actual owner of the machine even being aware of it. These zombie networks serve their criminal masters without question or hesitation. The criminals control them completely, and can use them directly for distributed denial of service attacks (DDOS) attacks, phishing, spam, or malware distribution. They also rent them out to others for cash.

Terrorism Enabled by Cybercriminals: Most Likely Cyber Threat

There is no doubt that terrorists want badly to hurt the modern Western and Western-leaning nations. The numerous dead and wounded, the horrific damage of past successful attacks, and the multiple foiled plots all make the deadly intent of the terrorists abundantly clear to all. This cannot be denied. Their continuing efforts to acquire and develop weapons of mass destruction for use against civilian targets are also prima fascia evidence of this burning desire to do harm in any way possible. I believe they will turn to our technological Achilles' heel, cyber.

Terrorist organizations can surely find a number of highly trained, intelligent, and computer literate people who are in agreement with their cause. These people can be taught to develop code, write malware, and hack as well as anyone else can. That will not be enough. They cannot, in a timely manner, develop the kind of large-scale operational capabilities that even a small nation-state possesses. This is what they need to make a truly effective assault on the West in the cyber realm. Two factors give them another option. First, they do not really need to attack an entire nation to achieve success. The capability they need is large, but not really "nation-state" size. They desire to create a large event, but it does not necessarily need to be as extensive as a full nation-state attack. The second factor is that some of these groups have abundant funds and potential access to even more. These funds open up the criminal option, which will give the terrorists the capability to be extraordinarily destructive.

The West has a huge number of intelligence and law enforcement assets dedicated to stopping the proliferation of weapons of mass destruction. Any movement of these devices or materials related to them will sound the alarm across the world. Numerous arrests of people attempting to traffic in weapons of mass destruction (WMD) or related materials have been made. This effort has nullified the effect of the excellent financial assets some terrorists have, and has frustrated their efforts to acquire WMD capabilities. The United States does not have the same type of watch-dog systems in place to prevent cyber enablement from occurring. Complicating interdiction is the nonphysical movement of malware—there are no borders to cross on the Internet.

If a cash-rich terrorist group would use its wealth to hire cybercriminal botnets, or criminal code writers, for their own use, then terrorists could take a shortcut to becoming cyber empowered, thus creating problems for societies dependent on modern communications and the Internet. A terrorist group so enabled could begin to overwhelm the cyber defenses of a specific corporation, a single government organization, or a regional infrastructure sector, and could do much damage. It could destroy or corrupt vital data in the financial sector, cripple communications over a wide (but circumscribed) area to spread panic and uncertainty. Similar to the nation-state attack scenarios discussed earlier, terrorists could use botnet-driven DDOS attacks to "blind" security forces at a border crossing point as a means of facilitating an infiltration operation, or a cyber attack in one area of a country to act as a diversion so a "conventional" kinetic terrorist attack can occur elsewhere. They could even conduct SCADA attacks on specific sites and use the system to create "kinetic-like" effects without the kinetic component. A good example would be to open the valves at a chemical plant near a population center, creating a Bopal-like event. The permutations are as endless as one's imagination. The 2009–10 Stuxnet worm attack that afflicted Siemens software present in factories, power plants, and water treatment plants will likely inspire terrorist groups to acquire and use the tools of cyberwar. The cyber capabilities that the criminals could provide would in short order make any terrorist organization infinitely more dangerous and effective. Metropolitan-area police officials are very concerned that their 911 systems will be hacked, allowing bad guys to reroute responders away from actual incidents and into ambushes. This would have the dual effect of harming the precious response assets a country has and undermining public confidence in a government's ability to respond to public emergencies. A scenario like this would create the fear that terrorists strive to inflict.

Some have opined that cyber attacks are not suitable as terror tactics because they lack the drama and spectacular effect of, say, a suicide bomber. This does not take into account the ability of the terrorists to adapt and the real fear created when bank accounts are zeroed, electricity is absent, or water does not flow. As intelligence and law enforcement agencies continue to effectively combat the terrorists, they will continue to evolve. The terrorists' old methods of inspiring fear will be augmented and improved. They will need to develop more imagination and versatility if they are to conduct successful operations. This evolutionary capability has not been in short supply among terrorist leadership. They will not define "spectacular" so narrowly. Imagine the operational elegance of simply hitting the return key and seeing thousands of enemies die a continent away, or watching a bank go under due to the destruction of all its data by an unknown force. This will be enormously attractive to terror groups. Additionally, the combination of cyber methods and kinetic strikes could be spectacular regardless of one's definition.

Criminals for their part are motivated by greed and power. Few of the leaders of the enormous cyber organized-crime world would hesitate to sell their capabilities to a terrorist loaded with cash. That fact, combined with the ever-growing terrorist awareness of cyber vulnerabilities, makes this set of scenarios not just likely but nearly inevitable.

There is one "near" proof case of this sort of cooperation. In the most recent Israeli incursion in to Gaza, the Israeli Civil Defense Network was hit with a massive DDOS attack. The forensic investigation showed it to be nearly identical (techniques, servers exploited, etc.) to the 2007 Estonia attack. It is very unlikely that the so-called patriotic hackers chose to do an encore on Israel several years later. I believe it is highly likely that the same criminal organizations that were enlisted to go after Estonia were hired by Hamas and Hezbollah (and their financial backers) to go after Israel. Clearly this is a supposition, but I feel it is a sound one.

As we progress along some of the obvious trend lines in the tech world, we will actually become more vulnerable. Three major trends that will contribute to this are mobile computing, cloud computing, and the use of smart-grid technology. All three of these developments are frankly unstoppable. They are happening today and will only grow in size and importance. They also all expand the potential attack surface of our digital world. Every day, more and more people begin to operate in a mobile mode. Smartphones and netbooks without sufficient malware protection; ubiquitous, often unsecured wireless connectivity; and highly distributed operations all contribute to this, and grow every day. Cloud computing and smart-grid technologies are enormously beneficial developments that will help the environment and save huge amounts of money. The security of these systems is still being developed, but much more slowly than the systems are being deployed. The bad guys will exploit these. This essay is not the place for a definitive discussion of these subjects, but they must be noted as future issues to be addressed.

Conclusion: Prepare for the Dangerous, but Know the Likely Is Coming

Terrorists will recognize the opportunity the cyber world offers sooner or later and will seek to act upon it. They will also recognize that they need help to properly exploit vulnerabilities. It is unlikely they will have the patience to develop their own completely independent capabilities. At the same time, the highly developed, highly capable cyber criminal networks want money and care little about the source. This is a marriage made in hell. Even if one dismisses the evidence of radical group and criminal collusion in the DDOS that targeted Israel, this possibility must be considered by planners and policymakers.

The threat of a full nation-state attack, either cyber or cyber-enabled kinetic, is our most dangerous threat. We pray deterrence will continue to hold, and we should take all measures to shore up that deterrence among nation-sates. Terrorists, however, will never be deterred in this way. They will continue to seek ways to successfully harm us, and they will join hands with criminal elements to do so. A terrorist attack enabled by cybercrime capabilities will now be an eighth group of cyber threats, and it will be the most likely major event we will need to confront.

Some would say that cybercrime is a purely law enforcement issue, with no national security component. That is a dubious "truth" today. This is not a static situation, and it will definitely be more dangerously false in the future. Unless we get cybercrime under control, it will mutate into a very real, very dangerous national security issue with potentially catastrophic ramifications. It would be far better to address it now rather than in the midst of a terrorist incident or campaign of incidents against one of our countries. Terrorism enabled by cybercriminals is our most likely major cyber threat. It must be met with as many assets as possible.

Notes

1. NATO, "Active Engagement, Modern Defence: Strategic Concept for the Defence and Security of the Members of the North Atlantic Treaty Organisation Adopted by Heads of State and Government in Lisbon," November 19, 2010. www.nato.int/cps/en/natolive/official_texts_68580.htm#cyber.

2. Ibid.

3. Author interview.

PART II

Armed Conflict and Cyber Defense

CHAPTER 5

Inter arma silent leges Redux?

The Law of Armed Conflict and Cyber Conflict

David P. Fidler

Introduction

For YEARS, EXPERTS HAVE PREDICTED that states will become increasingly interested in and adept at using computers and the Internet as weapons of war. Recent developments indicate that countries and their capabilities in cyberspace have entered a more serious dimension concerning competition and conflict in and through cyberspace. The 2010 establishment of US Cyber Command (USCYBER-COM) with the mission to "conduct full-spectrum military cyberspace operations" illustrates the shifts taking place.[1] These changes have stimulated concern about how the law of armed conflict (LOAC) applies to cyber operations.[2] This chapter explores the relationship between LOAC and the use of cyber technologies by states and nonstate actors.

Existing literature contains divergent views on this relationship, ranging from arguments that applying LOAC to cyber operations poses few difficulties to assertions that existing rules do not function well in cyberspace, producing the need to negotiate rules for this dimension of conflict. Debate between different perspectives is healthy, and I do not attempt to adjudicate among competing positions. Rather, I identify four problems that arise in evaluating the use of cyber technologies under LOAC—the problems of application, attribution, assessment, and accountability.

The problem of application identifies the difficulty of characterizing the use of cyber technologies by state and nonstate actors. Whether an event constitutes an armed attack, espionage, terrorism, or a crime is not always clear when computers and the Internet are used. Thus, putting the event into a specific legal category—a critical step of legal analysis—proves problematic. The problem of attribution arises when victims of cyber acts cannot identify the perpetrators with confidence. Not being able to attribute the cyber event to specific actors makes application of law difficult, if not impossible.

The problem of assessment occurs when analysts evaluate a cyber act under rules within LOAC. The assessment task confronts problems that arise with the legal principles as applied in noncyber contexts, such as controversies about the meaning of rules (e.g., the scope of the right of self-defense). Finally, the problem of accountability relates to the law's imperative to assign responsibility for regulated acts and consequences for violations. Cyber operations can dilute the ability to assign legal responsibility by creating ambiguities that undermine confidence in imposing consequences and create incentives that deter completion of accountability analysis.

To facilitate a comprehensive approach, LOAC is defined broadly to include the rules that address when states can resort to force (*jus ad bellum*), how states and non-state actors engage in armed conflict (*jus in bello*), development and use of weapons (arms control and nonproliferation), and the criminal culpability of individuals for violating international law during conflict (international criminal law). The problems of application, attribution, assessment, and accountability arise, in some form, in these areas in the cyber context. Thus, these problems constitute dilemmas for LOAC's regulation of cyber conflict.

The cumulative effect of these problems threatens to create a cyberspace version of the ancient warning about the impact of law during war—*inter arma silent leges*.[3] In cyberspace, competition and conflict transpire in a peculiar dimension that challenges the assumptions that legal analysis of armed conflict relies upon to evaluate behavior. Such disrupting challenges have happened in other contexts, as illustrated by the post-9/11 debates about whether an attack by a terrorist group triggers a state's right to use force in self-defense. However, cyber conflict creates a range and diversity of confounding questions that threaten the ability to speak authoritatively about the role of LOAC in the cyber context.

In this realm of confusion and controversy, additional efforts to show the relevance of LOAC will not make more headway than those already attempted. More important, the confusion and controversy provide cover for the cyber machinations of states, which are still feeling out the possibilities of cyber technologies. For the foreseeable future, LOAC will be difficult to use effectively in cases of actual or alleged cyber conflict, and states keen on being cyber powers will not seriously negotiate new rules until they better grasp the capabilities of cyber technologies in their pursuits of power and influence.

From Geekfare to Warfare: Developments Implicating the Law of Armed Conflict

The possibility that governments, terrorists, and criminals would weaponize computers has been fodder for science fiction writers and policy wonks for decades. Events within the past ten years, however, have revealed the potential of using computers as weapons, exploiting the Internet for mayhem, and targeting governmental and social vulnerabilities created by dependence on information technologies. The world has transitioned from computer geeks going "rogue" by releasing viruses or worms, to security threats created by organized, sophisticated, and pervasive uses of computers and the Internet by states and nonstate actors in their competition for money, information, advantage, influence, and power.

This trajectory accelerated in the past five years because of specific events and developments. The suspected Russian-instigated cyber attacks against Estonia and Georgia; mounting concerns about Chinese-linked hacking and infiltration of foreign government computer networks and companies (e.g., Google); the apparent targeting of Iranian nuclear centrifuges in the Stuxnet episode; the declared US intentions to "make cyberspace safe"; and the scaling-up of cyber capabilities by other governments have contributed to the sense that cyberspace is more seriously becoming a domain of competition and conflict, meaning that cybersecurity as a policy realm, now more than ever, includes cyber conflict as a threat (on China, see chapter 12, this volume).[4]

This shift creates problems and raises questions, which include the relevance of LOAC to cyber operations by state and nonstate actors. The need to revisit LOAC in light of novel technologies is nothing new. Chemical and biological weapons, air power, nuclear weapons, "smart" weapons, "nonlethal" weapons (e.g., directed-energy weapons), and unmanned aerial vehicles (UAV) have caused states and nongovernmental actors to think through the LOAC implications of new technologies. Conundrums have appeared in these contexts, perhaps best captured in the *Legality of the Threat or Use of Nuclear Weapons* case. Here, the International Court of Justice (ICJ) ruled that use of a nuclear weapon would generally violate international humanitarian law, but the ICJ could not "conclude definitively whether the threat or use of nuclear weapons would be lawful or unlawful in an extreme circumstance of self-defence, in which the very survival of a State would be at stake."[5]

Mapping cyber operations against the application of LOAC to other technological developments proves awkward because this exercise reveals the range of possibilities concerning how states and nonstate actors might use cyber technologies. Some experts have argued that cyber operations have the potential to cause the kind of damage associated with weapons of mass destruction (WMD).[6] However, existing experiences make cyber technologies look more analogous to nonlethal weapons than to WMD because, to date, cyber events have not caused the damage or death associated with armed conflict. In between WMD and nonlethal weapons exist other possibilities. Cyber technologies create the potential for cyber operations to exhibit characteristics akin to smart weapons that permit militaries to deliver munitions more accurately, and to robotic systems, such as UAVs, that allow operators to trigger payloads against targets remotely.

Thus, the implications of cyber operations for LOAC are broad, but analysis by analogy to other weapons tells us more about the other weapons than about the challenges that cyber operations pose. If a cyber attack produces an outcome similar to the use of a nuclear weapon, then how we think about LOAC vis-à-vis nuclear weapons is relevant. However, analogies grounded in analysis of other technologies do not get to the heart of the cyber challenge to LOAC. When analysis targets this challenge, problems multiply, especially the problems of application, attribution, assessment, and accountability.

The Problem of Application

When a cyber event occurs, commentary often focuses more on who was behind the event than what happened. Although attribution is important (discussed later), how to characterize the cyber event is equally significant. This step is particularly germane to LOAC, which, by definition, applies in times of "armed conflict." Thus, a threshold question exists before one can apply LOAC to a cyber event. Similarly, other areas of international law contain definitions that determine what rules apply. In law, definitions create categories of rules, and legal analysis slots facts into such categories in order to determine what rules apply. In a cyber event, what happened and to what category of rules the event belongs are often confusing and controversial.

War, Espionage, Terrorism, Crime, or Digital Riot?

The cyber attacks against Estonia in 2007 illustrate the problem of application (see chapter 11, this volume). Estonian officials characterized the distributed denial of service (DDOS) attacks as an armed attack that triggered Estonia's right of self-defense under LOAC.[7] Other countries, including Estonia's NATO allies, did not define the event in this way, with some likening it to a "cyber riot" or disturbance of the peace.[8] Cyber events complicate the need to slot the events into legal categories because such events and the technologies exploited make understanding what happened difficult. Legal analysis does not face the same problem with the detonation of a nuclear weapon, the use of a chemical weapon, or an attack using smart weapons.

The application problem also arises in the diverse ways allegations against Chinese cyber acts are described. Chinese infiltration of US government computers has been described as "attacks," "warfare," and "terrorism."[9] However, China is conducting espionage with the latest technologies, as other countries do. Claims that China rerouted or "hijacked" a substantial portion of Internet traffic in April 2010 raise the same problem—if true, what, besides espionage, would such an action constitute legally?[10] Using more dramatic monikers to describe what is essentially espionage reflects political agendas (e.g., hyping the China threat) that have little to do with characterizing actions for purposes of applying international law.

Although cyber technologies allow governments to conduct espionage at a new level of pervasiveness, such activity constitutes high-intensity espionage as opposed to low-intensity conflict—as these concepts have traditionally been understood. LOAC does not apply to espionage conducted during peacetime, and international law on espionage contains minimal, if any, constraints because most, if not all, states gather intelligence against other countries.[11] This reality persists even though espionage, even of the low-tech variety, can cause significant political, economic, national security, intelligence, and physical damage to a country and lead to the punishment, torture, and death of people caught spying.

Cyber Attacks in Armed Conflict

The problem of application does not arise when cyber operations occur in conjunction with actions that cross the line demarcating armed conflict from peaceful relations. For example, the cyber attacks Georgia experienced during its conflict with Russia in 2008 constitute part of that conflict. However, compared to the attention paid to the DDOS attacks on Estonia, cyber elements of the Georgia–Russia conflict received less attention because LOAC concerns focused on the conventional fighting and the threats it posed to noncombatant populations.[12] The cyber piece was a sideshow because more serious *jus in bello* issues arose.

What happened in the Georgia–Russia conflict does not mean that cyber operations within armed conflicts will be marginalized in the future. The main point is that the recognized existence of an armed conflict lessens the problem of application. Pursuing the cyber elements of such conflicts under LOAC still confronts the problems of attribution, assessment, and accountability (explored later).

The Zone of Ambiguity

Experience to date suggests that much cyber activity occurs, and will continue to occur, in contexts where the participants do not acknowledge application of LOAC. In these contexts, the problem of application illuminates a zone of ambiguity with technological and political features. Technologically, computers and the Internet constitute flexible, scalable, and integrative capabilities that users can manipulate to cause confusion about what happened and to complicate the task of "virtual forensics" during and after an event. The nature and ubiquity of cyber technologies mean that arms control and nonproliferation approaches used in other "dual use" contexts, such as those involving WMD, are not feasible to keep cyber technologies out of the hands of states and nonstate actors and prevent their hostile use.

Politically, the zone of ambiguity provides states and nonstate actors with incentives to engage in or tolerate a range of activities in cyberspace, such as hacking, espionage, crime, digital protests, terrorism, asymmetrical conflict, or low-intensity conflict, that do not clearly trigger LOAC. These activities face a lack of rules (e.g., espionage), controversies about what rules apply (e.g., asymmetrical and low-intensity conflict), or difficulties in making harmonized rules function (e.g., cooperation on cybercrime and cyberterrorism). The technological ability to obfuscate the origins of cyber operations enhances these incentives in the zone of ambiguity.

Lowering the Threshold for Applying the Law of Armed Conflict

One response to the zone of ambiguity is to shrink it by lowering the threshold for LOAC application to cyber acts. A precedent for such a move comes from arguments that attacks on a state by terrorists supported or harbored by another state trigger the right to use force in self-defense. This shift of the threshold triggering the right to use force in self-defense brings terrorism, previously categorized as a criminal law issue, within LOAC. The United States used this reasoning to justify attacking Libya in 1986, bombing Sudan in 1998, and invading Afghanistan in 2001.

In the cyber context, shifting the threshold could, for example, permit a state to use active defenses against computers located in another country that supports, harbors, or tolerates cyber attacks by nonstate actors.[13] The justification for active defenses would be the right to use force in self-defense, and the use of such defenses would be subject to *jus in bello* principles, such as proportionality and discrimination. The shift could mitigate the problem of application by expanding when states could rely on LOAC to justify responses to cyber attacks from state or nonstate actors. However, this strategy would face challenges related to the problems of attribution, assessment, and accountability.

The Problem of Attribution

Literature on crime, terrorism, and war in cyberspace often identifies the difficulty of attributing actions to specific actors as a technological, policy, and legal problem. The attribution problem derives from technological capabilities (e.g., creating botnets using zombie computers to launch DDOS attacks), but it creates headaches for legal analysis. Laws regulate the behavior of specific actors, be they individuals, groups, or governments. Assessing whether an act complied with laws requires attributing the act to actors subject to those laws. In this respect, LOAC is no different from other legal rules.

Attribution and the Law of Armed Conflict

LOAC has faced attribution issues in noncyber contexts. In *Nicaragua v. United States*, the ICJ had to determine whether it could attribute acts of different insurgent groups supported by Nicaragua and the United States to the Nicaraguan and US governments.[14] In *Prosecutor v. Tadic*, the International Criminal Tribunal for the Former Yugoslavia (ICTY) addressed whether actions by paramilitary groups were attributable to the Serbian government.[15] However, in these cases, the identities of the groups and their state benefactors were clear, as was the support the states provided, meaning that analysis could focus on whether international law shifted responsibility for the acts to states.

This clarity has not been present in cyber events that have caused international concern. First, the actions reviewed by the ICJ and the ICTY fell within LOAC, where, as discussed earlier, debate continues on how to categorize cyber events, most of which have not triggered application of LOAC (as Derek Reveron argues in chapter 14 of this volume, no one has died in a cyber attack). Second, although many people believe Russia was behind the Estonian DDOS attacks, analyses have not been able to detect direct Russian government involvement.[16] The groups and individuals who were involved remains a matter of speculation, as illustrated by Estonia's frustrations with trying to bring criminal charges against perpetrators.[17] Analysis of China's alleged rerouting of Internet traffic raised doubts not only about what happened but also about who or what caused this incident.[18] Who disseminated the Stuxnet worm that appeared to target Iranian nuclear centrifuges continues to be the source of conjecture.[19]

The attribution problem created by cyber technologies also arises in recognized armed conflicts, as illustrated by the Russia–Georgia conflict. To analyze the cyber attacks that took place during this conflict, being able to attribute them to Russia is critical for determining whether the Russia violated *jus in bello* principles of military necessity and proportionality. Although aspects of these attacks, such as their timing, suggest Russian involvement, this incident does not exhibit the clear linkages that made attribution analysis in *Nicaragua v. United States* and *Prosecutor v. Tadic* possible.[20] Pursuing nonstate actors for violating *jus in bello* in connection with these attacks also would require identification of the perpetrators. Strategies to mitigate the attribution problem identify technological, legal, and behavioral possibilities.

Technological Mitigation

Whether the attribution problem looms as large in the future remains to be seen. Technological developments, including changes in the way the Internet functions, could increase the ability to identify initiators of cyber attacks more rapidly and with more confidence. However, skepticism about a technological solution pervades proposals for strategies not dependent on law's need for attribution. These proposals include designing cybersecurity strategies around the tenets of public health or principles of maritime distress and assistance, neither of which require attributing responsibility for incidents before engaging in prevention and response activities.[21]

Legal Mitigation

Mitigation of the attribution problem could occur by broadening the rules used to impute to state responsibility for actions of nonstate actors during armed conflict in order to reflect the realities of cyber technologies. This approach would overlap with the strategy discussed earlier of lowering the threshold for applying LOAC, but it would also address *jus in bello* issues that arise during armed conflict. Taking this approach would require moving away from the higher standard for attribution found in the ICJ's *Nicaragua v. United States* decision (complete dependence on a state[22]) and toward the lower attribution threshold established in the ICTY's *Prosecutor v. Tadic* holding (overall control by a state[23]). This move could occur through customary international law or negotiation of a treaty designed to address cyber conflict.

Behavioral Mitigation

Another way for the attribution problem to recede involves governments becoming more transparent about their cyber operations during armed conflicts. Experts expect such operations to become more prominent in future armed conflicts, which would reduce the "plausible deniability" problem seen in the Russia–Georgia conflict. In establishing USCYBERCOM, US military leaders stated that US cyber operations will comply with LOAC, which indicates that the United States does not intend to hide behind a digital "fog of war" when it uses cyber technologies during armed conflicts.[24]

This approach treats cyber operations like any other method of armed conflict. In such cases, the problems of application and attribution are no longer relevant, and analysis concentrates on assessing cyber operations under LOAC (explored later). Similarly, insurgent groups waging noninternational armed conflicts could become more adept at using cyber technologies and more willing to acknowledge their cyber attacks. Such acknowledgment would remove the attribution problem and permit examination of cyber operations under the rules regulating the conduct of noninternational armed conflicts.

The Problem of Assessment

The problem of assessment arises when we evaluate the compliance of cyber operations with LOAC. Engaging in this assessment proves difficult for two reasons. First, the use of cyber technologies in armed conflict creates questions that complicate LOAC application. Second, the meaning of LOAC rules is often not settled, which creates controversy. This issue is not specific to the cyber context because it appears in other situations involving LOAC (e.g., does sabotage constitute an armed attack or merely an illegal use of force?). These problems combine to make assessment of cyber operations under LOAC frustrating and sometimes futile.

Rules on Permissible Weapons

Cyber operations disrupt information systems, and such disruptions might, or might not, cause intended or unintended effects that produce physical damage, human suffering, or loss of life. LOAC predominantly addresses weapons that employ kinetic or other physically damaging violence against people. The prohibition on the use of weapons that cause superfluous injury or unnecessary suffering captures this focus.[25] Cyber operations do not directly employ kinetic or other physical violence, and do not directly cause injury or suffering. Thus, cyber operations appear to be a new form of information operations that LOAC does not regulate, or a new kind of "nonlethal" technology, which does not resemble the weapons LOAC outlaws.

Leaving aside whether cyber technologies can launch "weapons" within the mean-ing of LOAC, cyber operations do not necessarily violate the prohibition on indis-criminate weapons that are not capable of being targeted at a military objective, or the effects of which cannot be limited as required by LOAC.[26] Cyber operations can target military objectives, as illustrated by espionage targeting of computers at the US Department of Defense (DOD) or the precision seen in the Stuxnet attacks. Although some have argued that the effects of a cyber operation's payload cannot be controlled, foreign-source infiltrations of US military computers do not indiscrimi-nately infect civilian computer systems, which illustrates that all payloads are not indiscriminate by their nature. Certain payloads, such as malicious code, might spread indiscriminately, but if the collateral damage is temporary or not severe, these limited effects might mean the payload does not breach LOAC rules on indiscrimi-nate weapons.

Jus ad bellum and Cyber Operations

The key question under international law regulating the use of force by states is whether a cyber operation constitutes a use of force, which violates the prohibition on such uses, or an armed attack, which triggers the right to use force in self-defense.[27] Assessing a cyber operation under these rules proves difficult because con-troversies surround these principles that developed in noncyber contexts. Whatever the context, analysis will focus more on consequences than on the means used.[28] A consequence-centric analysis might explain why many countries did not think that the DDOS attacks on Estonia constituted an armed attack. One can imagine a cyber operation that causes severe physical damage to critical infrastructure, which would violate the prohibition on the use of force and qualify as an armed attack. However, states and nonstate actors will engage in a range of cyber operations, many of which will not obviously be uses of force or armed attacks.

For example, determining whether the Stuxnet attack was a use of force or armed attack confronts long-standing problems experienced with *jus ad bellum*. Clarity on the meaning of "use of force," "armed attack," and "aggression" in international law has never been achieved, leaving countries with discretion in interpreting what these concepts mean. Thus, interpretations differ, such that the same event could be assessed as an armed attack, a use of force not amounting to an armed attack, or an unlawful intervention not constituting a use of force.

Cyber operations do not create this assessment problem, but they add to the interpretive complexity. Stuxnet was specifically designed to damage and did damage Iranian nuclear centrifuges physically, effects that indicate the episode involved an illegal armed attack.[29] However, the use of a computer worm rather than a smart bomb creates additional space for interpretive controversy concerning *jus ad bellum* because the means used potentially influences the perception of the effects caused. In the case of Stuxnet, state practice about this seminal cyber event is far from clear as to what it represents under international law on the use of force.[30] In addition, not knowing the worm's source eliminates including political context in the assessment (e.g., Israel as the source versus an anti-Iranian dissident group). The Stuxnet example not only highlights the *jus ad bellum* assessment problem but also connects to the problems of application (categorizing this incident legally proves difficult) and attribution (who disseminated Stuxnet remains unknown).

Jus in bello and Cyber Operations

International law requires combatants to comply with many rules potentially relevant to cyber operations, including the principles of military necessity, the distinction between combatants and noncombatants, proportionality, respect for specifically protected persons and objects, neutrality, and prohibitions on certain methods of war (e.g., perfidy).[31] Although few doubt these rules apply to cyber operations during armed conflict, differences exist about the ease or difficulty of assessing such operations under the rules. DOD has opined that *jus in bello* "is probably the single area of international law in which current legal obligations can be applied with the greatest confidence to information operations."[32] However, other experts have expressed doubts about how well the laws of war apply to cyber operations.[33]

As with *jus ad bellum*, assessment of *jus in bello* does not start with clarity on the meaning of applicable rules. Determining whether combatants comply with the principles of military necessity and proportionality faces controversies in every war. Throwing cyber operations into the mix increases the problems assessment confronts. For instance, cyber operations that degrade civilian information systems might not constitute an "attack" on a civilian target because the rules define "attack" as "violence against the adversary" and might be permissible if enemy forces utilize those systems for military purposes because of the interconnectedness of military and civilian information technologies.[34]

Although opposites, these two outcomes mean that cyber operations against civilian systems could be, simultaneously, information operations aimed at civilians not regulated by *jus in bello* and legitimate attacks on military targets subject to *jus in bello*. This scenario might worry those concerned about armed conflict's impact on civilians. Others might argue that the largely nonlethal nature of cyber operations is preferable, especially for civilians, than more kinetic attacks on civilian information systems used by military forces.[35]

Finally, difficulties applying *jus in bello* to cyber operations have to be kept in perspective. Assessment of cyber operations will draw on experiences applying *jus in bello* to predominantly kinetic military operations. This guidance demonstrates that the rules allow militaries to engage in serious violence and cause significant destruction, death, and suffering from direct military action or collateral damage. Thus, the range of impacts that cyber operations could cause and still be within the laws of war is considerable. This context might make assessment of many types of cyber operations easier because their impacts will not match or exceed what *jus in bello* permits in terms of conventional military violence.

The Problem of Accountability

LOAC's history reveals efforts to hold combatants accountable for their behavior during armed conflict. From reprisals to ad hoc tribunals, to the International Criminal Court (ICC), states and nonstate actors have created rules that assign responsibility for illegal acts and create mechanisms to impose consequences for their commission. Although these efforts connect to the general international legal principle of state responsibility, LOAC's concern with accountability runs deep because LOAC rules are violated, often on a massive scale, with impunity in many armed conflicts. Concerns about cyber operations in armed conflict create new accountability problems for LOAC that existing rules and mechanisms only awkwardly address, if at all.

In law, accountability requires high levels of certainty in assigning responsibility for acts because of the potential seriousness of the consequences. This need for certainty exists in deciding what rules apply to an act, who is responsible, and whether the responsible party violated the rules. In LOAC, for example, determining that a cyber operation constituted an armed attack triggers the victim state's right to use force in self-defense, which could escalate hostilities. Prosecuting an individual for committing a war crime by participating in a cyber attack raises human rights issues that the accountability process must not take lightly in order to retain legitimacy.

A Triple Burden for Accountability Analysis

Reaching the needed level of certainty with confidence faces difficulties in the cyber context. The problem of accountability arises from a triple accountability burden produced by the problems of application, attribution, and assessment *before* accountability analysis begins. Controversies about whether cyber operations fall within or outside LOAC represent differences in interpreting potentially applicable rules, but these controversies also provide ways to avoid accountability for cyber acts by keeping the controversies alive. In this respect, international law's lack of rules regulating espionage provides an elastic and expansive "accountability-free zone" for a vast array of cyber operations. The intensity of cyber espionage, documented by massive efforts to penetrate DOD and other US government computers, suggests that states are taking advantage of this "accountability-free zone" despite serious political, security, and economic damage caused by this behavior.

The attribution problem also feeds the potential for impunity if those responsible for cyber acts cannot be identified. The impunity that anonymity provides creates incentives to keep the attribution problem robust through technological means, potentially fueling an offensive–defense cyber arms race. The problem of assessment demonstrates that determining whether cyber operations violate LOAC rules can be difficult, perhaps encouraging tolerance for subjecting cyber activities to less scrutiny under LOAC, which undermines the need for accountability. The problems of application and attribution might feed this tolerance because getting past these two obstacles and the problem of assessment to reach actionable accountability will remain daunting without technological, policy, or legal breakthroughs that improve clarity of analysis and confidence in conclusions, especially in the area of attribution.

Cyber Accountability, Existing Mechanisms, and International Criminal Law

The accountability problem in the cyber context confronts other issues that exacerbate the difficulty for LOAC regulation of cyber operations. First, LOAC accountability rules and mechanisms have struggled to improve accountability in conventional conflicts. Over time states rendered reprisals illegal. Collective security and international judicial organs in the League of Nations and United Nations proved vulnerable to international politics. Ad hoc tribunals for prosecuting crimes committed in armed conflicts occurred after World War II but not again until after the Cold War. Experiences with such tribunals have been controversial, whether the problem has been accusations of "victor's justice," inconsistent usage, exorbitant costs, or failure to build rule-of-law capacity in postconflict nations. The latest mechanism, ICC, has yet to prove its sustainable effectiveness, especially with respect to the great powers. Seeking accountability in connection with cyber operations thus faces a sobering inheritance bequeathed by efforts to mitigate impunity in conventional conflict.

International Criminal Law and Cyber Operations

The nature of cyber operations raises difficulties for the criminal law approaches to accountability used in ad hoc tribunals and the ICC. For example, under the ICC's definition of the crime of aggression, would release of the Stuxnet worm qualify as an act of aggression? The ICC defines "act of aggression" as "the use of armed force by a State against the sovereignty, territorial integrity or political independence of another State, or in any other manner inconsistent with the Charter of the United Nations."[36] Analyzing whether dissemination of Stuxnet constituted the use of armed force in the definition of an act of aggression repeats the problems of determining whether the release of this worm qualified as a use of force or an armed attack under *jus ad bellum*.

Even accepting that consequences matter more than the means used, many cyber operations, like the Stuxnet episode, might produce limited impact because of their nonlethal nature, certainly compared to use of conventional lethal weapons. Further, the ICC's crime of aggression requires identification of "a person in a position effectively to exercise control over or to direct the political or military action of a State" who planned, prepared, initiated, or executed the act of aggression.[37] The same difficulties would arise in linking a cyber operation with other ICC crimes, such as the war crime of attacking civilian objects. Hence, with the international criminal law approach, we replay the problems of application, attribution, and assessment in the specific accountability context but with the knowledge that the imposition of criminal sanctions on individuals leaves less legal leeway for uncertainties in analysis.

Building Accountability into Emerging Cyber Operation Capabilities

States can address the accountability problem by building mechanisms in their cyber capabilities that heighten the level of LOAC evaluation of cyber activities by military, intelligence, and civilian entities. LOAC requires states to ensure that their armed forces are educated and trained in LOAC and that they can investigate and prosecute their nationals for violations.[38] USCYBERCOM has stated that operations under its command shall respect LOAC, which requires the new command to integrate LOAC-vetting processes into its full spectrum of military cyber operations.[39] The same requirement applies to all countries undertaking efforts to add, improve, and scale-up their offensive and defensive cyber capabilities. Guidance from the International Committee of the Red Cross, which is aware of the threat posed by cyberwar to LOAC, on accomplishing this national-level accountability task might be useful.[40]

Conclusion

As a "fifth dimension" of warfare, cyberspace represents a new dimension for LOAC. This chapter analyzed how cyberspace weakens the ability to speak authoritatively about LOAC concerning cyber operations in armed conflicts. These problems create the specter of a cyberspace version of Cicero's warning about law and war—*inter arma silent leges*. The threat does not arise from an absence of laws or analyses of how the rules translate in the cyber realm. The threat emerges from difficulties that arise in the controversies about how to categorize cyber operations in LOAC, the obstacles created by the inability to identify initiators of cyber acts, disagreements about the meaning of LOAC rules as applied to cyber actions, and challenges faced in ensuring that impunity does not characterize cyberwar. Underneath these problems, states and nonstate actors are accelerating development of offensive and defensive capabilities to engage in cyber operations as part of armed conflict.

As has happened before, a new technology of war is racing ahead of rules designed to regulate warfare. Experience with this phenomenon is not reassuring because new technologies of demonstrated utility can create lasting conundrums for LOAC. According to the ICJ, the use of nuclear weapons would violate LOAC; yet a growing number of states have nuclear weapons. "Smart" weapons allow for more discriminate uses of force, but the use of smart weapons with UAVs has stimulated LOAC and other legal controversies.[41] Nonlethal technologies have produced arms control disputes (e.g., concerning incapacitating chemical agents and the Chemical Weapons Convention[42]) and ethical challenges to LOAC (e.g., arguments that LOAC frustrates use of nonlethal technologies in civilian-dense contexts in favor of "lethal" weapons[43]).

The conundrums for LOAC related to cyber operations are in many ways deeper and more problematical than those described earlier. Only cyber technologies appear capable of producing both indiscriminate WMD-scale damage, which causes fear, and precise and nonlethal consequences, which creates fascination. Further, unlike many advanced weapons, cyber technologies are universally available and are beyond arms control or nonproliferation approaches. No other technology troublesome for LOAC has such a close relationship with information operations, intelligence gathering, and espionage—none of which LOAC regulates. Unlike other nonlethal weapons, cyber weapons do not operate directly against people or property, which makes any antipersonnel or antimateriel impact dependent on multiple intermediary mechanisms involving software-hardware-people/property interfaces.

Consequence-driven analysis of LOAC allows "what if" analogies using familiar LOAC scenarios. Although helpful, the utility of these analogies is limited for handling the cyber challenge to LOAC. People have imagined cyber attacks as devastating as nuclear attacks in order to apply LOAC, but this approach often fails to note that the relationship between LOAC and nuclear weapons remains controversial and that the greatest utility of nuclear weapons is deterrence not actual use. By analogy, then, states will want to possess awesome cyber capabilities to deter rivals, but the actual use of such capabilities in armed conflict will be more limited in line with the strategy and tactics guiding application of force in the conflict. Those more limited cyber operations are where the problems of application, attribution, assessment, and accountability have their biggest impact on LOAC.

Looking into the future, a cyber version of *inter arma silent leges* remains likely because the three dominant normative strategies described in the literature do not promise to clarify LOAC's relationship with cyber conflict. One strategy asserts that applying the existing body of LOAC to cyber operations presents no serious difficulties, meaning that we apply these rules to cyber events on a case-by-case basis. The four problems analyzed in this chapter and their cumulative impact on LOAC in cyberspace make this status quo strategy complacent for reasons that go beyond the attribution problem. However, this attitude is attractive if the purpose behind it is to leave LOAC in the background while states explore what cyber technologies can accomplish in armed conflicts.

The second approach argues for development of new rules because LOAC does not function well in cyberspace. This approach assumes that states know what rules to negotiate, which is not clear given the multiple challenges cyber operations present to LOAC, and that states are interested in negotiating new rules before they have advanced their cyber capabilities in a more fluid and conducive context. The third argument counsels abandoning the LOAC-centric framework because this approach, especially its need for attribution, will never provide guidance for improving cybersecurity in the context of armed conflict.

Perhaps the best prospects for developing and sustaining a more authoritative voice for LOAC in cyber conflict rest in current and emerging cyber powers. It is essential that these powers understand the promise and problems of cyber operations better and decide that both the promise and the problems require revisiting LOAC within their national contexts and at the international level through cybercentric refinements of existing approaches and rules. In the end, for law not to be silent when arms clash, those wielding the arms must be willing to have law heard in their battle cries.

Notes

1. US Strategic Command, "US Cyber Command Fact Sheet," current as of December 2011, www.stratcom.mil/factsheets/Cyber_Command.

2. See, e.g., William A. Owens, Kenneth W. Dam, and Herbert S. Lin, ed. *Technology, Policy, Law, and Ethics regarding US Acquisition and Use of Cyberattack Capabilities* (Washington, DC: National Academies Press, 2009), 241–82; and David E. Graham, "Cyber Threats and the Law of War," *Journal of National Security Law & Policy* 4 (2010): 87–102.

3. Cicero, *Pro tito annio milone oratio*, §IV ("In time of war, laws are silent"), *The Latin Library*, accessed December 14, 2010, www.thelatinlibrary.com/cicero/milo.shtml.

4. On Estonia, see Scott J. Shackelford, "From Nuclear War to Net War: Analogizing Cyber Attacks in International Law," *Berkeley Journal of International Law* 27, no. 1 (2009): 203–10. On Georgia, see US Cyber Consequences Unit, "Overview of the US-CCU of the Cyber Campaign against Georgia in August of 2008," US-CCU Special Report, August 2009, www.registan.net/wp-content/uploads/2009/08/US-CCU-Georgia-Cyber-Campaign-Overview.pdf. On Chinese-linked hacking and infiltration, see Adam Segal, "The Chinese Internet Century," *Foreign Policy*, January 26, 2010, accessed December 14, 2010, www.foreignpolicy.com/articles/2010/01/26/the_chinese_internet_century. On Iranian nuclear centrifuges in the Stuxnet episode, see Mark Clayton, "Stuxnet Malware Is 'Weapon' Out to Destroy . . . Iran's Bushehr Nuclear Plant?," *Christian Science Monitor*, September 21, 2010, accessed December 14, 2010, www.csmonitor.com/USA/2010/0921/Stuxnet-malware-is-weapon-out-to-destroy-Iran-s-Bushehr-nuclear-plant. On US intentions, see William J. Lynn III, "Defending a New Domain: The Pentagon's Cyber-strategy," US Department of Defense—United States Cyber Command: Cybersecurity, accessed December 14, 2010, www.defense.gov/home/features/2010/0410_cybersec/lynn-article1.aspx. On the cyber capabilities of other countries, see Rex Hughes, "A Treaty for Cyberspace," *International Affairs* 86, no. 2 (2010): 523–41.

5. International Court of Justice, "Legality of the Threat or Use of Force of Nuclear Weapons, Advisory Opinion," *ICJ Reports 1996*, 266.

6. Shackelford, "From Nuclear War to Net War," 195.

7. "Marching Off to Cyberwar," *The Economist*, December 4, 2008, accessed on December 14, 2010, www.economist.com/node/12673385.

8. Shackelford, "From Nuclear War to Net War," 209.

9. See, e.g., Gerald Posner, "China's Secret Cyberterrorism," *Daily Beast*, January 12, 2010, accessed on December 14, 2010, www.thedailybeast.com/blogs-and-stories/2010-01-13/chinas-secret-cyber-terrori sm/.

10. Jaikumar Vijayan, "Report Sounds Alarm on China's Rerouting of US Internet Traffic," *Computerworld*, November 18, 2010, accessed on December 14, 2010, www.computerworld.com/s/article/9197019/Update_Report_sounds_alarm_on_China_s_rerouting_of_U.S._Internet_traffic.

11. Simon Chesterman, "The Spy Who Came in from the Cold War: Intelligence and International Law," *Michigan Journal of International Law* 27 (2006): 1071–1130.

12. Human Rights Watch, "Up in Flames: Humanitarian Law Violations and Civilian Victims in the Conflict over South Ossetia" (New York: Human Rights Watch, 2009), www.hrw.org/sites/default/files/reports/georgia0109web.pdf.

13. Matthew J. Sklerov, "Solving the Dilemma of State Responses to Cyberattacks: A Justification for the Use of Active Defenses against States Who Neglect Their Duty to Prevent," *Military Law Review* 201 (2009): 1–85.

14. International Court of Justice, "Military and Paramilitary Activities in and against Nicaragua (*Nicaragua v. United States of America*), Merits," *ICJ Reports 1986*, 14–150.

15. International Criminal Tribunal for the Former Yugoslavia, "*Prosecutor v. Dusko Tadic*," Case No. IT-94-1-A, July 15, 1999.

16. Shackelford, "From Nuclear War to Net War," 208.

17. Duncan B. Hollis, "Why States Need an International Law for Information Operations," *Lewis & Clark Law Review* 11, no. 4 (2007): 1026.

18. Greg Keizer, "China Did Not Hijack 15% of the Net, Counters Researcher," *Computerworld*, November 19, 2010, accessed December 14, 2010, www.computerworld.com/s/article/9197438/China_did_not_hijack_15_of_the_Net_counters_researcher.

19. Peter Beaumont, "Stuxnet Worm Heralds New Era of Global Cyberwar," *Guardian*, September 30, 2010, accessed on December 14, 2010, www.guardian.co.uk/technology/2010/sep/30/stuxnet-worm-new-era-global-cyberwar.

20. US Cyber Consequences Unit, "Overview by the US-CCU of the Cyber Campaign against Georgia in August of 2008," 3.

21. Greg Rattray, Chris Evans, and Jason Healey, "American Security in the Cybercommons," in *Contested Commons: The Future of American Power in a Multipolar World*, ed. Abraham M. Denmark and James Mulvenon (Washington, DC: Center for a New American Security, 2010), 151–72; and Duncan B. Hollis, "An e-SOS for Cyberspace," *Harvard Journal of International Law* 52, no. 2 (2011), accessed December 14, 2010, http://ssrn.com/abstract = 1670330.

22. *Nicaragua v. United States*, 62.

23. *Prosecutor v. Tadic*, 50.

24. Gen. Keith B. Alexander, Commander, United States Cyber Command, "Statement before the House Committee on Armed Services," September 23, 2010, 7. www.defense.gov/home/features/2010/0410_cybersec/docs/USCC%20Command%20Posture%20Statement_HASC_22SEP10_FINAL%20_OMB%20Approved_.pdf.

25. International Committee of the Red Cross, Customary International Humanitarian Law, "Rule 70: Weapons of a Nature to Cause Superfluous Injury or Unnecessary Suffering," accessed December 14, 2010, www.icrc.org/customary-ihl/eng/docs/v1_rul_rule70.

26. International Committee of the Red Cross, Customary International Humanitarian Law, "Rule 71: Weapons That Are by Nature Indiscriminate," accessed December 14, 2010, www.icrc.org/customary-ihl/eng/docs/v1_rul_rule71.

27. Charter of the United Nations, Article 2(4), www.un.org/en/documents/charter/chapter1.shtml, and Article 51, www.un.org/en/documents/charter/chapter7.shtml. Both accessed December 14, 2010.

28. Michael N. Schmitt, "Computer Network Attack and the Use of Force in International Law: Thoughts on a Normative Framework," *Columbia Journal of Transnational Law* 37 (1999): 914.

29. Nicolas Falliere, Liam O. Murchu, and Eric Chen, *W32.Stuxnet Dossier*, Version 1.4, February 2011.

30. See David P. Fidler, "Was Stuxnet an Act of War? Decoding a Cyberattack," *IEEE Security & Privacy* 9, no. 4 (2011): 56–58.

31. Michael N. Schmitt, "Wired Warfare: Computer Network Attack and *Jus in Bello*," *International Review of the Red Cross* 84 (2002): 365–99.

32. US Department of Defense, "An Assessment of International Legal Issues in Information Operations," May 1999, 11, www.au.af.mil/au/awc/awcgate/dod-io-legal/dod-io-legal.pdf.

33. See, e.g., Graham, "Cyber Threats"; Hollis, "Why States Need an International Law"; Schmitt, "Wired Warfare"; and Shackelford, "From Nuclear War to Net War."

34. On the rules of attack, see "Protocol Additional to the Geneva Conventions of 12 August 1949, and Relating to the Protection of Victims of International Armed Conflicts (Protocol I), June 8, 1977, Article 49(1)," *ICRC* website, accessed December 14, 2010, www.icrc.org/ihl.nsf/FULL/470?OpenDocument.

35. Graham, "Cyber Threats," 99.

36. International Criminal Court, "The Crime of Aggression, RC/Res. 6," June 28, 2010, 2, accessed December 14, 2010, www.icc-cpi.int/iccdocs/asp_docs/Resolutions/RC-Res.6-ENG.pdf.

37. Ibid., 5.

38. International Committee of the Red Cross, "Customary International Humanitarian Law, Rule 142: Instruction in International Humanitarian Law within Armed Forces," www.icrc.org/customary-ihl/eng/docs/v1_rul_rule142; and International Committee of the Red Cross, "Customary International Humanitarian Law, Rule 158: Prosecution of War Crimes," www.icrc.org/customary-ihl/eng/docs/v1_rul_rule158. Both accessed December 14, 2010.

39. General Alexander, "Statement before the House Committee on Armed Services," 7.

40. International Committee on the Red Cross, "Cyber Warfare," accessed December 14, 2010, www.icrc.org/eng/war-and-law/conduct-hostilities/information-warfare/index.jsp.

41. Mary Ellen O'Connell, "Lawful Use of Combat Drones," Statement before the House of Representatives Subcommittee on National Security and Foreign Affairs for Hearing, "Rise of the Drones II: Examining the Legality of Unmanned Targeting," April 28, 2010, accessed December 14, 2010, www.fas.org/irp/congress/2010_hr/042810oconnell.pdf.

42. David P. Fidler, "The Meaning of Moscow: 'Non-Lethal' Weapons and International Law in the Early 21st Century," *International Review of the Red Cross* 87 (2005): 525–52.

43. David P. Fidler, "'Non-Lethal' Weapons and International Law: Three Perspectives on the Future," in *The Future of Non-Lethal Weapons: Technologies, Operations, Ethics, and Law*, ed. Nick Lewer (London: Frank Cass, 2002), 26–38.

CHAPTER 6

The Emerging Structure of Strategic Cyber Offense, Cyber Defense, and Cyber Deterrence

Richard B. Andres

Aт THE HEIGHT OF THE COLD WAR IN JUNE OF 1982, an American satellite detected a three-kiloton blast emanating from Siberia. Upon examination, analysts discovered that the explosion was the result of a logic bomb implanted by the United States in the cyber physical control system that governed a Soviet natural gas pipeline. The malware was designed to reset the pump speeds and valve settings in order to increase the pressure in the pipe. The result, according to former air force secretary Thomas Reed, "was the most monumental non-nuclear explosion and fire ever seen from space."[1]

The 1982 incident represented the first cyber attack of its kind in history and demonstrated a radical new military capability. The event was not important because of its kinetic results; missiles or bombers probably could have achieved the same objective. Rather, the attack was important because it demonstrated the efficacy of a weapon that ignores both physical defenses and deterrent threats. Interestingly, the United States was willing and able to use malware against a hostile, nuclear-armed superpower without concern of attribution or threat of retaliation.

Cyberwarfare

Over the last few years, US policymakers have become increasingly concerned about US vulnerability to cyber attacks. In 2009 President Obama warned of cyber threats to US national security and described cyber attacks that crippled Georgia during its conflict with Russia.[2] In his 2010 annual threat assessment to the Senate, US Director of National Intelligence, Adm. Dennis Blair, listed cyber attacks first on his list of threats—before the economy, terrorism or even the wars in Iraq and Afghanistan.[3] In response to these growing threats, the Department of Defense created US Cyber Command in 2011, a military command on par with the regional combat commands.

President Obama's and Admiral Blair's public statements and anxiety over cyber threats reflect the latest phase in an evolving debate about US vulnerability to opponents' cyber capabilities and strategies. Pessimists have long argued that US systems are susceptible and that enemies could launch attacks to US infrastructure that would inflict massive financial and physical damage to the country.[4] Conversely, optimists argue that cyber threats are generally overstated and that US systems are for the most part secure.[5]

In the past there were good reasons to side with the optimists. Despite a few highly publicized incidents over the decades, such as the 1982 Siberia attack, the "cyber Pearl Harbor" that pessimists worry about has never occurred. While claims have surfaced that cyber attacks were behind various disasters, in most cases neither the victim nor the purported attackers have stepped forward to assign responsibility or blame, making even these claims difficult to verify.

Nevertheless, in this arena, it is not clear that history is a good guide to opinion. Cyberspace is a murky realm in which few participants announce their activities. Cyber technology is quickly evolving, the organizational incentives it provides are in flux, and even cyber optimists agree that the trend is toward more frequent and serious attacks. Computer technology that sounds like science fiction one year is often passé the next. The number and sophistication of attacks on financial, intelligence, and physical control systems are all increasing. While this sort of trend does not provide prima facie evidence that cyber disaster looms in the near future for the United States, it does mean that it is unclear how much weight should be given to the earlier record. In the case of cyber threats, the past is not necessarily prologue. Assessing future threats requires understanding the strategy that the United States uses to protect itself and understanding how well that strategy copes with changing cyber technology and the organizational techniques used by cybercriminals, cyber spies, and cyberwarriors.

The Dynamics of Cyber Defense and Cyber Deterrence

Historically, when nations begin to adopt radical new weapons technology, the political incentives for conflict often change. This dynamic may make war less tempting, as did nuclear weapons in the twentieth century, or more enticing, as did the development of national rail networks in late-nineteenth-century Europe. In some cases, technological innovation can even change who fights, as when the development of oceangoing shipping moved Europe's commerce offshore and gave rise to semi-autonomous pirate fleets in northern Europe and North Africa in the sixteenth century.[6]

Over the last few decades, the rise of cyber technology has radically changed the economic and industrial landscape of the global system. Most data, including corporate and state secrets, are stored digitally on Internet-connected computer networks. Financially, the vast majority of the world's money is stored and transferred across the Internet. Industrially, the systems that control most physical infrastructure have become largely automated and connected to the Internet. As Derek Reveron describes in chapter 1, "companies have harnessed cyberspace to create new industries, a vibrant social space, and a new economic sphere that are intertwined with our everyday lives."

The increasing Internet accessibility of secrets, money, and industry creates significant incentives for individuals, groups, and states to find ways to use offensive cyber capabilities. This motivation is heightened by the fact that attributing attacks from cyberspace is often impossible and the laws and social norms relating to cyber espionage, crime, and warfare are often weak or nonexistent (see chapter 5, this volume). As a result, those who profit from cyber attacks are unlikely to be apprehended and if caught seldom face punishment.

The Existing Mechanism

The incentives for cybercrime, cyber espionage, and cyberwarfare that emerged with the growth of cyber infrastructure have given rise to a wide range of actors who regularly attempt to profit from the vulnerability of computerized systems. The US government has responded to these groups largely using the same formula that protects the United States from noncyber attacks. For the most part, the United States delegates defensive and deterrent duties against small actors—such as lone criminals or small groups—to state and local police forces and only employs federal agencies against states and significant nonstate actors such as major terrorist groups.

The reluctance of the federal government to intervene against small actors makes sense in the noncyber arena. The federal government seldom intervenes domestically because federal departments and agencies are limited in their ability to reduce local crime. Moreover, any significant measures the federal government might take, such as deploying the armed forces as police, would likely violate the existing social contract between the US government and its citizens.

The noncyber division of duties between federal and local groups is relevant to understanding the cyber division as well. The traditional model creates a precedent for limiting the federal government's role in protecting civilian systems. While federal intervention on cyber issues would not involve stationing soldiers in residential neighborhoods, it would raise constitutional questions about granting the government more control over US businesses and greater access to citizens' private information.

At the national and international levels, the traditional US separation of authorities is also important. If the United States seldom suffers many deaths from other states or large nonstate actors, this says more about the United States' ability to deter these attacks than about the lack of hostile actors with the ability to harm US citizens. Over the years, numerous actors have declared their desire to attack the United States and possessed the capabilities to do so. The Soviet Union, China, North Korea, Vietnam, Iran, and Cuba, to name a few, have all at times viewed the United States as a mortal enemy and controlled weapons that could inflict serious damage on American infrastructure, particularly if used in a surprise attack.

Across history, the US government has primarily protected the country's infrastructure against attacks through deterrence. Deterring attacks has depended on convincing opponents that the costs of attacking would be greater than any benefits they might obtain. In general terms, this means attempting to deny benefits to attackers by defending America's most valuable targets and raising fears that the United States will retaliate using its military or other forms of national power. The United States has also constrained the behavior of many states through treaties and other international agreements meant to increase transparency and link national and international institutions to states' good behavior.

A number of experts have argued that the dynamics for deterring nations from using cyber attacks are the same. They point out that while it is difficult to attribute the source of a cyber attack, it is not impossible. Even if no cyber forensic evidence is available, it is likely the United States could attribute the attack based on contextual factors or noncyber forensic evidence.[7] Thus, the argument goes, countries that would be unwilling to risk US retaliation for launching a conventional attack would also be reluctant to launch a devastating cyber attack.[8]

Probably as a consequence of accepting the separation of duties between federal organizations and local law enforcement authorities, the United States has drifted over the three decades of the cyber age toward similar practices to defend itself against cyber attacks. Local authorities and private companies play the main role in protecting US citizens against cyber attacks from individuals and small nonstate organizations. The federal government accepts responsibility for defending the nation against large-scale cyber attacks from nation-states and significant nonstate actors on critical infrastructure but relies almost exclusively on the premise that it can deter major attacks by the same means it uses to deter conventional attacks.

Emerging Problems

There are reasons to believe that the traditional bifurcated defense and deterrence model is failing under threats created by emerging cyber technology. Some of these are described below.

The Attribution Problem

A good deal has been written about the attribution problem. Because of how the Internet was designed and has evolved, it is often possible for skilled hackers to conceal their identity and the origin of their attacks.[9] In this respect, illegal actions in and through cyberspace are substantially different from those usually countered by traditional law enforcement and military methods. The attribution problem makes it difficult for both federal and local organizations to deter attacks and consequently provides an incentive to engage in cyber attacks.

The Geography Problem

Connected to the attribution problem is the geography problem. The traditional formula for defending against criminals and other nonstate actors only authorizes authorities to act within a certain jurisdiction. Cyberspace, however, does not have well-defined borders and, as a general rule, distance and geography are irrelevant. As a result, most attacks originate outside the jurisdiction of local police, making it difficult to find and hold distant attackers to account. Meanwhile, the federal government seldom has the will or resources to pursue extra-geographical cybercrime.

The Code of Silence Problem

A third characteristic that accompanies cyber technology and cyber conflict is a code of silence problem. Cyber offensive and defensive techniques and capabilities are most effective when they are secret. Once a hacking technique is known, defenders can develop a counter. When a defensive vulnerability is discovered, attackers find ways to exploit it. Beyond this, organizations that suffer attacks often lose the confidence of stakeholders: when clients learn that a financial organization has been successfully hacked, they may take their business elsewhere; when boards of governors or politicians find that a utility has been penetrated, they often demand expensive reforms; when intelligence and military organizations are compromised, they risk losing credibility with their constituencies. Consequently, public and private organizations both have a significant incentive to prevaricate when their defenses are compromised. This reduces the ability of organizations to learn from their mistakes and raise their guard against future attacks and stifles private industry's ability to develop better defense techniques.

The Antiregulation Problem

In some cases, government regulation could do much to protect vulnerable industries from cyber attacks. This may include regulations that require better cybersecurity for firms that are likely targets for attacks by foreign countries, or that require firms controlling critical infrastructure to disconnect their hardware from the Internet. In the United States, the organizations that control critical infrastructure are typically privately owned and cyber regulation would impose significant economic costs upon them. Since there is little incentive for criminal organizations to attack such companies, it is often unclear to these industries why they should pay to protect themselves from cyber attacks. As a result, many of the most likely targets of devastating cyber attacks by states or terrorists consistently lobby against greater regulation.[10]

The Spy-versus-Treaty Problem

Related to the problem just described is the spy-versus-treaty problem that causes some democracies to reject international cybersecurity agreements. A promising remedy for cybercrime and espionage involves creating treaties and other international agreements designed to facilitate tracking attacks across borders. Such treaties could mandate technical methods of tracking attacks within and between countries and require law enforcement agencies and companies within countries to share information across borders with organizations in victimized states. The problem with this method is that government organizations are often reluctant to develop forensic methods within their own countries or share information on attacks with other states. One reason for this involves intelligence-gathering organizations. Few organizations benefit as much from cyberspace as intelligence agencies. In the pre–digital age, a spy's take was usually measured in individual sheets of paper smuggled at great risk to drop points by hand. Getting a document out of a country might require dozens of agents, millions of dollars, and years of planning. Today, spy agencies exfiltrate data by the terabyte (a terabyte is approximately 64 million pages), usually from the comfort of an office within their home country. The ability to spy via computer and the Internet has radically improved agencies' ability to collect information, but it also provides them with a powerful incentive to oppose legislation or regulation that might restrict their ability to use this new capability. This is particularly true for countries that follow through on their international agreements. In the United States, for instance, the Constitution gives international treaties the force of law. If the United States were to sign a treaty that restricted intelligence agencies from using the Internet to spy on other states or that required the United States to share cyber evidence, US intelligence agencies would be placed at a disadvantage compared to their counterparts in nations that do not honor their international commitments.

The Offensive Incentive Problem

Beyond the incentive to avoid international agreements, organizations with offensive cyber capabilities have incentives to conduct preemptive attacks on potential opponents. The incentives are obvious for criminal and intelligence organizations: the amounts of money and sensitive data that can be obtained through offensive cyber actions are significant. There is also a less often recognized incentive for militaries to act preemptively in cyberspace. One of the most noteworthy characteristics of cyber defenses is that they change rapidly. Practically speaking, the only way to maintain the ability to penetrate an opponent's cyber defenses is to continually probe and alter them. If a state wants the capability to penetrate an opponent's defenses in war, it must map them before the war begins; if it wants to be able to activate logic bombs in an opponent's weapons systems or electric power grid in the future, it must plant them in the present. However, these preemptive actions can have unanticipated and sometimes catastrophic consequences. Probing critical infrastructure can inadvertently disable it, and logic bombs may spread beyond the attacker's control.

The Social Norms Problem

A final dynamic making cyber attacks more difficult to deter than physical attacks is the social norms problem. Over the past few centuries the international community has developed social norms related to crime, espionage, and warfare. These norms infuse common understandings about proper and proportional behavior. Governments have precedents for distinguishing between crime and espionage, and there is some agreement about what sorts of measures are acts of war. In cyber conflict, traditional norms seldom hold and there is little agreement about the thresholds that separate crime, espionage, and acts of war. If private actors based in one country were to steal a million dollars worth of goods being transported on the high seas, most observers would consider it an act of piracy; if they stole ten million dollars worth of software from another state's computers, it is not clear the act would get much notice.

To provide another example, a state launching a cruise missile that destroyed a million dollars worth of another state's infrastructure would be considered an act of war, but a state launching a virus that destroyed a hundred million dollars worth of another state's infrastructure would not yield the same strong reaction. The lack of norms in cyber conflict creates ambiguities about deterrence thresholds and increases the odds that states will use cyber weapons to achieve objectives that they would be unwilling or unable to pursue using traditional military means. This type of uncertainty increases the chances that attackers and defenders' beliefs about thresholds will not match and thereby increases the odds that states or powerful nonstate attackers will cross defenders' red lines and invite retribution and escalation. (Herb Lin explores this in depth in chapter 3 of this volume.)

Recent History and Trends

The dynamics described earlier are creating challenges for traditional conceptions of national security. The incentive to use cyber weapons has proven irresistible to both private and governmental organizations. Over the last decade, the combination of private and public incentives for weaponizing cyberspace appears to have led states to adopt a two-tiered system. On the one hand, following the traditional model, governments sometimes act directly in cyberspace—stealing opponents' secrets and damaging each other's infrastructure but generally keeping attacks to a level that does not escalate to kinetic war. On the other hand, states empower private groups within their borders to take far more provocative actions while providing governments with plausible deniability.

State-on-State Cyber Attacks

The most obvious way that states are currently using cyber weapons is to directly attack each others' systems. Little is known about virtually any state's offensive campaigns, but several events have come to light that provide at least a glimpse into the world of state-versus-state cyber conflict. This look under the cyber veil suggests that the last two decades have seen significant escalation in the frequency and magnitude of state-sponsored cyber attacks.

A timeline of cyber conflict would show that following the 1982 attack on the USSR, the most common and well-known state-on-state cyber attacks involved espionage. *Newsweek* reported in 1999 that, in an operation labeled "Moonlight Maze," Russian hackers broke into government computer systems at the Pentagon, NASA, the Department of Energy, and many other locations. *Newsweek* quoted Deputy Secretary of Defense John Hamre as saying "we're in the middle of a cyberwar," which suggests that the attack was state-sponsored.[11] Beyond Hamre's remark, the incident does not appear to have risen to the level of a diplomatic incident. In a similar vein, *Time* reported that, in a series of coordinated attacks in 2003 labeled "Titan Rain," hackers operating out of China penetrated numerous sensitive, but not secret, US government and defense contractor computer systems.[12]

Over time, the scope and sophistication of these attacks has increased. In 2009 Canada's Information Warfare Monitor announced that it had discovered a China-based spy program (Ghostnet) that had penetrated ministries of foreign affairs and embassies in more than one hundred countries.[13] This time the worm not only permitted its designers to download files, it also allowed them to use the microphones and cameras in hacked computers to eavesdrop.[14] The following year, Google reported that China had hacked its servers attempting to retrieve information on human rights activists in China. Upon closer inspection the campaign, later termed "Operation Aurora," was discovered to have penetrated the networks of more than thirty major financial, defense, and technology companies as well as research institutions in the United States.[15]

For most of the cyber era, the US government had little to say about cyber attacks. In the fall of 2010, however, this changed when Deputy Secretary of Defense William Lynn dropped a bombshell in a *Foreign Affairs* article by admitting that between 2008 and 2010 the Department of Defense's classified and unclassified networks had been plundered by hackers. He termed the US response to the hacking campaign "Buckshot Yankee" and went on to say, "Over the past ten years, the frequency and sophistication of intrusions into US military networks have increased exponentially. Every day, US military and civilian networks are probed thousands of times and scanned millions of times. And the 2008 intrusion that led to Operation Buckshot Yankee was not the only successful penetration. Adversaries have acquired thousands of files from US networks and from the networks of US allies and industry partners, including weapons blueprints, operational plans, and surveillance data."[16]

Beyond mere espionage, there is evidence that states are sabotaging critical infrastructure in other countries. In 2009 the *Wall Street Journal*, quoting unnamed government officials, reported that both Russia and China had penetrated the US electric grid, inserting malware that could potentially destroy it. The article went on to say that US intelligence agencies had detected successful cyber attacks against other nations' critical infrastructures and that many US infrastructures were as vulnerable as their foreign counterparts.[17] In his *Foreign Affairs* article, Secretary Lynn stated that foreign governments are able to penetrate the systems that control critical civilian infrastructure such as the US electric grid, transportation networks, and financial systems and could cause massive physical damage and economic disruption.[18] Reports by the Department of Homeland Security have concluded that a successful cyber attack on the US electric grid could physically destroy generation and transmission equipment, potentially plunging significant portions of the country into darkness for months or longer.

Late in 2010 an example of a state-sponsored attack on physical infrastructure came to light when reports surfaced that Iran's nuclear facilities at Natanz had been damaged by the Stuxnet virus. Based on the complexity of the malware, analysts concluded that only a nation-state had the resources to write it. The worm appeared to be designed specifically to damage the centrifuges at Natanz, where Iran is believed to enrich uranium for nuclear weapons. Moreover, the software was designed to destroy the Iranian equipment without causing collateral damage elsewhere. Overall, experts have guessed that the worm set Iran's nuclear program back by at least two years, about the same result that airstrikes on Iran's dispersed and deeply buried infrastructure would achieve.[19] While the effects of the Stuxnet virus are not as flamboyant as the attack that took down the USSR's gas infrastructure in 1982, the actual fiscal and strategic impacts of the attack are probably far greater.

Two things stand out from the record of (apparently) state-sponsored attacks. First, despite the best efforts of the attackers to cover their tracks, cyber analysts and the media generally agreed on the sources of the attacks. While they did not claim that their evidence was sufficient to hold up in court, there was a good deal of consensus about which countries were responsible and whether attacks were sufficiently sophisticated to have required state support. Second, most attacks have been fairly moderate. In an era with a great deal of physical infrastructure vulnerable to physical destruction by cyber, most attacks have been constrained to espionage and denial-of-service attacks. Even in the case of Stuxnet, the worm appears to have carefully targeted Iran's secret and illegal refinement infrastructure, assiduously avoiding Iran's much more vulnerable and critical civilian infrastructure. By and large, where direct attacks by states are concerned, deterrence appears to be working.

Cyber Militias

If fear of retaliation limits states' willingness to attack each other directly with cyber weapons, it has done less to deter them from using groups of domestic semiautonomous hackers to attack one another. The concept of state-sponsored unflagged piracy is not new. In the sixteenth century, the government of Elizabethan England turned a blind eye and even actively supported raids by English pirates on Spanish treasure ships. In doing so, England enriched itself while weakening its foe and circumventing Spain's deterrent threats. The idea was, and is, to use plausible deniability to reduce the likelihood of retaliation while still gaining the fruits of attacking. In both high-seas piracy and cybercrime, states are aware that no nation can prevent all criminals within its borders from attacking other countries so countries cannot easily be held accountable for some attacks originating from their territory. Thus, aggressive states can play with thresholds by empowering autonomous groups to do things for them that they fear to do themselves.

In the cyber arena, cyber militias made their debut when patriotic Serbian and Russian hackers attacked and defaced US websites during Operation Allied Force (OAF) in 1999 when NATO fought Serbia over Kosovo.[20] During the same war, after the United States accidently bombed the Chinese embassy in Belgrade, Chinese citizens launched retaliatory cyber attacks on the United States after which pro-NATO hackers responded with attacks on Chinese sites. By the end of the year, the methodology had spread, the groups became more organized, and states began to play a greater role. During this period militias in China and Taiwan began to spar, as did groups in India and Pakistan, and Iran and Israel.

During the 2000s illegal cyber activity by civilians increased exponentially—largely driven by the profit motive. During this period the use of botnets, distributed denial-of-service (DDOS), malicious code on websites, software piracy, corporate espionage, and identity theft became more sophisticated. Numerous cyber-for-hire groups emerged, willing to sell criminal cyber capabilities to the highest bidder. Some of these groups appear to have resources rivaling major multinational corporations. Calculating losses due to cybercrime is difficult because losses are often unobserved and unreported. Nevertheless, by the end of the decade President Obama declared that $1 trillion was lost to cybercrime in 2009 alone, a figure larger than the global market for illegal drugs.[21] Representative Sheldon Whitehouse pointed out that cybercrime "is probably the biggest transfer of wealth through theft and piracy in the history of mankind."[22]

There is widespread evidence that numerous governments in countries benefiting from the massive transfer of wealth either regularly turn a blind eye to or actively support these groups. China and Russia are considered two of the biggest beneficiaries of cybercrime and are supporters of cybercriminal groups. Russian groups, such as the Russian Business Network, are part of an organized crime network closely tied to Russian politicians. China appears to have adopted a national strategy that views cyber corporate espionage as a key pillar of its economic policy.[23]

The profit motive for state support to criminal cyber groups overlays another motive for states to encourage cyber militias within their territory. The organizations created to steal money provide both cover and allies for state military-like cyber operations. In 2007, when Russia became involved in a political dispute with Estonia, cyber groups within Russia launched a large-scale DDOS attack on Estonia's networks. The attacks crippled the nation's communication infrastructure, prompting Estonia to petition NATO for intervention. In the wake of the attack, Russia refused to honor its treaty obligations to coordinate with Estonia on locating the attackers and is widely believed to have instigated and supported the attacks.[24] Groups in Russia again attacked an opponent the following year. During the weeks leading up to Russia's invasion of Georgia, Russian groups conducted DDOS attacks on Georgia and apparently rerouted Internet traffic through Russian telecommunications firms. During the invasion the groups conducted more concentrated cyber attacks.[25] Russia used similar cyber techniques in 2009 attacks against Kyrgyzstan, temporarily shutting down its two main Internet service providers and reducing the country's bandwidth by around 80 percent.[26] In each case the patriotic criminals proved enormously helpful to Russia, and in each case Russia refused to sanction its militias or to cooperate with other states to investigate their identities.

Although their actions up until now appear relatively benign when compared to kinetic wars, hacker militias probably represent the most serious cyber threat in the world today. Host states have developed militias in order to provide plausible deniability for their offensive cyber operations. In doing so, they have reduced opponents' ability to deter their predations. This strategy has allowed aggressive states to reap enormous benefits in dollars, intelligence, and even military power. Unfortunately, to be truly convincing, countries have had to provide their militias with a good degree of autonomy.

In a world populated by cyber–physical control systems such as those related to electric grids, chemical plants, gas pipelines, air traffic control systems, and train switching yards, empowering domestic criminal groups to make decisions about the use of cyber weapons is reckless. Broad unofficial statements to hackers about bounties for attacking other states are difficult to fine tune, and interpretations about what classes of infrastructure are within bounds are frequently grey.[27] The skill of those involved is uneven, with clumsy attackers potentially able to cause serious harm by accident. Monitoring and disciplining these groups is nearly impossible.

Because the victims of cyber attack seldom step forward to describe their shortcomings, it is difficult to know how much damage cyber militias have caused so far; but there are some clues. Joel Brenner, the senior US counterintelligence official under Director of National Intelligence Mike McConnell, pointed out in 2008 that the Chinese "operate through sponsoring other organizations that are engaging in international hacking, whether or not under specific direction. . . . It's coming in volumes that are just staggering."[28] There is some evidence that cyber hackers knocked out the Brazilian power grid in 2005, 2007, and 2009. Each of these was a major event, with the 2009 episode cutting power to half the country.[29] Some have speculated that the 2003 blackout in the Northeast United States, the largest in US history, and the great 2008 Florida blackout were caused, possibly accidentally, by Chinese hackers.[30]

Less speculatively, several senior US officials, including President Obama, have gone on record saying that other countries have had their power grids knocked offline by cybercriminals. In 2008 the Central Intelligence Agency announced that utility companies in a number of countries had been blackmailed by hackers operating through the Internet.[31] In a 2009 speech on America's cyber vulnerability, Obama said "we know that cyber intruders have probed our electrical grid and that in other countries cyber attacks have plunged entire cities into darkness."[32] So far no country that has experienced a major blackout has stepped forward to admit that it was one of those referenced by the president. In a study, the Department of Homeland Security concluded that a major attack on the grid had the potential to disable a third of the nation's power for a period of months, and that the economic cost of such an attack would rival the entire cost of World War II.

The heart of the problem is that although states can often be deterred by the threat of attribution and retaliation, militias are less susceptible to deterrence. During the 2008 attack on Georgia by Russian cyber militias, Georgian hackers did little to retaliate. Subsequently, however, Georgian hackers have become more organized, and groups have declared their intent to attack Russia's critical infrastructure in the event of a future Russian attack on Georgia. Groups in Latvia, Kyrgyzstan, Kazakhstan, Estonia, and Lithuania appear to be making similar plans.[33] How much provocation would be required to activate these groups and strategies is unknown, as is whether Russia could defend itself against such attacks. Troublingly, there is no reason to believe that patriotic hackers in other countries are not making similar plans to attack critical US infrastructure if the United States acts in ways opposed to those countries' interests, and reasonable worry exists about whether the governments in those countries could constrain their citizens if emotions ran sufficiently high.

Conclusion

Virtually no evidence regarding cyber conflict is indisputable and virtually no belligerent in this struggle is enthusiastic about discussing its operations or intent. Nevertheless, based on the events described in this chapter, the outline of the emerging character of cyber offense, cyber defense, and cyber deterrence is coming into focus and growing increasingly clear.

The incentives for when and how states use cyber weapons are significantly different from those involved with the use of conventional and nuclear weapons. When states bargain with conventional or nuclear weapons, they prefer to win via coercion without employing the weapons directly. On the cyber front, states prefer to use their weapons without announcing their intent to do so because, when used, cyber tools frequently bring in vast rewards without incurring retaliation or even discovery from defenders.

The nature of the technology is the root cause of the incentive system that encourages states to attack each other in cyberspace: attribution is difficult; cyber weapons easily cross borders; both civilian and government victims are reluctant to admit they have been attacked or penetrated; intelligence organizations within states benefit from the current system; the offense has distinct advantages over the defense; and the norms that determine thresholds for retaliation for noncyber attack do not apply well to attacks from cyberspace.

Based on the incentives created by this system, a number of states have begun to employ a two-part strategy. In the first part, they develop military grade cyber weapons and organizations and employ them directly. In the second, they empower civilian groups (cyber militias) in their countries to attack and loot civilian and government organizations in other states.

The first approach has much in common with traditional espionage and appears to be governed by many of the same rules and norms. While states have shown that they are willing to use their cyber capabilities to gather information, there are few known examples of states using cyber weapons to destroy physical or financial infrastructure (the 1982 attack on the USSR and the Stuxnet attack on Iran being apparent exceptions). This restraint is most likely due to fear of attribution and the risk of retaliation.

The second approach is more problematic. By allowing civilian cyber combatant–like groups to coalesce, providing them with resources, and encouraging them to attack opponents, states can benefit but do so at great risk. In 1999 civilian cyber groups could do little more than deface web pages. Ten years later cybercriminals were responsible for more than one trillion dollars worth of theft. To put this in perspective, in 2009 Russia's gross national product barely exceeded two trillion dollars. Beyond theft, states have begun to use civilian groups in support roles for kinetic wars. There is evidence that some of these groups are capable of overcoming states' defenses to destroy critical infrastructure. If such groups cannot yet do so, given the rapid improvement in offensive cyber technology, there are good reasons to fear that they will be able to do so in the near future. Most importantly, there is little reason to believe that the governments using these groups will have control over when or why they employ their military-grade software.

The nature of war does not change, but its character does. Cyber weapons are beginning to change the character of war in ways that would have been difficult to believe even a few years ago. It is incumbent upon today's thinkers and leaders to understand these changes and attempt to mitigate the potential risk they entail for those engaged in cyber conflict.

Notes

The opinions expressed here are those of the author alone and do not necessarily represent those of National Defense University, the Department of Defense, or the US government.

1. "War in the Fifth Domain: Are the Mouse and Keyboard the New Weapons of Conflict?," *Economist*, July 1, 2010, accessed July 4, 2010. www.economist.com/node/16478792?story_id =16478792&fsrc=rss.

2. Barack Obama, "Remarks by the President on securing Our Nation's Cyber Infrastructure," May 29, 2009, accessed February 25, 2011, www.whitehouse.gov/the_press_office/Remarks-by-the-President-on-Securing-Our-Nations-Cyber-Infrastructure/.

3. Dennis C. Blair, "Annual Threat Assessment of the US Intelligence Community for the Senate Select Committee on Intelligence," February 2, 2010, 3–4, accessed February 23, 2011, www.dni.gov/testimonies/20100202_testimony.pdf.

4. See, for instance, Richard A. Clarke and Robert K. Knake, *Cyber War: The Next Threat to National Security and What to Do about It* (New York: HarperCollins, 2010); and Bradley K. Ashley, "Anatomy of Cyberterrorism: Is America Vulnerable?" (Maxwell AFB, Montgomery, AL: Air War College, Air University, February 27, 2003), accessed February 24, 2011, www.au.af.mil/au/awc/awcgate/awc/ashley.pdf. These concerns are not new; see US General Accounting Office, "Information Security: Computer Attacks at Department of Defense Pose Increasing Risks," GAO/AIMD-96-84, (May 22, 1996), accessed February 24, 2011, www.fas.org/irp/gao/aim96084.htm.

5. Martin Libicki, *Cyberdeterrence and Cyberwar* (Santa Monica, CA: RAND, 2009); Stephen M. Walt, "Is the Cyber Threat Overblown?" *Foreign Policy*, March 30, 2010, accessed February 23, 2011, http://walt.foreignpolicy.com/posts/2010/03/30/is_the_cyber_threat_overblown; and Ryan Singel, "Is the Hacking Threat to National Security Overblown?" *Wired*, June 3, 2009, accessed February 23, 2011, www.wired.com/threatlevel/2009/06/cyberthreat/#.

6. On ways technology can affect international politics, see Emily O. Goldman and Richard B. Andres, "Systemic Effects of Military Innovation and Diffusion," *Security Studies* 8, no. 4 (September 1998): 79–125.

7. Richard Kugler, "Deterrence of Cyber Attack," in *Cyberpower and National Security*, eds. Franklin D. Kramer, Stuart H. Starr, and Larry K. Wentz (Dulles, VA: Potomac Books, 2009); and Will Goodman, "Cyber Deterrence: Tougher in Theory than in Practice?" *Strategic Studies Quarterly* (Fall 2010): 124–25.

8. Richard Clarke, *Cyber War*; and Clarke and Knake, *Cyber War*.

9. J. Hunker, "Roles and Challenges for Sufficient Cyber Attack Attribution" (Hanover, NH: Institute for Information Infrastructure Protection, Dartmouth College, January 2008), accessed February 25, 2011, www.thei3p.org/docs/publications/whitepaper-attribution.pdf; and Ron Keys, Charles Winsteas, and Kendra Simmons, "Cyberspace Security and Attribution," National Security and Cyberspace Institute, July 20, 2011, www.nsci-va.org/White Papers/2010-07-20-Cybersecurity%20Attribution-Keys-Winstead-Simmons.pdf.

10. David Powner, "National Cyber Security Strategy: Key Improvements Are Needed to Strengthen Nation's Posture," Testimony before the Subcommittee on Emerging Threats, Cybersecurity, and Science and Technology, Committee on Homeland Security, House of Representatives, March 10, 2009, accessed February 25, 2011, www.gao.gov/new.items/d09432t.pdf; and "Securing the Modern Electric Grid from Physical and Cyber Attacks," Hearing before the Subcommittee on Emerging Threats, Cybersecurity and Science and Technology of the Committee on Homeland Security, House of Representatives, July 21, 2009, no. 111-30, accessed February 25, 2011, http://frwebgate.access.gpo.gov/cgi-bin/getdoc.cgi?dbname=111_house_hearings&docid=f:53425.pdf.

11. Gregory Vistica, "Russian Hackers Cracked Defense and Energy Department Computers; May Have Snared Classified Naval Codes and Missile Information," *Newsweek*, September 12, 1999, accessed February 23, 2011, on *PRNewswire*, www.prnewswire.com/news-releases/newsweek-exclusive-were-in-the-middle-of-a-cyberwar-74343007.html. The *Newsweek* story was

later questioned. See Daniel Verton, "Russia Hacking Stories Refuted," *Federal Computer Week*, September 27, 1999, http://fcw.com/articles/1999/09/27/russia-hacking-stories-refuted.aspx? sc_lang = en.

12. Nathan Thornburgh, "The Invasion of the Chinese Cyberspies," *Time*, August 29, 2005, accessed February 23, 2011, www.time.com/time/magazine/article/0,9171,1098961-2,00.html. See also Nathan Thornburgh, "Inside the Chinese Cyber Hack," *Time*, August 25, 2005, accessed February 23, 2011, www.time.com/time/nation/article/0,8599,1098371,00.html.

13. "Tracking GhostNet: Investigating a Cyber Espionage Network," *Information Warfare Monitor*, March 29, 2009, www.nartv.org/mirror/ghostnet.pdf.

14. "Major Cyber Spy Network Uncovered," *BBC News*, March 29, 2009, accessed February 23, 2011, http://news.bbc.co.uk/2/hi/americas/7970471.stm.

15. Ariana Eunjung Cha and Ellen Nakashima, "Google China Cyberattack Part of Vast Espionage Campaign, Experts Say," *Washington Post*, January 14, 2010, accessed February 23, 2011, www.washingtonpost.com/wp-dyn/content/article/2010/01/13/AR2010011300359.html? sid = ST2010011300360.

16. William J. Lynn III, "Defending a New Domain: The Pentagon's Cyberstrategy," *Foreign Affairs*, September/October (2010), accessed February 23, 2011, www.foreignaffairs.com/arti cles/66552/william-j-lynn-iii/defending-a-new-domain.

17. Siobhan Gorman, "Electricity Grid in the US Penetrated by Spies," *Wall Street Journal*, April 8, 2009, accessed February 23, 2011, http://online.wsj.com/article/SB123914805204099085.html.

18. Lynn, "Defending a New Domain,"2.

19. "Stuxnet: Targeting Iran's Nuclear Programme," *IISS Strategic Comments* 17 (2011), accessed February 23, 2011, available at https://www.iiss.org/publications/strategic-comments/ buy-a-comment-now/?entryid9 = 56567&q = 0~Stuxnet~.

20. Cyber militias existed before 1999, but their involvement in Operation Allied Force was a seminal event. See, for instance, Robert S. Dudney, "Rise of the Cyber Militias," *Air Force Magazine* 94, no. 2 (February 2011), accessed February 25, 2011, www.airforce-magazine.com/ MagazineArchive/Pages/2011/February%202011/0211cyber.aspx.

21. Clarke and Knake, *Cyber War*, 25.

22. Tim Starks, "Cybersecurity: Learning to Share," *CQ Politics*, August 1, 2010, accessed February 25, 2011, www.cqpolitics.com/wmspage.cfm?docID = weeklyreport-000003716158& cpage = 1.

23. Jamil Anderlini, "Motorola Claims Espionage in Huawei Lawsuit," *Financial Times*, July 22, 2010, accessed February 25, 2011, www.ft.com/cms/s/0/616d2b34-953d-11df-b2e1-00144 feab49a.html.

24. Scott J. Shackelford, "From Nuclear War to Netwar," *Berkeley Journal of International Law* 27, no. 1 (2009): 207, accessed February 25, 2011, www.boalt.org/bjil/docs/BJIL27.1_ Shackelford.pdf.

25. John Markoff, "Before the Gunfire, Cyberattacks," *New York Times*, August 12, 2008, accessed February 25, 2011, www.nytimes.com/2008/08/13/technology/13cyber.html; and Dudney, "Rise of the Cyber Militias."

26. Dudney, "Rise of the Cyber Militias."

27. David Barboza, "Hacking for Fun and Profit in China's Underworld," *New York Times*, February 1, 2010, accessed February 25, 2011, www.nytimes.com/2010/02/02/business/global/ 02hacker.html?pagewanted = 1.

28. Shane Harris, "China's Cyber-Militia," *National Journal*, May 31, 2008, accessed February 25, 2011, http://nationaljournal.com/magazine/china-s-cyber-militia-20080531.

29. Michael Mylrea, "Brazil's Next Battlefield: Cyberspace," *Foreign Policy Journal*, November 15, 2009, accessed February 23, 2011, www.foreignpolicyjournal.com/2009/11/15/brazils-next-battlefield-cyberspace/.

30. Harris, "China's Cyber-Militia."

31. Andy Greenberg, "Hackers Cut Cities' Power," *Forbes*, January 18, 2008, accessed February 25, 2011, www.forbes.com/2008/01/18/cyber-attack-utilities-tech-intel-cx_ag_0118attack .html; and William Lowther, "CIA Launches Hunt for International Computer Hackers Threatening to Hold Cities Ransom by Shutting Off Power," *Daily Mail Online*, January 18, 2008, accessed February 25, 2011, www.dailymail.co.uk/news/article-509186/CIA-launches-hunt-international-hackers-threatening-hold-cities-ransom-shutting-power.html.

32. Barack Obama, "Remarks by the President on Security our Nation's Cyber Infrastructure," May 29, 2009, accessed February 25, 2011, www.whitehouse.gov/the_press_office/ Remarks-by-the-President-on-Securing-Our-Nations-Cyber-Infrastructure/.

33. Comments by Scott Borg, director and chief economist of the US Cyber Consequences Unit, quoted in Dudney, "Rise of the Cyber Militias."

CHAPTER 7

A New Framework for Cyber Deterrence

Jeffrey R. Cooper

Introduction: *"Si vis pacem, para bellum"*

INFORMATION HAS ALWAYS BEEN a key element of national power and influence. Enabled by modern digital technologies, worldwide communications and information networks have fundamentally reshaped patterns of international trade, finance, and global intercourse in general. These patterns affect not only economic relationships but also political and social relationships. Due to interdependencies created by these new patterns, even authoritarian regimes cannot maintain the closed autarchic economies of the past. New actors, many of them entities other than states, now interact in novel ways and play important roles in the international system. As a consequence, with the collapse of the Cold War's bipolar structure, forces enabled by digital technologies significantly refashioned international relations and created new national security challenges.

Importantly, digital information and the infrastructure that processes and carries it—what we commonly call "cyber systems"—have their own special characteristics and possess particular strengths and weaknesses. Cyber capabilities—with novel intrinsic properties—provide both powerful tools and weapons but also represent sources of great potential vulnerability. These conditions have created a powerful interest in better protecting our information and the cyber infrastructures through which it is processed and transmitted. As part of an effective and comprehensive security strategy to secure our cyber environment, deterrence merits attention as potentially one important component.

Understanding Deterrence

Deterrence was never an end in itself but rather a mechanism to forestall the Soviet Union from initiating destabilizing acts of aggression. The United States employed deterrence to support an overarching strategy of containment with the objective of allowing internal pressures to modify, over the long term, the dynamics of that regime. We can similarly employ deterrence as an element in implementing an overall national strategy for cyber; but without strategy, there is no effective way to assess the benefits and the costs of such an approach, other than by immediate consequences of the actions an actor takes.

Deterring cyber threats requires moving beyond the common proposition that deterrence rests solely upon the threat of punitive retaliation. Not only is that incorrect but it too tightly binds deterrence to solving the twin problems of attribution and identity—both of which may be very difficult for cyber attacks. Where direct retaliation can be effective, deterrence by threats of punishment can still be credible. But they may be less attractive to decision makers because the effects of retaliatory cyber attacks are likely to be less predictable and create more unintended consequences than other response options. Moreover, since credible attribution and identification may not be feasible for many cyber threats, this chapter proposes concepts for deterrence less reliant on direct retaliation.

The specific concepts of nuclear deterrence practiced during the Cold War were developed to suit the particular conditions of the contest between the United States and the Soviet Union—a Manichean struggle between nuclear-armed super powers within a bipolar structure that disappeared in 1991.[1] The new logic for deterrence flows from the realization that Cold War deterrence was formulated for conditions that no longer exist; disentangling the general principles of deterrence from those tied to that particular environment is essential.

For application to the emerging range of cyber threats, deterrence must now be rethought and adapted for the conditions of a distinctive cyber domain within a different geostrategic environment, including a far broader set of actors whose motivations and behaviors are much different than assumed for previous opponents. The logic of a new deterrence must address three important factors: (1) an international system with a wide range of actors who exist within complicated new contexts created by multiple relationships and roles; (2) a cyber environment with special characteristics; and (3) an understanding that networks, both physical and virtual, possess different properties than other forms of relationships and these can significantly impact the decision calculus.[2] This chapter introduces two new concepts that can serve as a basis for improving deterrence of threats to critical cyber capabilities: (1) the cooperation, competition, and conflict (3Cs) framework; and (2) networked deterrence.

Cyber Deterrence: Changing Logics

There are obvious inconsistencies between the foundational bases of traditional deterrence and the current conditions of the international system. Traditional US nuclear deterrence doctrine rested upon an intellectual foundation of an international system built on four Enlightenment-era pillars.[3] First, that international system was based on a Realist model of unitary state actors within an anarchic geostrategic environment pursuing national interest by increasing their own power or security. A second pillar was a Clausewitzian understanding of the purposes of conflict in which war was seen as a rational continuation of the political struggle for power. A third pillar was a perspective on the international system from classical Newtonian physics mirroring Newton's model of a "clockwork universe" in which forces were linear, deterministic, and predictable. Finally, the fourth pillar built on assumptions of classical economics (David Ricardo, Adam Smith, and Herbert Simon) for its understanding of behaviors by both human and state actors: rational value maximizing, within a competition often perceived to be zero-sum.[4] Anne-Marie Slaughter captured these assumptions when she wrote, "The twentieth-century world was, at least in terms of geopolitics, a billiard-ball world, described by the political scientist Arnold Wolfers as a system of self-contained states colliding with one another. The results of those collisions were determined by [tangible] military and economic power."[5] This was a world believed to be fundamentally knowable through rational thought based on universally applicable laws and observable phenomena; and the old calculus of deterrence included deeply embedded assumptions about the context, the decision makers, and the decision processes that no longer conform to present realities.

Changing Conditions and Assumptions

The new international system is no longer the province of self-contained state actors seeking to accumulate tangible power. The evolving system now involves a wide range of actors, all enmeshed in a range of relationships with other parties on a dynamic and continually changing international landscape. Moreover, unlike the key Realist proposition that tangible power is the central pursuit, many of the current actors are motivated by considerations other than traditional political, economic, and military factors and emphasize issues other than those of traditional "high politics."[6]

In this new environment, "value" by which power and influence is exercised and measured is far more a function of these networked relationships in which actors are enmeshed than a possession of traditional tangible sources of national power. Interactions among states and other actors are now likely to involve multiple relationships, to be conducted through many diverse channels cutting across various hierarchical levels, and to include actors exhibiting different personas in these relationships. And the effects of networks not only influence members within the network but also extend to those outside the network engaging with network participants.[7]

Further, the cyber domain exhibits some unique properties reflecting that it actually encompasses networks with two quite different sets of characteristics.[8] Connected by physical and logical resources of the cyber infrastructure, one type of network shares limited resources and operates as a "commons."[9] The other type comprises communities of interest that are linked by information and discourse, where information is nonrival and nonexclusive—like a true public good. While networks that share physical and logical resources must grapple with limited physical resources, virtual "communities of interest" may create a second type of "commons" in which the scarce resource is attention.[10]

These new conditions create a far more dynamic, more complex system than the classical physics concept of a relatively static, "closed" system normally in equilibrium that underlies the traditional balance of power model of international politics. These entangling networks, together with the intrinsic characteristics of cyber, introduce complex system properties. This new system resembles less a mechanical, deterministic artifact than a less predictable, dynamic, living ecology. Importantly, this reduced predictability arises not from an inability to measure or specify precisely the initial conditions but from inherent indeterminacy and uncertainty about the processes and consequences of interactions: complex systems exhibit the inherent property of "emergence." Previous presumptions about the nature of the international system—among them rationality, proportionality, predictability, and knowability—may no longer be operative in this new international system and are certainly not appropriate assumptions for policymakers.

Rethinking Key Deterrence Assumptions

Deterrence fundamentally remains a set of propositions about perception, decision making, and behavior—by others and by ourselves. Deterrence often appears to be purely abstract and a simple doctrine considered to be universally applicable;[11] but application and implementation are actually situational dependent and must correspond to the particular conditions of the international system, the players involved, their motivations and objectives, and the relevant technical factors related to targets and mechanisms of influence. The calculus of deterrence is a function of particular decision makers, within a matrix of idiosyncratic values and expectations, evaluating possible gain versus loss for specific opportunities involving expected consequences and perceived uncertainties. This evaluation rests on believing they understand the adversary's thinking and also appreciate the adversary's understanding of their beliefs and likely behaviors.[12]

In the past it was usually assumed (and almost always modeled) as if the behaviors of concern for deterrence were noncooperative. Classical deterrence targeted behaviors of autarchic unitary actors who were pursuing power measured in tangible factors through influencing decisions made by leaders "rationally" calculating costs and benefits within a narrow, abstract, isolated, game-theoretic construct.[13] The United States had to be able to ensure that the adversary—almost always identifiable and with physical assets that could be held at risk—perceived that retaliatory costs to be imposed by us outweighed any potential gains. Actions taken by us directly against them would deter their hostile acts. That model of deterrence now faces serious problems with respect to ambiguity of an attack, identity of the attacker, and finding value important to the attacker to hold at risk.

New capabilities for influencing behaviors now exist because participation in social relationships or networks in which all actors are enmeshed affects both motivations and patterns of behavior. Relationships create links and impose linkages that affect and constrain behaviors, including expectation of reciprocity among members of "communities."[14] More complex decisions result when there are multiple roles and mixed motives in shared environments reflecting differing cooperative, competitive, and conflictual objectives within various social relationships.[15] Effective deterrence now requires a significantly revised calculus that reflects a better understanding of human cognition and judgment, by both individuals and collectives, within these more complicated situations.[16]

Even with these substantial differences, deterrence still depends on two core factors—capability and credibility.[17] Deterrence works best when it is a self-reinforcing, nested, hierarchical structure—strategic/operational/tactical—with strong coupling between those levels. Credibility remains linked to the appropriateness and proportionality of our likely response, which is why "massive retaliation" was replaced by progressively more discriminating, even if still large-scale, response options. Strengthening the factors and mechanisms that create the linkages between these levels in the new digital environment would help create a coherent, more effective cyber-deterrence capability. And reduced reliance on retaliatory measures as the basis for effective cyber deterrence in this framework would allow deterrence to be improved without heightening concerns about increasing our cyber-attack capabilities that underwrite retaliation for offensive purposes.

Credible deterrence must create an overall reference frame for potential attackers that reinforces the belief that we will respond effectively; this cannot be done merely by declaratory statements of intent but must be demonstrated by tangible activities. It is not built just on willingness to carry out responses to a particularly flagrant provocation but by an opponent's belief that we are in fact prepared to respond across the range of behaviors of concern. Such beliefs are deeply conditioned by a wide range of our activities—high-level strategic policy through operational-level actions down to tactical, day-to-day reactions—not just by considerations of our specific response to the instant high-level exploit. Continued tolerance of provocations that we find aggravating but not lethally threatening may well induce potential adversaries to perceive that we will not respond to more threatening activities.

Rather than just threatening immense losses, deterrence is most effective when it operates against the entire decision calculus of a potential hostile actor, targeting all four factors—{Factor 1} Gain Value, {Factor 2} Gain Probability, {Factor 3} Loss Value, and {Factor 4} Loss Probability. Networked relationships in this more dynamic environment can be used to shape motivations and behaviors of participants by exploiting the effects relationships impose on these four factors, but improved knowledge of the effects of social context on collective intelligence and decision making is needed. These implications of membership and participation in groups must now be factored into our understanding of perception, decision making, and behavior as they impact deterrence and argue that we reexamine the factors affecting decision making within that context.[18]

A New Framework for Cyber Deterrence

Networks of relationships, whether formal or informal, are crucial mechanisms for fostering cooperative behavior, reflecting the important implications of social preferences.[19] Any new deterrence calculus should reflect a *"homo socialis"* rather than a *"homo economicus"* perspective: individual interactions may still be transactional and mostly benefiting one party, but social ties—necessarily bound by reciprocity—will fray if the balance is too consistently one-sided.[20]

Cooperation, Competition, and Conflict: The 3Cs Framework

The cooperation, competition, and conflict framework explicitly recognizes that nonstate actors and networks of actors (among them "virtual communities") conduct multiple but distinct relationships with each other across numerous and diverse channels of interaction and have emerged as important players in international relations.[21] Actors participating in networks composed of a diverse range of entities perform different functions, assume different personas, and often exhibit substantially different behaviors at the same time. Consequentially, "role" is no longer tightly or uniquely bound to "identity," but is rather a characteristic of a particular transaction or a set of relationships in which an actor is involved, and both attribution and identification become very complicated for cyber threats.

The 3Cs framework remains firmly within the Realist construct since it continues to see the actors driven by and pursuing self-interest, whether in terms of security or other measures of power and influence (see table 7.1). However, it extends Realism by explicitly recognizing that networks of relationships affect actor's motivations and behaviors—in a networked environment, actors perceive their self-interests within a larger social frame and may see their self-interests best served by a mutuality of benefits. Actors pursuing their self-interest can seek different objectives within the different networks, and such distinct relationships can exist simultaneously. This introduces the notion of multiple parallel "decision frames," resulting in complex behaviors creating "mixed-motive games."[22] Defining these behaviors and distinguishing among the players' decision frames can offer insight in understanding how such players may approach complex choices.

This environment, with multiple roles and sets of relationships involving unstable preferences and non–zero-sum outcomes, introduces complex phenomena such as intrinsic indeterminacy and incalculable uncertainty. These features represent sharp breaks from the past, requiring new ways of thinking about the world around us and about how we pursue our national security interests, and how we impact actors' decision making. They create limits on what we know, what we can know, what we can predict, and what we can control; yet there seems to be little appreciation of these limits within the national security community.

The Networked Deterrence Concept

By using a range of indirect methods that are not dependent on attribution, networked deterrence intends to influence actors and behaviors that we could otherwise

TABLE 7.1
Understanding Cooperation, Competition, and Conflict

	Objective	*Example*
Cooperation	"Positive-sum" outcome for the participants as a whole and mutuality of benefits so that no participant is worse off.[a]	A novel production technology that, because of significant efficiencies, produces a substantial consumer surplus that can be shared by both producers and consumers.
Competition	Improved relative position, but one that can often produce an increase in overall welfare.	A novel production technology similar to that for cooperation but one where the inventor can exploit "first mover" advantage to take significant market share from his competitors while still increasing overall welfare through cost savings to consumers.
Conflict	Improved relative position, without concern for absolute welfare consequences ("zero-sum" orientation). This reflects a classic game-theoretic outcome with noncooperative players and often occurring in real conflicts.	A novel production technology where the winner could end up being worse off in absolute terms due to reduced profit margins.

[a] Technically this is a Pareto optimal distribution. This mirrors Friedberg's concept of a "plus-sum" outcome for a mutually beneficial US–China relationship. Aaron L. Friedberg, "Ripe for Rivalry: Prospects for Peace in Multipolar Asia," *International Security* 18, no. 3 (Winter 1993).

not deter; it is based on two important notions. First, it posits that networks themselves are increasingly the key underpinning international power and influence and therefore represent the real source of value. Joseph Nye and others posit that "soft power" and "smart power" (the ability to build, enrich, and employ networks) are now recognized components of international power and influence.[23] As noted by Anne-Marie Slaughter, "We live in a networked world. War is networked. . . . Diplomacy is networked. . . . Business is networked. . . . Media is networked. . . . Society is networked. . . . Even Religion is networked. . . . In this world, the measure of power is connectedness."[24] Indeed, Slaughter argues that the network connections themselves create the most important source of value for actors seeking power and influence.[25] Therefore, the value by which the calculus of deterrence is measured should be a function of these networked relationships in which actors are enmeshed rather than direct control of tangible resources or assets.

Second, networked deterrence presumes that the multiplicity of relationships and roles demands a different approach to assessing implications of potential deterrence actions due to the differential and very complex effects such actions may create within multiple network contexts. It rests on an understanding, building on research on cooperative relationships done by social scientists, that these entangling relationships powerfully affect every actor's motivations and behaviors, and, hence, their decision calculus. It argues consequentially that affecting (or threatening to affect) those relationships can influence the behaviors of an actor and should be generally applicable to forestalling a wide range of potential threats.

While directly "holding at risk" such networks may be an outdated concept, networked deterrence seeks to influence actors, directly or indirectly, and to create restraining forces through these networks to enhance deterrence. Deterrence here is exercised indirectly through our actions affecting the network of relationships in which the potential challenger is involved—even where we may not know the exact identity of the actor causing the problem—and focuses more on affecting networks of relationships than the actors as independent entities.[26] The implications of social relationships and networks have been widely recognized in areas such as public health and criminology, but integrating them into a coherent framework for cyber deterrence and developing appropriate mechanisms present new challenges. Implementation of deterrence in this new strategic environment requires innovative adaptations of the fundamental concepts of deterrence.

Entangled relationships argue against the ability or desirability of trying to alter them all in reaction to changes in one channel, thus requiring us to reexamine our traditional responses to threats in which transition from peace to crisis to conflict significantly altered every aspect of the relationship. Responses to particular activities should be taken not as specific, case-by-case reactions but within a much broader, coherent strategic framework that allows balancing a wide range of factors and equities. Thus, one might tolerate a single particularly provocative action in a relationship that overall provides significant benefits, but one might also be far less tolerant of a series of low-level activities that are merely annoying in a relationship that has only marginal utility. Clearly communicating the reason for our response to the counterparty is important for maintaining reciprocity and encouraging not only mutually beneficial behaviors but also respect for appropriate norms.

A Financial Services Approach

In order to deter attacks, we propose to adapt and extend an approach from the financial services sector to reduce their cyber risks that exert influence on potential attackers through these networks of relationships, including dependencies with us and our partners. Traditional thinking by the national security community about cyber deterrence has not usually exploited such network effects.

The financial services sector includes many diverse participants, comprises a very complex series of relationships, and must contend with a wide range of potential threats to its important cyber systems. Because trust and credibility of information, participants, and processes are essential to the proper functioning of this community, the threats below represent serious challenges to the collective interests of this community. These threats, which can come from both inside and outside, can be malicious or accidental. Threats to the financial industry include the following:

◊ Unauthorized and illicit access to and misuse of sensitive information to protect both client and firm confidentiality.
◊ Unauthorized information sharing.
◊ Theft and embezzlement.
◊ Theft of intellectual property and other unique process data.
◊ Access to sensitive financial information.
◊ Illicit credentialing and violation of employee privacy.
◊ Disruption of communications.
◊ Disruption of systems.
◊ Corruption of data.

To help manage these risks within this complex environment, some of the more vigilant financial services firms employ a deterrence approach incorporating four elements—penalty, futility, dependency, and counterproductivity.[27]

Penalty corresponds to the traditional deterrence focus on imposing costs, either by increasing loss value or loss probability. Private parties cannot themselves impose penalties such as criminal sanctions, nor do they possess the authority to strike back and retaliate in kind, which is clearly subject to strict legal constraints. Firms can, however, threaten referral for criminal prosecution or civil legal actions for recovery of damages, or can impose financial or transactional constraints on the perpetrator. Private actors can also employ other forms of retaliation that impose costs—such as refusal to engage in subsequent transactions with transgressors, subject to legal constraints on boycotts and embargoes.

Futility refers to protective measures taken to make cyber attacks more difficult, more costly to the attacker, more sporadic, or less effective. Making it technically or economically more difficult for the adversary to attack you alters the potential attacker's perception of relative gains versus costs. To the degree that successful access is less predictable, risks increase and confidence in potential gains are reduced. Futility also operates on the attacker's perceptions of "opportunity costs"; by making the effectiveness of protective processes salient, alternative targets become more attractive.[28]

The attractiveness of futility measures is reinforced because they often impact several factors in the adversary's calculus simultaneously. They can raise the potential costs to the attacker by forcing more or higher-quality resources to be committed for the same gain; they can increase the likelihood of being caught; they can reduce probability of success; and they can decrease the value of possible gains. Moreover, by creating effective barriers, these measures can improve the likelihood that attacks will be detected, will force disclosure of intent, and will increase the probability of adverse reaction. Additionally, effective protective measures create thresholds of capability necessary for successful attacks, not only reducing likelihood of success but also increasing the risks of attribution by narrowing the population of capable perpetrators—which increases the likelihood that penalties could be imposed. Another byproduct is that by increasing the security or resilience of one's systems and operations, the perceptions of risks are reduced, altering the decision calculus and increasing willingness to take responsive actions.

Dependency creates a direct link between the value that a target creates for the potential attacker from their relationship and puts that value at risk from attacks. Some actors may be clients of the financial services community, and their ability to make transactions or investments could itself be put at risk by attacks they stage or permit (even when attribution is impossible) or by responses to the attack—such as cutting off the relationship—when their role can be identified. While such dependent relationships by themselves may not prevent attacks, they may significantly affect the perpetrator's calculus of risks versus benefits from these attacks.

Although counterproductivity is similar to dependency, it operates indirectly by affecting wider sets of relationships, including those of the party attacked as well as those in which the attacker participates. Reactions could include public outrage that occurs after an attack because of the impacts on related members or simply because the attack is perceived to violate norms of acceptable behavior. It may make those related to the party attacked more willing to provide information about the attacker or reduce tolerance for bad behaviors. If networks in which the attacker participates perceive potential costs because of the attack, or feel their norms have been violated, they may become less willing to facilitate or to tolerate offensive behaviors. Especially to the degree that the attacker's capabilities rely on task interdependencies with these networks, these impacts affect his perceptions of benefits and costs. These considerations suggest that deterrence efforts should not generally focus on the attacker but rather should emphasize influencing the trust networks on which the attackers depend; "it follows that if we identify and destroy that network, we destroy the ability of the individual attacker."[29]

Exploiting the Financial Services Approach

The range of cyber threats to national security is broader than that faced by the financial community, but they are similar in character and source, even if the targets and scale might be considerably different. Exploiting these effective measures provides a useful starting place for constructing an effective national security cyber-deterrence framework, and governments can strengthen them given the additional powers they possess. A cyber-deterrence framework that places far more emphasis on protective measures and network influences than direct retaliation should create a "plus-sum" outcome, offering improved resilience and confidence without creating concerns over a cyber "security dilemma."

It is worth emphasizing, however, that of the four components in this approach, only penalty specifically demands identifying the attacker, thus supporting the networked deterrence objective of minimizing reliance on attribution. Protective activities undertaken to increase futility do not generally require that the identity of an attacker be known to be effective, although characteristics of likely attacks themselves are extremely useful.[30] One type of "self-initiating" response would trigger alerting procedures and force generation measures that significantly increase readiness and capability. These measures could include adopting polymorphic protective operations or increasing the stringency of security procedures.[31] They could change the default options on a variety of security settings or procedures, tightening down access or inducing significantly more mindful attention by system operators, among other commitment devices.[32] The utility of "zero-day exploits" requires that they do not prematurely reveal attack signatures prior to actual operational employment. The obverse is that the attacker must have very high confidence that he can predict the actual conditions that his attack will encounter. Polymorphic operations introduce a high degree of uncertainty into predictions about future state conditions.

Because dependency operates from the potential attacker's perspective, it also is not reliant on attribution. Even counterproductivity does not require knowing the identity of the attacker, although it may be more effective if the matrix of relationships from which the attack is carried out is known. Counterproductivity is effective if the networks from which the threat emanates believe that the threat itself—or the responsive deterrence measures—might pose significant adverse effects for them, and participants in the potential attacker's networks are better positioned to take effective action if they can be induced to do so.

Bringing pressure on subordinate entities by influencing their superior partners must be an element of networked deterrence. Despite claims that they lack the capability to control inimical activities, states claiming sovereignty still have a duty to exercise control; international law recognizes the rights of parties harmed by uncontrolled activities to apply pressure to force the dominant entity to exert control or assume liability for failing to do so. The objective is to force the dominant party to assess their overall costs and benefits in tolerating such activities, although within the current more complicated context of multiple relations and objectives, it may take more effort to assist them in understanding this balance.

Penalty and futility have been part of classic deterrence thinking. They do not depend on the existence of dependencies or social relationships for their effects, but using social connections can significantly amplify their effectiveness by spreading knowledge throughout the networks of interested parties. Disseminating knowledge of attack signatures and methods, as well as information about effective protective measures, can increase the speed and effectiveness as well as lower the costs of these protective measures. Communicating to and among potential attackers that this target is "too tough" may dissuade some potential attackers. Networked deterrence exploits dependency and counterproductivity, not part of the traditional deterrence toolkit, to amplify the effects of social entanglements for deterrence leverage.

Neither futility nor counterproductivity relies on identifying the attacker, which highlights the need to rethink the presumed dependence on attribution for effective cyber deterrence. A robust futility posture will include a range of protective measures that require only recognition of inimical activities, not by knowing the identity of the attacker or the objective of the attack. They are triggered by the act itself and might be termed "self-initiating" responses. The use of an electrified fence for perimeter security is a good analogy: the fence shocks an attacker simply by being touched; it does not shock because it knows the identity of the attacker. With counterproductivity, influences on adversary behavior are exercised by members of the groups in which the attacker participates, not by defenders directly. They may operate indirectly by exerting pressure on all group members by enforcing norms that minimize tolerance of bad behaviors and reduce willingness to cooperate in those activities—without necessarily knowing specifically who is guilty of a triggering act. Those members may know who an attacker is and, because of pressures applied on the group, may decide to sanction the offender or take other actions in order to minimize additional adverse consequences. Where these networks include participants linked to the attacker by "task interdependence," counterproductivity may offer especially effective leverage.

Extending the Financial Services Approach

To provide a more comprehensive platform to implement a collective security approach to networked deterrence, two additional measures—intolerance and cooperative security—are suggested to augment the existing components. These measures help foster the development of appropriate norms of cyber behavior and improve the opportunities for effective collective action by concerned parties. Stress on collective action to improve security is intended to foster recognition by all parties that activities by government alone are neither sufficient nor appropriate to address the wide range of cyber challenges to our national security interests. These two additional measures leverage government's unique authorities and exploit its legitimate capabilities.

For the financial services community, the importance of interrelationships and dependencies to their common interests was self-evident. Given the broader range of parties affected by cyber threats from a national perspective, it is essential to make more explicit the relationships and dependencies that affect and bind government entities at all levels, participants in the commercial sector, private organizations, and individuals. As with other "commons," activities disruptive to the globally networked cyber environment reduce benefits for and impose costs on all. Unfortunately, the current default attitude to cyber by the general population and by users who should be more concerned is usually one of sloppiness; too often little care or attention is given to what should be common "public health" measures for the cyber environment. Highlighting the common interests by all parties in a properly functioning cyber environment is a crucial first step in the creation of appropriate norms in a process intended to spur effective collective action that is in the interest of almost all parties.

Fostering a greater intolerance for "unacceptable" behaviors exploits the importance of norms in shaping social behaviors. By creating more explicit expectations and by strengthening norms, if not more formal rules and constraints, against activities considered unacceptable by members of the group, damaging cyber activities as well as tolerance for committing them may be subject to constraining influences by the group. A necessary counterpart to creating intolerance is fostering a more mindful attitude toward use of cyber systems and shifting the default attitude to one of careful employment. Although no change in norms and their enforcement will induce perfect compliance with models of good behavior, they can be an important component of behavioral constraints imposed by social relationships.

First, relying on its legitimate role in national security, the government, through policy, legislative, educational, and leadership activities, can assist in fostering, promulgating, and enforcing norms appropriate for a society critically dependent on cyber environment; raising awareness and mobilizing public support are crucial elements of an effective cybersecurity strategy. The government can help educate the general population about good cyber practices and the importance of obeying norms. As a first step, the government can encourage through its own activities the use of good practices that help build norms, demanding far more discipline in its own actions than previously.

Second, by removing regulatory and legal barriers, the government can enable or facilitate cooperative behaviors and support more effective collective action by private parties. The government can bring capabilities and authorities to create rules and norms not available to private parties, including using civil and criminal penalties as a start on norm-building and enforcement. By strengthening legal penalties where necessary, the government can directly impose costs through more vigorous prosecution of criminal activities and help set an example for societal norms. But while black-letter law may define legally impermissible activities and the government can enforce sanctions, community norms and individual assumption of responsibility are essential for creating a culture and behaviors appropriate to the real dependencies of our cyber environment. Legal penalties, however, can serve as important markers of culturally acceptable behaviors and strengthen societal norms against those activities. Influencing attackers by threat of imposing ex post penalties for illicit activities requires specific knowledge of the identity of the attacker, but affecting behaviors through the creation and enforcement of norms is less subject to this constraint.

Other government measures can alter the fundamental financial or economic attractiveness of certain harmful cyber activities or the costs in tolerating them. Many cyber attacks, like other criminal activities, appear to have mixed motives or at least serve multiple purposes; criminal activities can be precursors or enablers of threats with serious national security consequences. Reducing potential gains by attacking the back-end financial transactions through which the illicit gains are extracted appears to be worthwhile.

To support cooperative security, the government can create incentives for and can cooperate with private actors in their norm-building and cooperative enforcement efforts. It can encourage private action against illicit cyber activities through the use by commercial entities of terms and conditions through underwriting standards and by relaxing certain antitrust restrictions against collaborative activities in this area. Moreover, the government possesses authorities well beyond private entities in many areas, such as sharing information or sanctioning illicit activities; although some activities are under way, they would be significantly more effective if they were part of a more coherent national strategic framework.

That we are attempting to foster collective action in what Lewis termed a "pseudo-commons" suggests that we should look at the Nobel prize–winning research on managing common pool resources and shared environments by Elinor Ostrom and colleagues.[33] This work showed first that neither a "Leviathan" nor formal institutions were necessary to address these problems, and, second, that cooperative actions by self-interested parties through their own actions could achieve the desired goals. It brought into play the powerful motivations created by social relationships and communities with shared interests and concerns.[34] The focus on collective action, by strengthening cooperative mechanisms in shared environments rather than by centralized authority, provides important lessons for developing an effective cyber-deterrence framework.

Implicit in the research on managing commons is a conclusion that collective action, like a policy of engagement, must create a set of conditions in which all parties to the relationship understand that reciprocity is important. The injunction by Robert Keohane is worth emphasizing: cooperation should be understood "not as harmony but as an intensely political process of mutual adjustment in a situation of actual and potential discord."[35] Having said that, futility remains the most high-leverage place to start effective efforts within a new cyber-deterrence framework, and more emphasis on cyber "public health" measures would be a useful first step in initiating effective collective action.

Notes

1. Frank C. Zagare, "Classical Deterrence Theory: A Critical Assessment," *International Interactions* 21, no. 4 (1996): 366.

2. Many networks, for example, exhibit power law distributions and show increasing returns to scale—for example, social networks, which obey Metcalfe's Law.

3. For a more detailed explanation why this foundation is now less relevant, see Jeffrey R. Cooper, *New Approaches to Cyber-Deterrence: Initial Thoughts on a New Framework* (SAIC, December 29, 2009). Prepared under contract number N65236-08-D-6805, Under Secretary of Defense for Intelligence, Joint & Coalition Warfighter Support, Cyber, Information Operations

and Strategic Studies Task Order, DWAM80950. Available at AmericanBar.org, www.american bar.org/content/dam/aba/migrated/2011_build/law_national_security/new_approaches_to_cyber_deterrence.authcheckdam.pdf.

4. See Thomas J. Christensen, "Fostering Stability or Creating a Monster? The Rise of China and US Policy toward East Asia," *International Security* 31, no. 1 (Summer 2006): 81–126, for a discussion of perspectives other than a competitive game-theoretic construct, including "positive-sum" (or "plus-sum") objectives.

5. Anne-Marie Slaughter, "America's Edge: Power in a Networked Century," *Foreign Affairs*, January/February (2009), www.foreignaffairs.com/print/63722.

6. Hans J. Morgenthau, (rev. by Kenneth W. Thomson), *Politics among Nations: The Struggle for Power and Peace*, brief ed. (New York: McGraw-Hill, 1993), 5; Joseph S. Nye Jr., *Soft Power: The Means to Success in World Politics* (New York: Public Affairs, 2004); and Joseph S. Nye Jr., *The Powers to Lead* (New York: Oxford University Press, 2008).

7. The effect on behavior—such as the "broken windows" phenomenon, for example—has been recognized in law enforcement research and practice. See George L. Kelling and James Q. Wilson, "Broken Windows," *Atlantic*, March 1982, www.theatlantic.com/magazine/archive/1982/03/broken-windows/4465/.

8. The inhabitants of cyberspace also often manifest novel behaviors as well. See Sherry Turkle, *Life on the Screen: Identity in the Age of the Internet* (New York: Simon & Schuster, 1995).

9. Or often termed "common pool resources" by natural resource economists.

10. I am indebted to discussions with Anthony Olcott, officer in residence at the Institute for the Study of Diplomacy, Georgetown University, for this insight.

11. In some unfortunate aspects, the use of abstract, game-theoretic approaches for modeling deterrence mirrors some of the more unsettling aspects and mistakes in risk modeling, leading to the recent financial catastrophes.

12. In cognitive psychology, this ability to recognize and take into account the thoughts of the other is known as "theory of the mind"; it "allows one to attribute thoughts, desires, and intentions to others, to predict or explain their actions, and to posit their intentions." See Simon Baron-Cohen, "Precursors to a Theory of Mind: Understanding Attention in Others," in *Natural Theories of Mind: Evolution, Development and Simulation of Everyday Mindreading*, ed. A. Whiten, 233–51 (Oxford: Basil Blackwell, 1991).

13. These included decision makers as rational actors based on a "*homo economicus*" perspective; the actors and decision makers operating from an autarchic perspective; and a game-theoretic framework employing Nash equilibria based on noncooperative actors.

14. This is different from the "group think" pressures highlighted by Janis.

15. The research on cooperative decision making in shared environments such as common pool resources is the basis on which Ostrom and Williamson won the 2009 Nobel Prize in economics, formally known as the Bank of Sweden Prize in Economic Science in Honor of Alfred Nobel.

16. The corpus of judgment and decision making, including recent research on cognitive and neuropsychological factors, needs to be better accounted for generally in national security decision making, and in deterrence thinking in particular.

17. Keir A. Lieber and Daryl G. Press, "Nukes We Need: Preserving the American Deterrent," *Foreign Affairs*, November/December (2009): 41.

18. Robert Jervis, *The Meaning of the Nuclear Revolution: Statecraft and the Prospect of Armageddon* (Ithaca, NY: Cornell University Press, 1989), 52.

19. Robert O. Keohane, *After Hegemony: Cooperation and Discord in the World Political Economy* (Princeton, NJ: Princeton University Press, 1984), xiii.

20. Ernst Fehr and Simon Gächer, "Fairness and Retaliation: The Economics of Reciprocity," *Journal of Economic Perspectives* 14, no. 3 (Summer 2000): 159–60.

21. The concepts for cooperation/competition/conflict grew out of a series of the Office of Secretary of Defense–sponsored Highlands Forum meetings starting in 2007 that was initially focused on issues and problems related to identity in the cyber domain and discussions about the changing nature of conflict in the emerging international environment.

22. The notion of multiple parallel decision frames is similar to what Keohane suggested in "going beyond Realism" by stressing the role of institutions within the Realist construct. See Keohane, *After Hegemony*, 16. On mixed-motive games, see Thomas C. Schelling, *Strategy of Conflict* (Cambridge, MA: Harvard University Press, 1960).

23. For example, see Joseph Nye, *Soft Power*; and Nye, *Powers to Lead*.

24. Slaughter, "America's Edge." Slaughter, formerly dean of the Woodrow Wilson School at Princeton, was the director for policy planning at the US Department of State.

25. Ibid.

26. Lewin's two concepts of fate interdependence and task interdependence create opportunities that we can exploit: for example, in the networks that we affect, we can influence their members without us necessarily knowing the identity of the particular member.

27. With permission, this discussion draws on a presentation by Phil Venables, director of cyber security at Goldman Sachs, at the Highlands Forum Enrichment Session on Deterrence, March 10, 2008.

28. Such "impact shifting" may be useful for private parties seeking to protect their own equities in a sea of similar targets, but it may be less useful for governments seeking to protect specific assets or operations, or as a matter of public policy.

29. Comment by Venables during the Highlands Forum, March 10, 2008.

30. There are some exceptions, of course, such as security measures, including noncooperative biometric identification, that use signatures of potential attackers to protect against intrusions.

31. "Polymorphic operations" are a shifting set of state configurations and operating procedures that decrease an attacker's ability to know what specific posture or procedures he will actually face for his attack.

32. See Richard H. Thaler and Cass R. Sunstein, *Nudge: Improving Decisions about Health, Wealth, and Happiness* (New York: Penguin Books, 2009). One of the significant findings from behavioral finance is the ease with which humans can be induced to make choices or execute behaviors by presentation and default settings.

33. James A. Lewis, "The 'Korean' Cyber Attacks and Their Implications for Cyber Conflict," *CSIS*, October 2009; and Elinor Ostrom, James Walker, and Roy Gardner, "Covenants with and without a Sword: Self-Governance Is Possible," *American Political Science Review* 86, no. 2 (June 1992): 404.

34. Ernst Fehr and Urs Fischbacher, "Why Social Preferences Matter—The Impact of Non-Selfish Motives on Competition, Cooperation and Incentives," *Economic Journal* 112, no. 478 (March 2002): C1.

35. Keohane, *After Hegemony*, 52.

CHAPTER 8

Cybered Conflict, Cyber Power, and Security Resilience as Strategy

Chris Demchak

National Surprise from a Densely Populated Cybered World

THE UBIQUITY, CONNECTIVITY, AND CRITICALITY of cyberspace changes national security balances throughout the globe. Cyber power transcends geography's natural barriers and can cause harm to others on varying scales while the cyber actors remain safely a long distance away.[1] Among the concepts requiring adjustment for this emergent age are cyber war, cyber power, and the appropriate reach of effective national security strategy. This chapter makes two arguments. First, "cybered conflict" is a better term than "cyberwar" for the kinds of national-level struggles endemic to the interdependent complexity and scale of the world rising up around us.[2] The term helps frame the complexity of conflict involving cyberspace, especially for those making decisions about how to develop a strategic response to threats. Actions meant to harm another nation will not stay contained within legacy military notions of a battlefield "domain" or even within the networks that enable global attacks.

Second, national cyber power and its associated strategy for national security must include internal societal preparations for surprise as much as external disruptive projections to avert offensive cyber asymmetries. The new normalcy of cybered conflict is its enduring potential for cascading unexpected outcomes anywhere across the deeply interconnected and complex critical systems of a modern society. A national security resilience strategy offers the necessary composite framework to guide and explicitly coordinate society's cyber resilience with the national military capabilities developed to secure national borders. Recognition of this new composite form of national power and the corresponding security resilience strategy is emerging indirectly across the policies and institutions of westernized nations, but these are early days yet.

Cybered Conflict, not Cyber Domain or War

For an emerging variety of human conflict across a densely connected digital globe, "cyberwar" is too narrow a term.[3] In the emerging cybered age, cyberspace is a ubiquitous substrate, not merely one domain among many others. Any conflict of concern to a nation-state is likely to develop far beyond the purely electronic hostilities occurring entirely within electronic networks of a "cyberwar."[4] Rather, "cybered conflict" better captures the ambiguities and extends the national security dilemma today. A cybered system is more than its cyber underpinning; it includes all sorts of systems of people, things, processes, and perceptions that are computer-related but not necessarily purely computerized.[5] Phishing can be an attack even if it simply sends information to bad actors through the foolishness of the email recipient.[6] The purely cyber portion could constitute a preparatory phase, a main avenue of attack, a central campaign element, a large-scale deception and espionage operation, an episodic enabler, a foregone set of activities, or all of these at different times in a long-term cybered conflict.[7] The entire conflict, however, is cybered if the exchanges of weapons and damage do not stay within the networks but rather seep or explode beyond the technical into the wider organization or society.

In fall of 2010 the broader, inclusive cybered conflict emerged explicitly in the international system. With the damaging attack on critical Iranian nuclear reactors, a malicious piece of software called Stuxnet became the first publicly known cyber weapon to cross over from the bytes of electronic networks into direct physical sabotage of large-scale industrial systems. Its success heralded the arrival of the era of cybered conflict. This particular malicious worm struck Iran's nascent and internationally contested nuclear reactors in situ in Iran far from any foreign military installation. Even though the reactors were disconnected from the internet, the software directly disrupted the process of moving the reactors into full operations.[8] Unlike other viruses and malware, Stuxnet matters globally because it showed the path of preference for future attackers on all sides in the emerging era. From here on, every fight will be cybered at key points before, during, and after the main effects.[9]

The Stuxnet designers demonstrated to the rest of the world how the attack advantages of a globally unfettered, easily accessed, and readily used cyberspace can be employed against enemies. Over the course of about two years, the Stuxnet application on innocent USB mobile drives copied itself often and spread far enough to end up where the iterative designers wanted—inside a large-scale technical plant not connected to the internet. If it traveled to an internetted machine, the code opened a backdoor to two URLs and requested an update. For those infected systems without an internet connection, the program had to be able to deliver its final payload without an update. As a result, the payload was buried in code that also hid its activities from the operator. While the operator stared at a screen whose code said the machine tests were within expectations, the actual commands changed by Stuxnet ordered the centrifuges to oscillate wildly with no human in the loop. Ultimately, despite Stuxnet having wandered into thousands of other systems in India and

China, for example, the damaging payload was delivered as planned and the Iranian nuclear reprocessing program was delayed for at least one to two years.[10]

Stuxnet also showed how state-level conflict and criminality are and will be intricately linked in the cybered conflict age. The bundled modules harnessed the delivery and stealth skills of exquisitely good cybercriminals to the intents and probably state-sized funding of cybered warriors to produce a physical effect. In the Stuxnet case, there was no downside for the attackers in borrowing the cybercriminal's delivery methods or types of covert infection codes. Furthermore, intelligence was automatically acquired as the Stuxnet worm wandered around, checking for updates from two key URLs if an internet connection was available. Not only did these callbacks tell the owners of the URLs where Stuxnet had landed, they also provided critical operational system data about every other nontargeted system the worm passed through in its search for its target. Until the two websites were closed down in summer 2010, the designers of this cyber weapon obtained a great deal of information about thousands of infected systems that could prove useful in later conflict operations or even business competitions.

Stuxnet did not need to be connected to the internet to cause the intended damage. This "fire and forget" aspect of a cyber attack represents the increasing levels of ongoing threatening surprises inherent in future cybered conflict. For the future, it will not be wise to assume the odd bit of seemingly innocuous code that has floated into one's computer system from all directions is safe because it has no obvious effects or infection pattern.[11] What may have seemed safe in the neighbor's systems might find in one's own computer its specific target, the computer DNA the small bit of software targeted for harm. The benign lost code might suddenly then issue its disable, disrupt, deceive, or destroy command.[12] The innocence of the utopian cyber prophets from the 1990s is now firmly gone.[13] The same people who orchestrated this industrial level of sophisticated application development are today still out there, able to do it again, for whatever reason or for whichever employer. Variations of the Stuxnet worm are in the wilds of the hacker international world now. It is almost certainly the target of reverse engineering all over the world by thousands of computer hackers, government scientists, cyber warriors, or commercial consultants. "Son of Stuxnet" is inevitable as an employed tool, along with its cousin or distantly related code attempting to replicate the demonstration event of the original.

While it is now relatively easy to find a Stuxnet infection, its children and look-alikes will not be so easy to locate. The follow-on worms are likely to be repurposed for any number of targets and delivery systems. Stuxnet floated around for at least a year before even being noticed and largely ignored by the major antivirus firms. It is easy to imagine a campaign of many Stuxnet-like variations released all over the world in a sort of "tailored DNA swarm" that floats for some time without apparent effects. Today this kind of assault can begin with all sorts of actors and reasons, challenging societies across all sorts of connections that reach deeply into their internally critical spaces.[14]

What is emerging is not the traditional environment of war for which most modern militaries prepare. Cyberspace does not fit into the framework of a military "domain," a term used by the US military in particular to blend cybered conflict into the traditional molds of competitive armed struggles. As a global, synthetic substrate, cyberspace is an arena, tool, weapon, and enabler of conflict with implications in threat and harm beyond the normal military four fields of battle: land, air, sea, and space.[15] In 2009 the US military officially declared cyberspace a military domain, immediately spawning a large number of repetitive conferences trying to fit cyberspace into concepts derived from existing air, land, sea, and space domains.[16] The domain designation may be useful for parsing the lines of authority among military services, at least bureaucratically, and it also may make for more accustomed objectives if a national military seeks to dominate the enemies in the cyber domain. Cyberspace is not, however, a conveniently bounded fifth domain offering some kind of limit of action, knowledge, operational effect, or even conflict.

Nor does cyberspace demonstrate attributes equivalent to those of the nuclear domain in weapons, deterrence, or systems. Nuclear weapons are highly specialized and centrally developed. As topics of deterrence, the technology is the central point of intensely debated international regimes and its proliferation both reviled and inhibited. As systems, they are remarkable in their (fortunate) lack of use. The cybered substrate is dual-use, wantonly proliferated without identification of locations or owners, and used continuously. It stretches ubiquitously into, across, and throughout the society that the military is trying to protect as well as outward to the world from which the attackers may come. No identified domain of war offers the equivalent scale and complexity of cyberspace as a globally shared system that consistently intrudes into, connects at long range, and induces behaviors transcending traditional boundaries of land, sea, air, institution, nation, and social or technical medium.[17] In the same way the term "cyberwar" fails to capture the true complexity of the challenge, the designation of a cyber "domain" does not help guide any national leader in dealing with the cybered conflict age.

From here forward in the digitally connected globe, conflict will be cybered. Cyber networks will always be involved state-level conflicts, whether with another state, nonstate actor, or both, but conflict of national significance will not stay purely within the networks. The cybered age has been built up under the collective feet of westernized societies focused on ecommerce and communication without borders. In the cybered world, humans in their own groups have engaged in a process well known in ecological systems studies as *autopoiesis*. Like ants dumping their debris out their front door and creating ant hills they then have to climb up and down, modern societies collectively built the big security obstacles to which each society now must individually adapt.[18] Conflict will travel along any path of human or machine exchange enabled by cyberspace.

In the modern world, one cannot leave cyberspace and go home.[19] Cyberspace never evolved into a sort of information-enabled Eden filled with nice, sharing people who recognized and ethically supported the desire of information to "be free."[20] Rather, a good analogy may be that cyberspace is a globally unfettered exchange space more like an enormous, muddy, colorful, moderately chaotic, annual medieval fair without adequate security from an overlord or the town leaders and with all the human energy and pathologies possible in shared space.[21] One can even associate archetypes. While offering great and new resources, the fair exchange stalls and spaces (cyberspace's e-commerce and social websites) were also replete with conniving paupers (script kiddies), pickpockets (small-time credit card thieves), con artists (phishers, social engineers, ID thieves), and organized competing gangs of muggers (huge professional botnet masters), along with occasional wholesale attacks by armed brigands (organized cyber gangs, national-level covert cyber units).[22] Occasionally overwhelming force by an opposing or angry aristocrat would crush the entire event physically, if necessary.[23] In short, while the fair was always an economically energizing place, it was never safe. Always present was a good chance of dangerous surprises for individuals and less powerful groups set upon by others known or unknown to be enemies in advance. Cyberspace goes much further than the medieval fair in its continuousness, more like the medieval age in its ubiquity, and its corollary cybered conflict flows into the same places as cyberspace. A globe's volume of human pathologies can operate all the time using cyber means to reach and harm others anywhere, through any mode of access into the internet, and for whatever enduring or spontaneous purpose.

Put more formally, cybered conflict is distinguishable from cyberwar by the course and national significance of effects beyond the functions of the network. A cybered conflict is any conflict of national significance where success or defeat critically depends on cyber means in key activities over the course of all relevant events. A purely cyber conflict or war, in contrast, stays largely within the technical networks of cyberspace. Combatants of all levels and numbers gain access, steal data, and leave destroyed but quickly replaceable computer hard drives behind. Beyond the networks, little else happens in the wider society that is clearly disabling either widely or for long. The hard drives are replaced, backed-up data is reloaded, and a new round of spy/criminal-versus-malicious-spy/criminal begins. Cybered conflict may not involve any direct harm to any machine on any network. The major thrust of the attackers' operations could be quite covert and yet could leak outside the networks with serious effects. A major attack campaign could rest on a small set of independently spread, singularly covert pieces of software, each of which ultimately spreads across a limited or large number of critical nodes in a key system and changes their functioning in nonobvious ways. The resulting inaccurate operations could continue over long periods without recognition, especially if the changes across several critical values in internal but basic transactions vary erratically enough and the harm seems more a high level of normal accidents. Yet, in the process and over time, crucial decisions across the wider societal institutions could be misdirected, enfeebling defenders and the wider society.

Owing to its emergence in and through a global cyberspace, cybered conflict has distinctive characteristics that include universality and high tempo in participation across widely dispersed populations, ubiquity in intrinsic surprise potential across sectors and levels of society, and indeterminateness in its duration. First, its volume of attack tempo is high due to the massive number of potential bad actors anywhere in the globe who, with limited skill, can easily access and abuse the openness of the internet.[24] Any individual can for any reason use scale, proximity, and precision advantages formerly only open to either close neighbors or super powers. That is, all along the passageways of cyberspace, individuals can organize an attack organization at a scale from five to five thousand co-combatants. The same bad actor operating on the internet can plan to attack from a safe location ranging from five miles to five thousand miles within proximity of the targets. Finally, that actor, group, or state and fellow travelers can select with standardized cyber weapons and an unprecedented range of precision any set of targets from one state, group, or individual to combinations of whole regions, communities, or societies. Normal barriers to entry to this kind of pathological behavior do not operate in the current topology of cyberspace, making very small the likelihood of being able to stop bad actors or their attacks before the operations are launched.

Second, cybered conflict will always involve a large number and wide range of surprises across integrated networks. Either these will be foreseeable (in form or frequency) or rogue (unforeseeable) surprises, but they will always be present due to the intrinsic complexity of the streaming and converging globally cybered systems and the attack advantages given to bad actors anywhere around the globe today.[25] Unexpected nasty events will come by accident, by intention, by opportunism, or all three simultaneously. Outcomes will embody the full variety of what complex systems, including people, can perpetrate on one another at a distance, thus ensuring the safety of attackers. For example, hurricanes can destroy electrical grids, and so might hackers. Hurricanes, however, will not change their strategies in order to make the damage and suffering even more debilitating when the responders show an ability to recover quickly. Moreover, others not involved as central parties to a conflict will often enough use the cyber substrate to act maliciously as well, to "pile on" in others' conflicts without much risk or even a clear objective. A world in which global climate change is making climate turbulent and more dangerous now offers a global passageway by which others could conceivably reach inside a nation responding to a natural disaster and worsen the cascading harm for whatever reasons that may motivate their decision to act.

Cybered conflict thus presents a new form of normalcy in its imposition on national systems of this increased potential for nasty surprise across a society. Nationally critical systems can no longer depend on obscurity or the goodness of strangers in order to be left alone to operate safely. Such a level of uncertainty is unprecedented in its near ubiquity across all levels of society, but it is far from historically unknown. Facing daily insecurity has been a well-known situation for most individuals throughout history. For pioneers in the 1860s in the United States, for example, nothing one needed could be presumed to be safe. From the safety of the dried food, to drinking water, to the companions on the trail, to the path through the wilderness that a scout directed—all could deceptively look robust and yet fail at any moment, and do so critically. What the spread of the cybered world has done is reintroduce modern societies by their own actions to a much older "frontier" level of insecurities.[26]

Third, cybered conflicts are uncomfortably indeterminate in how the participants' struggles for control of outcomes begin, endure, or end—if ever they ever do. Many conflicts will begin with no particular warning and no clear indicators of how long, far, or deeply this particular struggle might progress. With global scale, at any given moment some actors somewhere will be trying to change the allocation of—or access to—physical, reputational, or even projected resources in ways they desire and for rationales they may alone accept. With ubiquitous access to the global cyber passages, a vast number of actors at any given moment will employ any cyber means available to them at costs and risk levels they can accept in pursuit of the outcomes they seek. There are currently no natural barriers to entry in this bubbling competitive struggle for preferred outcomes. The flood of attacks can come from anywhere for literally any reason and can last as long as the rationale, the means, or the lack of personal risk exists. At any given time, thousands of such actors are operating through cyberspace precisely because it is so easy, useful, and accessible without the local societal constraints developed over centuries by modern societies.

As a result of these attributes the combinatorial possibilities of cybered conflict are exceptionally difficult to accommodate, making the current focus of more democratic national strategies on the technical aspects of cyber attacks misplaced and even dangerous. The concept of a cybered conflict is necessary to move national security focus to a more integrated system approach consistent with the challenges cyberspace actually imposes. The enormous scale of material traveling through cyberspace is such that small campaigns with swarms of such small changes, perhaps inserted by hijacked updates, can be routinely conducted unnoticed as a whole, each time adding a bit more to the troubling variability threatening wider critical national systems. The effect could be to continually sow distrust, inefficiencies, losses, and harm to a society, perhaps in conjunction with a planned military action or perhaps merely to attrite the defending nation's economic strength over time so as to make the planned action much easier to persuasively pursue. Far from the networked nodes affected, national leaders could make inaccurate or ineffective decisions based on distorted guidance about the reliability of the nation's GPS system or electrical supply, or the integrity of data driving targeting in military operations, or massive capital flows in national financial calculations. They could focus on the cyber aspect of the conflict but miss the wider ripple effects of the cybered struggle and its effects beyond a cyberwar in breadth, extent, and significance.[27] Beyond the term's conceptual advantage in understanding what is changing for security in a cybered world, using the term "cybered conflict" allows both technical and nontechnical experts to sit at the same table to collectively design national policies for cybersecurity. The more comprehensive "cybered" adjective moves the national security debate beyond defending networks or attacking back through them. Policymakers are better able to jointly see the emerging security dilemmas of large-scale complex societal-technical systems across the entirety of a modern nation.

The adjustment in concepts is critical across a wider range of concepts and terms of art in order to make them more congruent with the emerging world. With the "cybered" characterization, the cybered conflict aspects of other well-known forms of struggle such as hybrid warfare, asymmetric conflicts, and counterterrorism campaigns are easier to integrate with the cybered age. Even in these forms of struggle and defense operations, key events will depend on the cyberspace substrate for completion.[28] Furthermore, the internationally accepted rules of war are now under debate, appearing to have trouble in application to cyberwar. With a broader, more systemic notion of conflict as cybered, these rules would find more resonance with much of what happens to the overall system before and during a struggle that has not quite broken out into kinetic exchanges.[29] Even experts in the history of traditional war and those in the development of social media networks could avoid having endless debates in their own communities about whether cybered conflict is or is not relevant to their area of expertise.[30] The systemic nature of threats forces each community to link to other areas of expertise to address the ubiquity of cyberspace, its complexity in reach and unprecedented intrusions, and its unpredictably tough dual-use nature. In the developing age of cybered conflict, national power depends on how all the skills sets work together against nasty surprises that travel far beyond the underlying cyber networks.[31]

Cyber Power and a National Security Resilience Strategy

In a deeply cybered world, notions of national power and the content of national security strategies need to change if the well-being of the nation is to be maintained. Cyberspace as a globally unfettered system alters the relative distribution of international influence available for state or nonstate actors. National cyber power will have to address global complexity directly throughout its wider arena of operations and threat assessments. Definitions and institutionalized implementation of national power will perforce begin to reflect a more systemic, less traditional war-related framework if one is to face successfully the wide variety of surprising threats that could emerge from widely connected, asymmetric actors.[32]

In particular, the dual-use nature and ubiquitous reach of cyberspace push a nation's national security concerns to widen and to be more inclusive in order to effectively anticipate and respond when the society is surprised. In the emerging cybered age, cyber power for a nation will always rest on the nation's coordinated abilities both to disrupt likely and ongoing incoming cybered surprises and to be resilient through systemic internal preparations against the inevitability of successful attacks. When the attacker can use the cyberspace substrate in unprecedented, novel ways, society's security will depend on its already well-embedded abilities to hit and heal in ways commensurate with the significance of potential harm.

Cyber power today is defined as the ability of a nation's leaders and institutions facing cybered conflict to keep the overall uncertainty across nationally cybered systems down at levels tolerable for their citizens' expectations of normal well-being. In practice, dissipating disabling threats internally means creating national "breathing space" against the harm planned by remote cyber bad actors or the damage emerging in current attacks that have already gotten inside the nation's systems. Cyber power based on a dual-robustness in responses to impede in advance or endure in response will be tailored over time in the relative emphasis given each component according to the circumstances of vulnerability of the nation at risk. Nonstate actors could conceivably have as much cyber skill as the defending state actors, or more. A rather common outcome of a narrow focus on cyberwar is developing cyber-attack means without commensurately developing the resilience of systems that attackers will target in the wider society. Effective national power will depend on the ways in which internal and external national actions and abilities in cyberspace are balanced and sustained over time and experience.

One indicator of a nation's cyber power is the effective reduction of the advantages that cyberspace affords attackers even if they do not solely use cyber means to cause harm.[33] In some cases, attackers may only be able to organize a sufficiently large number of fellow actors or infected computers as long as they are insulated from discovery by local police or even from networked retaliating defenders.[34] In other cases, the attackers may be able to persuade opportunistic fellow travelers to pile on in such numbers that personal identification becomes irrelevant. In these circumstances, negating the effects by being internally quite resilient dampens the enthusiasm to keep up the attacks across large numbers of loosely affiliated bad actors. If one cannot find or reach the attackers, a state with a great deal of cyber power can frustrate them with additional emphasis on resilience, producing the same effect as having individually silenced each attacker. The nation sustaining the dual aspects of cyber power continually disrupts efforts at attack where possible but always ensures that it survives well through any attack successes.[35]

National security strategies designed for a cybered age must develop this dual set of capabilities for effective cyber power. A security resilience strategy combines both traditional notions of security with nontraditional notions of resilience. No longer can a nation have its security agencies only look outward to possible enemies and avenues of response when, using the access and three attack advantages of cyberspace, attackers can bypass military forces and physical borders completely. Unlike the terrorists of al-Qaeda, the cybered conflict attackers do not have to physically enter the targeted nation, group, or community. The emerging densely populated, unequally resourced international system poses composite security challenges inside nations, requiring national security organizations to have key multilevel roles that they have not had since before the Cold War.

First, in a complex social system under threat, national-level agencies will have to engage in coordinating and guiding redundancy, slack, and continuous trial-and-error learning across critical internal national systems as much as identifying specific hostile foreign actors and attacking or negotiating with them across national borders. These policy challenges of cybered conflict might well be captured with two critical adages for the security strategist at any organizational scale: beware and prepare. The national security strategy must orchestrate the natural tendencies of its

society to do both to meet surprise in its critical systems. If organizations are digitally and globally connected to each other to obtain something critical to their
respective ability to operate, then one cannot sensibly fully trust anything reachable
from those connections, or any aspect of the larger systems to which they link.
National security rests on a shared public–private organizational recognition of the
deep penetration of cyberspace's global scale and complexity into all critical societal
systems. As easily as the great benefits of economic efficiencies and knowledge
exchanges come throughout the internet, likewise come all the traditional forms of
human greed, pathologies, and cruelty—only more subtle and persistent.[36] The
national security strategy needs to encourage instinctive and dedicated wariness.
Cyberspace is the same old medieval fair, but it now includes mercenaries, lords,
scalpers, and grouped predators that come from near and far, and can all operate on
the same set of targets simultaneously and suddenly. For the same level of security
of thirty years ago, the national security policy must be able to interdict the worst
aspects of this behavior at greater distance, higher levels of unexpectedness, and
fantastically accelerated speed in a cybered globe.

Second, national policies must prepare its home society for the reality, however
infrequent but inevitable, that their critical systems will fail at some point. The origins may be accidental or deliberately instigated, but the nation's responses must
expect that the harm can be exploited, extended, or exacerbated by attentive attackers operating safely immune across open cyber passageways from somewhere around
the globe. For example, in early 2011 Libyan rebels fighting the forces of the dictator
Muammar Gaddafi found that the social media sites they were using to organize
operations were under intense disabling cyber attacks by Serbian ultraconservative
groups far from North Africa. The Serbian groups' rationale for this "pile-on" was
that they hated NATO for helping Kosovar rebels in 1999, and attacking the Libyans
was a way to make things hard for NATO. They were not materially involved in the
Libyan struggle, nor did they care about the consequences for the Libyans themselves. Rather, in a demonstration of the variety of likely combatants in any future
cybered conflict, the Serbians joined in simply because they could express their grievances using the attack advantages of cyberspace.[37] National security policies need to
develop the national understanding that organizations and individuals so deeply
connected must practice in advance to operate without the benefits or the machines
involved with possibly little or no notice.[38]

For post-Cold War modern democracies, having a national security policy address
domestic security issues is normatively, institutionally, and legally troubling, but the
circumstances of the unbounded cybered world require it for strategic well-being.
The complexity and scale of cyberspace do not stop at national borders today. Securing complex interdependent and critical systems requires extraordinary knowledge
about large-scale societal systems at home as well as all those between the defending
nation's outer limits and likely sources of any attack.[39] Before the Cold War era,
military writers (outside of nations with large strategic buffers such as oceans) recognized that wars on one's home soil inherently blended two external and internal
imperatives—externally repel and internally endure. War of existential consequence

was always going to be total, if for at least one state-level combatant. Every nation needed to have forces and policies to deflect attackers from national territory and to be prepared to withstand the attacks inside the borders. Indeed, historically, such a level of internal as well as external insecurity usually meant that military forces operated both inside and at the border. Police forces did not emerge until later in the development of the modern state, when enemies as the main source of societal insecurities could reliably be pushed physically outside recognized limits to national territories.[40] Police forces are more efficient forces when the society is largely socialized into accepting the societal control regimes. However, when internal insecurity rose to require coordination across a large number of actors to develop resilience against large-scale disabling surprise, usually in times of war, then history suggests national security institutions were more often the mechanism by which the nation balanced its outward-looking security and its inward-looking resilience capabilities for survival.[41]

During the Cold War era, however, the stable westernized nations disconnected national security cognitively and institutionally from internal resilience largely because recovery in the face of a nuclear war seemed both undoable and unthinkable. What the total war needs of World War II had pushed together, the Cold War consensus between superpowers about staying away from mutual nuclear destruction separated profoundly. Especially in the United States, national security grew to focus uniquely on significant aggressive actors acting from areas outside one's border.[42] Conversely, the concepts of resilience (viewed more as robustness) became the province of strictly domestic national disaster and emergency institutions.[43] Its central concepts and policies were associated with protecting large interdependent societal systems in the face of engulfing environmentally natural surprises. Active enemies have not been included among the possible instigators of a natural disaster, and hurricanes are not seen as national security threats. Therefore, military involvement in natural disaster responses has been routinely relegated to enhancing the normal abilities of domestic services and providing backup capabilities to be used only if the local or domestic authorities are overwhelmed. Bad actors in the geographically bordered world have had to pass borders to cause significant internal harm; therefore, internal security has been left to domestic police forces and external security kept strictly to the military and foreign office domains.[44]

Over the past ten years the external threats to internal systems posed by terrorism and transnational criminal organizations have challenged this artificial domestic versus national security cognitive, legal, and institutional barrier. In the early 2000s key terrorist leaders made explicit declarations of war on whole societies, not just their military or overseas representatives.[45] Threats from cyberspace similarly reach directly into societies. Nonetheless, it has been difficult to overcome the deeply embedded presumptions that external threats should be met by entirely different concepts, strategies, and institutions from those dealing with internal threats to critical national systems. American security studies literature in the United States over the past twenty years shows exceptionally limited use of the term "robustness," or its equivalent. Even today, senior scholars in international relations have been publicly unconvinced of the national security threat from cybered attack, referring to the possibilities of disabling cyber attacks on a westernized nation as "hyperbole" or "threat inflation."[46] The national security versus domestic safety distinction continues formally today the area of cybered conflict, with internal resilience and responses to international cyber crime dissociated from national security concerns of signatory nations. As long as this distinction holds, the integration of crime with conflict will continue to pose exceptional surprises to nations inside their traditional borders. The global "university of cybercrime" routinely innovates techniques appropriated for effective use by state and nonstate actors who then use the massive noise of cyber criminal operations as cover for their more malicious operations.[47] National strategies for survival and well-being in a ubiquitously cybered world will only be effective when security and resilience concerns blend strategically at the national level. The gap is precisely what enables the harm to enter national systems from the globe's bad actors at every level from criminal to peer state.

Cybered Conflict Age: Rise of Cybered State Borders and National Security-Resilience Strategies

Today the automatic barrier between national and domestic security has thinned; however, more explicit embrace of the possibility of nationwide significant cybered surprise is needed. Given the triple onslaught of transnational criminals, terrorists, and now cyber attackers coming virtually and physically inside traditional national borders from all corners on a global scale, leaders in modern democratic states are moving step by sometimes halting step to develop their nation's ability to repel and endure the harmful surprises of cyberspace.[48] While not explicitly declaring an intent to sieve the walls between the two security policies and communities, key westernized states are iterating toward this recognition in their various expressions of their own cybersecurity strategies.[49] Without using the term in so many words, the recognition of the need to both prevent the attacks and endure the inevitable surprises is present in the US 2009 cyber policy declaration by President Obama, in the 2009 French defense paper that details changes to its national cybersecurity organizations, and in the 2010 British national defense and security strategy.[50] The institutions being established across these nations for the purposes of national cybersecurity vary a good deal, but they begin to demonstrate a nascent recognition of the old–new dual nature of conflict via cyberspace. Across these and other westernized nations, the new strategies and institutions have begun to show interesting similarities in what critical national functions are to be protected, how actors are to be made aware of threats and responsibilities, and how each national government intends to support security from cybered attacks both internally and externally.[51] For example, while only applying to the US military, the new Department of Defense Strategy for Operating in Cyberspace (DSOC) is about resilience of the forces and even the wider nation.[52] The DSOC requires more clarity, conceptual and institutional development, and the grounding of experience fed back into thinking. However, when the central arguments of the DSOC are combined with the normative and protective language of the US International Strategy for Cyberspace (ISC), the rudiments of a future explicit national security-resilience strategy guiding national capabilities in both resilience and disruption seem to be present.[53]

A security-resilience strategy will take time to evolve in the format necessary for the circumstances of each nation. Only the United States has formally established a military cyber command, but one may argue that the new authorities and institutions put in place in other nations are likely to act as cyber command equivalents over time. While the United States has emphasized the hit capability over the heal requirements of a security-resilience strategy, France and the United Kindgom have focused on the heal component over the hit abilities. However, both the security and resilience components are critical to national cyber power in the emerging cybered age. In each nation connected to other like-minded groups of nations, eventually some set of balanced institutional mechanisms to achieve national security resilience against cybered conflict will emerge commensurate to the vulnerabilities and likely harm to the nation at risk. Given the advantages of scale, proximity, and precision afforded the attacker today, it is likely that the cyber command as a generic response will be seen in future as the hallmark of a state's willingness to defend its cyber territory as well as endure attacks inside the nation. Similarly, the surprise-embracing aspects of the present across the DSOC and ISC documents are likely to serve to mark the beginning of a wider transformation process in the United States and other westernized states in their efforts to maintain their well-being against the surprises of a heavily integrated, existentially competitive cybered world. The evolutionary twists and turns of national power, strategies, and institutions lie before us. Welcome to the early days of the cybered conflict age.

Notes

Publisher's note: At the request of the author, the term internet is not capitalized.

1. John Markoff, "Cyberwar: Old Trick Threatens the Newest Weapons," *New York Times*, October 27, 2009.

2. Excellent discussions of complexity and its inherent surprises across large-scale systems can be found in the following sources: T. R. LaPorte, *Organized Social Complexity: Challenge to Politics and Policy* (Princeton, NJ: Princeton University Press, 1975); M. R. Lissack, "Complexity: The Science, Its Vocabulary, and Its Relation to Organizations," *Emergence* 1, no. 1 (1999): 110–26; J. L. Casti, *Complexification: Explaining a Paradoxical World through the Science of Surprise* (New York: Abacus, 1994); C. S. Holling, "Understanding the Complexity of Economic, Ecological, and Social Systems," *Ecosystems* 4, no. 5 (2001): 390–405; and John H. Miller and S. E. Page, *Complex Adaptive Systems* (Princeton, NJ: Princeton University Press, 2007).

3. Parts of this argument in an earlier form can be found in the author's "Cybered Conflict" blog on the Atlantic Council website, www.acus.org/tags/cybered-conflict. The concept of security resilience is also much more extensively discussed in C. Demchak, *Wars of Disruption and Resilience: Cybered Conflict, Power and National Security.* (Athens: University of Georgia Press, 2011). On the term "cyberwar," see R. Hughes, "Cyber War: Bits, Bytes and Bullets," *The World*

Today 63, no. 11 (November 2007), www.chathamhouse.org/publications/twt/archive/view/167215.

4. Kenneth J. Knapp and William R. Boulton, "Ten Information Warfare Trends," in *Cyber Warfare and Cyber Terrorism*, ed. L. Janczewski and A. M. Colarik (New York: Information Science Reference, 2007).

5. M. Mueller, *Ruling the Root: Internet Governance and the Taming of Cyberspace* (Cambridge, MA: MIT Press, 2002).

6. N. Kshetri, "Pattern of Global Cyber War and Crime: A Conceptual Framework," *Journal of International Management* 11, no. 4 (2005): 541–62.

7. Josh Rogin, "Attack by Korean Hacker Prompts Defense Department Cyber Debate," *Federal Computer Week Online*, February 9, 2007, http://fcw.com/articles/2007/02/09/attack-by-korean-hacker-prompts-defense-department-cyber-debate.aspx?sc_lang=en.

8. David E. Sanger, "Iran Fights Strong Virus Attacking Computers," *New York Times*, September 25, 2010.

9. Isaac Porche, "Stuxnet Is the World's Problem," *Bulletin of the Atomic Scientists*, December 9, 2010, http://thebulletin.org/web-edition/op-eds/stuxnet-the-worlds-problem.

10. Nicolas Falliere, Liam O Murchu, and Eric Chien, "W32.Stuxnet Dossier: Version 1.4, February 2011," *Symantec*, www.symantec.com/content/en/us/enterprise/media/security_response/whitepapers/w32_stuxnet_dossier.pdf.

11. John Leyden, "FBI 'Planted Backdoor' in OpenBSD—Break Out the Code Auditing Kit," *Enterprise Security*, December 15, 2010, available at *The Register*, www.theregister.co.uk/2010/12/15/openbsd_backdoor_claim/.

12. Michael J. Gross, "Stuxnet Worm: A Declaration of Cyber-War," *Vanity Fair*, April 2011, www.vanityfair.com/culture/features/2011/04/stuxnet-201104.

13. M. Benedikt, *Cyberspace: First Steps* (Cambridge, MA: MIT Press, 1991).

14. Riva Richmond, "The RSA Hack: How They Did It," *New York Times*, April 2, 2011.

15. John Markoff, David E. Sanger, and Thom Shanker, "Cyberwar: In Digital Combat, US Finds No Easy Deterrent," *New York Times*, January 26, 2010.

16. William Lynn, "Introducing US Cyber Command," *Wall Street Journal*, June 3, 2010.

17. John Markoff, "BIT: The Asymmetrical Online War," *New York Times*, April 3, 2011.

18. G. Morgan, *Images of Organization* (Santa Monica, CA: Sage Publications Inc., 2006).

19. Economist Staff, "The Future of the Internet: A Virtual Counter-Revolution," *Economist*, September 2, 2010.

20. Benedikt, *Cyberspace*.

21. J. F. Brenner, "Why Isn't Cyberspace More Secure?" *Communications of the ACM* 53, no. 11 (2010): 33–35.

22. Dan Goodin, "Upstart Crimeware Wages Turf War on Mighty Zeus Bot: All Your Bots Belong to Us," *El Register*, February 9, 2010; and A. A. Cárdenas, S. Radosavac, J. Grossklags, J. Chuang, and C. Hoofnagle, "An Economic Map of Cybercrime," Paper presented at the 37th Research Conference on Communication, Information and Internet Policy 2009, George Mason University Law School, Arlington, VA, September 2010.

23. C. Tilly, *Coercion, Capital, and European States, Ad 990–1992* (Cambridge, MA: Blackwell, 1992).

24. Elinor Mills, "Insecurity Complex: In Their Words: Experts Weigh in on Mac vs. PC Security," *CNET online*, February 1, 2010, http://news.cnet.com/8301-27080_3-10444561-245.html?tag=contentMain%ntentBody;1n.

25. Louise Comfort, Arjen Boin, and Chris Demchak, eds., *Designing Resilience: Preparing for Extreme Events* (Pittsburgh: University of Pittsburgh Press, 2010).

26. John Leyden, "Monster Botnet held 800,000 People's Details: Fourth Zombie Admin Could Be in South America," *El Register*, March 4, 2010, www.theregister.co.uk/2010/03/04/mariposa_police_hunt_more_botherders/.

27. Richard A. Clarke and Robert Knake, *Cyber War: The Next Threat to National Security and What to Do about It* (New York: Ecco Books, 2010).

28. G. Todd, "Cyberlaw Edition: Armed Attack in Cyberspace: Deterring Asymmetric Warfare with an Asymmetric Definition," *Air Force Law Review* 64, no. 65: 65–211.

29. S. J. Shackelford, "From Nuclear War to Net War: Analogizing Cyber Attacks in International Law," *Berkeley Journal of International Law* 27 (2009): 192.

30. Richard Baskerville, "Hacker Wars: E-Collaboration by Vandals and Warriors," *International Journal of e-Collaboration* 2, no. 1 (2006): 16. doi:10.4018/jec.2006010101.

31. P. Gao, "Using Structuration Theory to Analyze Knowledge and Process Management in a Consortium: a Case Study," *Knowledge and Process Management* 14, no. 2 (2007): 104–16.

32. Joseph Nye Jr., *The Future of Power in the 21st Century* (Cambridge, MA: Public Affairs, 2011).

33. John Leyden, "DNS Made Easy Rallies after Punishing DDoS Attack: 50Gbps of Botnet-Powered Badness," *The Register*, August 9, 2010, www.theregister.co.uk/2010/08/09/dns_service_monster_ddos/.

34. R. Young, "Hacking into the Minds of Hackers," *Information Systems Management* 24, no. 4 (2007): 281-87.

35. Shane Harris, "The CyberWar Plan, Not Just a Defensive Game," *National Journal*, November 14, 2009.

36. K. J. Knapp and W. R. Boulton, "Cyber-Warfare Threatens Corporations: Expansion into Commercial Environments," *Information Systems Management* 23, no. 2 (2006): 76-87.

37. Tanjug, "Libyan Opposition Accuses '50,000 Serb hackers,'" *B-92 News*, March 24, 2011, www.b92.net/eng/news/society-article.php?yyyy=2011&mm=03&dd=24&nav_id=73415.

38. Josh Rogin, "Cyber Officials: Chinese Hackers Attack 'Anything and Everything,'" *Federal Computer Week Online*, February 13, 2007, http://fcw.com/articles/2007/02/13/cyber-officials-chinese-hackers-attack-anything-and-everything.aspx.

39. Jennifer Baker, "EU and US join NATO Cyber Security Pact," *Computerworld UK online*, November 23, 2010, www.computerworlduk.com/news/security/3249914/eu-and-us-join-nato-cyber-security-pact/.

40. D. H. Bayley, *Patterns of Policing: A Comparative International Analysis* (Piscataway, NJ: Rutgers University Press, 1990).

41. R. L. O'Connell, *Of Arms and Men: A History of War, Weapons, and Aggression* (London: Oxford University Press, 1989).

42. C. S. Gray, "How Has War Changed since the End of the Cold War?" *Parameters* (Spring 2005), 14–26, at 21.

43. Note that the former West Germany did retain an interest in national resilience as a Cold War frontline state but, nonetheless, strongly separated its military from the internal decisions of the society. Its national leaders have assigned national-level protections in cyberspace to the Ministry of Interior with little to no role for the national security services of the Ministry of Defense, whose role in cyberspace is solely to protect its own classified networks.

44. F. P. Harvey, "The Homeland Security Dilemma: Imagination, Failure and the Escalating Costs of Perfecting Security," *Canadian Journal of Political Science/Revue canadienne de science politique* 40, no. 2 (2007): 283–316.

45. Gil Ariely, "Knowledge Management, Terrorism, and Cyber Terrorism," in *Cyber Warfare and Cyber Terrorism*, ed. L. Janczewski and A. M. Colarik (New York: Information Science Reference, 2007).

46. Stephen Walt, "Is the Cyber Threat Overblown?" in *International Security*, ed. J. Joyner (Washington DC: Atlantic Council of the US–New Atlanticist).

47. See, for example, the International Convention on Cybercrime as amended 2006. http://conventions.coe.int/Treaty/Commun/QueVoulezVous.asp?NT = 189&CM = 8&DF = 17/02/2006&CL = ENG.

48. Cheryl Pellerin, "DOD, DHS Join Forces to Promote Cybersecurity," *American Forces Press Service US Department of Defense*, October 13, 2010; and D. E. Bambauer, "Cybersieves," *Duke Law Journal* 59, no. 3 (2009): 377–595.

49. Ellen Nakashima, "Pentagon's Cyber Command Seeks Authority to Expand Its Battlefield," *Washington Post*, November 6, 2010.

50. William J. Lynn, "Defending a New Domain: The Pentagon's Cyberstrategy," *Foreign Affairs*, September/October 2010; Government of France, "The French White Paper on Defence and National Security," Office of President Nicolas Sarkozy (Paris: Govournement de France, 2009); and Richard Norton-Taylor, "The UK Is Under Threat of Cyber Attack, the National Security Strategy Says—Home Secretary Outlines Priority Threats Facing Britain ahead of the Publication of the National Security Strategy Today," *Guardian Online*, October 18, 2010.

51. J. Rollins, and A. C. Henning, "Comprehensive National Cybersecurity Initiative: Legal Authorities and Policy Considerations" (Washington, DC: CRS, March 10, 2009), www.fas.org/sgp/crs/natsec/R40427.pdf; and Thom Shanker, "Pentagon Will Help Homeland Security Department Fight Domestic Cyberattacks," *New York Times*, October 20, 2010.

52. DOD, "Department of Defense Strategy for Operating in Cyberspace," July 14, 2011, www.defense.gov/news/d20110714cyber.pdf.

53. The White House, "International Strategy for Cyberspace: Prosperity, Security, and Openness in a Networked World," May 2011, www.whitehouse.gov/sites/default/files/rss_viewer/international_strategy_for_cyberspace.pdf.

PART III

National Approaches to Cybersecurity and Cyberwar

CHAPTER 9

Persistent Enemies and Cyberwar

Rivalry Relations in an Age of Information Warfare

Brandon Valeriano and Ryan Maness

Introduction

IN OCTOBER 2010 THE US CYBER COMMAND was constituted as an active military four-star command. The 2010 National Intelligence Annual Threat Assessment states that the United States is "severely threatened" by cyber attacks.[1] With the increased importance of wars involving nonstate actors, the increase in the number of internal conflicts, and the scope of globalization, some scholars conclude that war and foreign policy have changed since 9/11.[2] The belief that war has changed is bolstered by the conjecture that cyberspace is now an important military battlefield. The field of security studies might be considered to be at a crossroads due to these perceptions.

Since the beginnings of armed conflict, enemies and combatants have always used the latest technology available to them to gain an advantage. Examples abound of states using technology, digital communication, and scientific espionage to challenge rivals. The difference now is that technology is the battlefield and the tactic at the same time. There is little to disconnect the means and objectives of cyberwar and cyber combat. This potential shift or revolution in foreign policymaking has to be evaluated on these terms. Has cyberspace become the battlefield, and what evidence do we have that this shift has changed relations between states? Yet very little has been done to study the actual impact of new tactics and weapons in the modern international battlefield. What is the true impact of cyberwar on the dynamics of conflict and interstate relations? This important question motivates our study in this volume.

This chapter focuses on persistent enemies or rivals. Interstate rivals are those states that perceive the other state as a threat and view interstate relations as a zero-sum game.[3] Vasquez defines rivalry as a "relationship characterized by extreme competition, and usually psychological hostility, in which the issue positions of contenders are governed primarily by their attitude toward each other."[4] To this point the data suggest that such pairs of states have experienced the most war in the interstate system since the end of the Napoleonic wars.[5] If one were to predict who will fight whom in the future and which states have realistic security threats, then scholars should rightly focus on rivals as the main unit of interest.[6] This study follows this advice and examines the impact of cyberwar or cyber tactics on the dynamics of rivalry.

This chapter examines the theoretical and empirical impact of cyber strategies on rivalry relations. What sorts of behavioral expectations can we derive from a theory of information warfare during a rivalry? Our research path follows two lines of questioning. First, which rivals have cyber capabilities? To examine to the extent that informational battle tactics have changed diplomacy and military relations in the modern era, we must first examine the state of actual cyber capabilities. Do rivals have cyber-combat units, and if so, are these units tasked to target rivals or possible inflated threats?

Our second question is what impact cyber capabilities have on rivalry relations. If a state has a cyber unit tasked to target a rival, does this operation actually affect interstate relations? To accomplish both tasks we present an examination of a few cases that explore the reach of cyber strategies in modern military structures among the rivalry population. How deeply have cyber capabilities and tactics penetrated rivalry dynamics? If there are cyber capabilities evident, do these tactics escalate tensions?

These research questions are important if one is to examine and theorize about the extent and impact of cyber tactics in modern international relations. Before policymakers can discuss the need for cybersecurity or the coming danger of cyberwar, we must first understand the true nature of cyber conflict against dangerous and long-standing enemies. The study of cyberwar must move away from the study of conjecture and fears of the possible and into the study of actual modern enemies' capabilities. This step is important, and this research effort is the first to examine both the theoretical and empirical impact of cyber technologies on conflict dynamics.

The chapter proceeds to define the domain of our analysis—cyber conflict—and then moves toward an examination of the importance of rivalry studies. Based on other models of conflict, we theorize about the impact of the cyber tactics of rivals. Finally, our study answers the critical question of who has cyber capabilities and what impact these capabilities have on modern rivalry relations at this point.

Cyberwar and International Relations

For our purposes, cyberspace is physical; that is, it has defined boundaries of mainframes, wires, hard drives, and networks. Herb Lin explains the technical dimension of cyber attack in chapter 3, but it is important to know that the cyber world is restricted to the domains of human thought. Computer science and math can only provide so many avenues of storage and information processes (despite the view of movies such as *Tron* and its sequel). Software tends to persist despite its faults; hence, we see the constant use of common programs (Windows) and platforms (Macs).

Perhaps the most important distinction of cyberspace is between the physical layer and syntactic layer.[7] These layers are not collapsed together. The danger coming from cyber invasions can only apply to the knowledge existing in the information world and not to all knowledge. In other words, a state is only as vulnerable as it allows itself to be.

The common usage of the term cyberwar seems to indicate direct battle between computational technologies and actors. The term's true intent is to suggest there is an ongoing technological battle in the context of a foreign policy interaction. This point is critical because we are talking about cyber technologies as used in war, battles, and foreign policy interactions rather than a futuristic war to take informational territory or further a cyber ideology. Cyberwar is generally the term used for a state's offensive capabilities and actions in cyberspace.[8] Hersh defines cyberwar as the "penetration of foreign networks for the purpose of disrupting or dismantling those networks, and making them inoperable."[9] Therefore, we define cyberwar as the use of computational technologies on the military or diplomatic battlefield of international affairs and interactions, whereas cybersecurity is the term used for a state's defensive (and sometimes offensive) capabilities in cyberspace.

As discussed in chapter 1, cyber attacks take the form of denial-of-service attacks, website defacement, and malicious code. All of the methods have the potential of doing real physical damage to states' infrastructure, secure government sites, or military operations. Malware is the most potent form of cyber warfare and should be the type most commonly used by rivals. But malware typically can only be used as a tactic if the target allows access. Malware generally works hand in hand with phishing attempts to gain passwords to access systems. Other forms of malware, such as the 2008 thumb-drive attack on the US Department of Defense network, require the physical insertion of the software into a disconnected network.

Most scholars suggest that cyber techniques change the character of war. Their line of logic is that the type of tactic or weapon used changes the nature of war because of its potential for devastating effect. What scholars must study is the impact of techniques on relations or outcomes rather than the possible impacts of said tactics. The focus must be made toward the observable and quantifiable rather than the suggested, inflated, or perceived fears that come from modern technologies.

To this point, studies about the impact of cyber technologies on foreign relations are purely speculative (as Patrick Jagoda writes in chapter 2). When one wants to advocate a position, the cyber challenge is put as a life-or-death struggle with immense implications for the modern nation-state. As Lynn puts it, "a dozen determined computer programmers can, if they find a vulnerability to exploit, threaten the United States' global logistics network, steal its operational plans, blind its intelligence capabilities, or hinder its ability to deliver weapons on target."[10] One can take such quotations and imagine the nuclear fallout created by self-aware artificial intelligence made famous by *The Terminator* franchise. Our view is much different. Rather than suggest that the nature of combat has changed, we are interested in measuring if, how, and why it has changed.

Theoretically, our concern is with how cyber tactics are perceived in the enemy and the impact of the use of these tactics. Cyber tactics could destroy command-and-control structures in the military, wipe out the media apparatus of a state, destroy financial memory and wage economic combat, target the health industry and hospitals, or wither the ability of domestic units to protect the citizenry by eliminating technology used by police and the FBI. However, all these impacts are purely speculative. We do know, however, that there is a value to chaos in the enemy. By potentially destroying one's ability to respond, coordinate, and reciprocate attacks, intensive damage is done. Fear is the motivating mechanism for much of what occurs in the international arena, and cyberwar is no different. Cyber tactics could do damage, but the fear that these technologies engender is probably more important than any theoretical conjecture a pundit can make.

The real utility in cyberwar seems to be much more benign than is usually believed. The added value of cyber tactics is that these options tend to be low-penalty options. Information can be stolen, money can be moved around electronically, chaos can ensue through the activation of computer viruses, but these outcomes fail to compare to damage done by large-scale military options or even economic sanctions. Since most military networks are decentralized, the installation of malware is a difficult proposition. The question is really whether, in the future, military networks are going to strive for more integration or move prudently toward a path of isolation. The 2010 Stuxnet worm that seems to have hit the Iranian nuclear program had to be planted from the inside with traditional intelligence operatives, and most people overestimate hackers' ability to carry out large-scale attacks from a single computer.

In terms of conflict operations, the attractiveness of the target in relation to the capability used is a critical equation rarely examined. What good would a cyber attack be if it does little actual damage to a rival state? Much is made about the secret nature of cyber operations, but this can only be true in nonwarfare, nonrivalry situations. If Russia is invading Georgia and the entire information infrastructure of Georgia is destroyed, it is pretty clear who the aggressor is. Risk to the attacker in relation to the impact of the tactic does not make the use of cyber strategies a very rational option on the battlefield.

The Importance of Interstate Rivalry

The concept of rivalry brings history and historic interactions back into the study of political science. War is obviously not an isolated event that arises from a discrete set of events, yet this is how the field studies the event statistically. To understand why wars or crises develop, one must look at the entire past history of interactions at the military, diplomatic, social, and cultural levels. Rivalry is simply defined as long-standing conflict with a persistent enemy.

Time is a key consideration for a rivalry. For a rivalry to exist, there must be a long history of events leading up to the situation. Rarely in international history do wars arise out of thin air or from quickly sparked events. When conflict does occur, there is likely a long-standing ancient and recent history of animosity that pushes both sides toward combat.

The next important consideration for rivalry is relative positions. As evidenced in the Vasquez definition of rivalry provided earlier, the issue positions of the contenders engaged in a rivalry are made in relation to the attitude of the other side.[11] Foreign policy perspectives during a rivalry are not made out of self-interest or rational planning but out of the simple consideration of denying a gain to the enemy. Rivals are in some ways addicted to perpetual conflict because of their singular outlook targeting the enemy. This perpetual competitive relationship is a dangerous situation in international affairs due to the buildup of hatred and tension over time.

The singular focus on the enemy also leads to another important consideration: the tendency of rivals to seek to "burn" the other side.[12] In a rivalry, the phrase "to cut off the nose to spite the face" comes to mind. A state engaged in a rivalry will likely harm its own security or people in order to support a wider collective struggle against an enemy.

Statistically, rivals tend to experience the most amount of conflict in the international system.[13] Whether this is an artifact of dataset construction is a debate that is ongoing, but William Thompson gives us greater confidence in the proposition that rivals are likely to fight again in the future.[14] But it is clear that a small amount of dyads in the interstate system experience an increased rate of warfare and conflict.

It then must be asked why rivals are so important in international relations. Rivals can tell us who will fight in the future but also—and more importantly—who to focus conflict reduction and resolution practices on in the present. These rival states are those that are most "at risk." Diehl and Goertz identify rivals as those states that have experienced a certain amount of militarized interstate disputes (either three or six disputes, depending on the level of rivalry under consideration).[15] William Thompson codes rivals based on historical sources and the mutual recognition of the other as an enemy. Much work has been done on why rivals fight or how rivalries start, but little work has been done on the changing nature of warfare and rivalry.[16]

The Theoretical Impact of Cyberwar on Rivalry

During a rivalry, tensions are heightened and conflict is likely when there is a disagreement about the fundamental issues at stake in a foreign policy portfolio. The question for this chapter is what might be the impact of cyberwar on rivalry relations? Cyberwar is a tactic used to gain an advantage either diplomatically or militarily against a target. During a rivalry, all options should be on the table. Even war becomes a viable foreign policy option, but here we are more interested in what the impact of cyber tactics will be on the escalation toward war.

Escalation to war in a rivalry typically occurs after a certain number of high-tension events occur in a rivalry relationship. The interesting thing about rivals is that they tend not to like launching offensive operations first, lest they be accused of starting a conflict in the first place. The normal relations range for rivalry interactions tends to take the form of espionage, war games, brinksmanship, and economic warfare.

Due to the nature of rivalry, we should expect that cyber tactics are frequently used because these options are short of war and allow for plausible deniability as to the origin of attacks. While everyone might know where the attack is coming from, few have direct evidence of cyberwar as a foreign policy choice when compared to more overt military options. Cyber tactics will tend to be the "first shot fired" in a rivalry relationship. Due to the low cost of operations and advantage they might gain for the offensive side, the use of these tactics should be widespread in a rivalry relationship. Yet the challenge of attributing a cyber attack may facilitate covert actions against rivals.

Our theory is that cyberwar tactics are used during a rivalry. When these tactics are used, they should exacerbate the rivalry and result in the escalation of tensions between the states engaged in the operations. The value of chaos and fear is a key issue for cyber strategies in international relations. The ability to launch offensive cyber attacks alone might be enough to modify the behavior of a state. Attaining a minimal level of security to deter a large-scale cyber attack could motivate an enemy to launch a cyber technology arms race to gain the upper hand. The cyber race, like other arms races, reduces confidence and escalates tensions in a dyad.[17] Cyber rivalries should heighten tensions and lead to the breakdown of cooperation. Cyberwar is unlikely to trigger conventional war, but these operations could be leading sources of discontent between enemies and could lead to the escalation of conflict between the states engaged in such practices.

The counter hypothesis is that cyber tactics as used in a rivalry neither exacerbate tensions nor degrade confidence in the states engaged in the action. Cyberwar might be part of what Azar called the normal relations range for a rivalry.[18] Cyberwar is expected to occur and even tolerated as long as total offensive operations are not conducted. By total offensive operations, we mean direct attacks that might lead to the destruction of the energy infrastructure of a state or attacks meant to take control of army units. These options should be off the table for rivals because they will lead directly to war and therefore must never be tolerated; generally neither rival wants to be seen as the aggressor. The surprising finding in relation to conventional wisdom could be that rivals will tolerate cyberwar operations if they do not cross a line that leads directly into the loss of massive life.

"The Heavyweights"

There are only a few cyber "heavyweights" recognized by cyberwar experts of the international community.[19] Among these are the United States, China, Russia, Iran, and Israel.[20] The United States is the most "plugged-in" when it comes to reliance on the Internet for infrastructural and governmental services. Therefore, the United States is most frequently attacked by potentially malicious software. Furthermore, as the world's hegemonic power, the United States is also the main target state that dissident groups, terrorists, and rogue states wish to damage. Almost all Internet infrastructures are now connected to the web in the United States, thus making the number of targets for cyberwar activity nearly unlimited. The United States is also one of the leading states in terms of the number of active rivals.[21] Thus, the expectation is that the United States, with its dependence on the web, would have advanced cyber defenses, with the government playing a leading role in the protection of both private and public domains. However, this is not the case.

The United States is also known as the most offensively capable state in the realm of cyberwar.[22] American hackers are heavily recruited by government agencies such as the Department of Defense and Department of Homeland Security. There are also numerous private employment opportunities. This is not to say that the United States is free of cybercriminals; rather, the options for Americans with these skills to find legitimate work are more prevalent than in other nations with cyberwar capabilities. Russia and China, for example, do not have the number of high-tech jobs available as in the United States, nor do they have the American Constitutional constraints that a free society may have. The expansive capabilities of American cyber agents are a frightening enemy for any state that chooses to pursue a cyberwar with the United States.

As Nigel Inkster highlights in chapter 12 of this volume, China has been gaining clout on the international stage in recent decades, and sees itself as a new force with which to be reckoned. Because China is aware that it is no match for the United States in conventional military terms, China has turned to a policy of managing this asymmetric gap by alternative means with the capabilities it has at hand. Some of these capabilities lie in cyberspace, and the Chinese have proven their worth in this domain. Chinese hackers are both homegrown and specially trained in universities.

Along with offensive cyber capabilities comparable to those of the United States, the Chinese government also has complete control of its Internet infrastructure.[23] If China were to come under a serious cyber attack, the government could shut off access to all international web portals, thus containing and suppressing the attack. This capability is not something that the United States can claim because the multiple access points are privately owned by a number of diverse firms over which the government has no control. Therefore, in terms of cyberwar capabilities, it can be argued that China has a definite advantage over the United States.

Nevertheless, we have a problem with a potential cyber conflict between the United States and China; these two countries are not considered to be rivals under any rivalry dataset. There is no history of serious disputes on the level of historic examples such as the United States and the Soviet Union or India and Pakistan. Despite claims by pundits, China and the United States are not on a collision course. China's main foreign policy objective seems to be economic expansion, and there is little chance it will be able to compete militarily or economically with the United

States in the near future.[24] If the two main heavyweights often thought to be likely to fight in the near future are not rivals and are thus unlikely to fight, what danger is there from their immense cyber capabilities?

Russia is another state that has ambiguous cyberwar capabilities and policies. Russia boasts a highly educated and technically skilled workforce; however, the number of jobs that cater to these skills are few and far between. Furthermore, Russian culture demands a high degree of nationalistic pride, as the glory of the recent Soviet past still looms large in the hearts and minds of most Russians. Therefore, this combination of few jobs in the Russian private economy for high-tech skills along with Russian national pride has created a black market of hacking communities that have a potent ability to inflict damage on states. Nick Gvosdev offers a good explanation of this in chapter 11 of this volume. The potential of offensive Russian "hacktivism" is thus real, and its potential to do great damage is apparent.

The Islamic Republic of Iran is a semiclosed state that has great control over content of the Internet channels coming in and out of the country.[25] During the mass protests over the controversial 2009 elections, the Iranian government was successful in shutting out the opinions from the outside world on the Web, especially from the West. Iran is a state that can and will use the Web to control and censor its people. Iran is clearly a rival of the United States, at least in terms of foreign policy objectives.

Iran does have cyberwar capabilities but perhaps not as advanced as those from the United States, China, Russia, and Israel. Because Iran is a fundamentalist state that supports the expulsion of the Zionist state from the Holy Land, the country has been known to help Hamas and Hezbollah with their cyber campaigns against Israel. The Ashiyane Security Group is a covert Iranian hacking community that has hacked into more than four hundred Israeli websites, including those belonging to members of the Israeli Defense Ministry.[26] However, these attacks have only been distributed denial of service (DDOS) and website defacement attacks, which cause mischief and disruption but are nowhere near as potent as the various types of malware.

Israel is becoming known as the most advanced cyber-capable state in the world.[27] The Israeli government has extensive networks of both offensive and defensive cyberwar technologies. It also actively supports Israeli "cyber patriots," private citizens with necessary technical skills who wish to help protect Israeli cyberspace from attacks by its many enemies in the Middle East, including Iran.[28] Israel's most recent and most infamous cyber attack is the September 2010 Stuxnet worm, which targeted the Iranian nuclear facilities as well as other important plugged-in infrastructure facilities. There is speculation on Israel's guilt in this attack; the United States has also been blamed, but neither country has claimed responsibility. However, behavior by diplomats from both Israel and the United States suggests that they are not denying responsibility either.[29]

Cyberwar between rivals may be more covert than vocal, and the data presented in the next section will help answer our primary question of how cyber capabilities are used in interstate rivalries. Table 9.1 is an outline of cyber capabilities as adapted

TABLE 9.1
Overall Cyberwar Strength among Key Countries

Nation	Cyber Offense[a]	Cyber Dependence[b]	Cyber Defense[a]	Total Score[c]
Iran	4	5	3	12
United States	9	2	4	15
Israel	8	3	4	15
China	5	4	6	15
Russia	7	5	4	16

[a] On a scale of 10, with 10 being the strongest.
[b] On a scale of 10, with 10 being the least dependent.
[c] On a scale of 30, with 30 being the most vulnerable.

Source: Adapted and modified from Richard A. Clarke and Robert K. Knake, *Cyber War: The Next Threat to National Security and What to Do about It* (New York: HarperCollins, 2010), 148.

from Clarke and Knake. This table ranks on a scale of 10 each country's offensive and defensive capabilities as well as its dependence upon cyberspace. Cyber dependence is ranked in reverse order; the higher the number, the less dependent the state is on computer technologies. The United States gets a low score because of how "plugged-in" it is to the Web for important infrastructural needs such as electricity and water. Therefore, the more dependent a state is on cyber technology, the more vulnerable it is.[30]

The football proverb "you can't have a good offense without a good defense" comes to mind here. The United States has the most powerful cyber arsenal in the world, but at the same time is heavily dependent upon the Internet and has relatively weak defenses from attack because it is not possible to "shut off" the Internet. Israel is similar to the United States in most respects but overall is not as dependent on cyber technologies as the United States is. Russia and China, on the other hand, are more balanced in terms of offensive and defensive capabilities. Although these states are not as offensively capable as the United States is, they are able to defend themselves more readily against attack due to the fact that the government controls the important infrastructural lifelines of cyberspace. Iran falls somewhere on the lower end of the scale because it has very few offensive capabilities but is also less dependent overall and remains in control of access points. With capabilities defined, we will examine two case studies where capable rivals could wreak havoc on their adversaries.

Cyberwar in Rivalry: Case Examinations

The states mentioned earlier have robust, advanced cyber capabilities. Therefore, it is expected that these countries would use these capabilities against their rivals as part of their foreign policy to weaken or destroy the capabilities of their adversaries. Rivals might wish to embarrass or demoralize their adversary publicly so that the adversary knows exactly where the attack comes from, and to claim credit, thus exerting power over the adversary. Animosities between rival states are largely vocal and exposed; thus, it would be expected that cyber attacks between rivalries would not be covert but rather open and public. Furthermore, it would also be expected that cyber attacks during a rivalry would increase tensions and push the states toward war.

Two ongoing and well-established contemporary rivalries that are chosen for this chapter are the dyads of Russia–Georgia and Israel–Iran. These rivals were extracted from the datasets on rivals by Klein, Goertz, and Diehl and by Thompson because they represent some of the heavyweights mentioned earlier, and because these dyads are the most often discussed by news pundits as being engaged in cyber combat.[31] It is important to study rivals who have cyber capabilities so that the possible effects of cyberwar are observed because we theorize that rivals will be more willing to use these capabilities on each other.[32]

Russia and Georgia

Russia and Georgia have been through many disputes since the fall of the Soviet Union. Tensions came to a head when Russia invaded Georgia on August 8, 2008.[33] The war lasted five days and ended with an overwhelming Russian victory.[34] There were many events leading to Russia's invasion, which centered on South Ossetia and Abkhazia. First, the nature of South Ossetia and Abkhazia were disputed. Second, there were minor skirmishes between Russian and rebels troops; eighteen events have been counted during the five days.[35] Third, Russia has used its energy policy to throw its weight around with the countries of Europe, including Georgia.[36] Finally, it has been argued that because of the uncertainty of the Black Sea Fleet's fate in Crimea, Russia was looking for a new Black Sea port through Abkhazia.[37] Given that the 2008 war occurred in the information age, it is important to examine the role cyber capabilities played in this rivalry.

As the data show, although these adversaries have advanced and potentially catastrophic cyber capabilities, use of these weapons has been minimal and the credit claimed for the attacks has not been from the governments of these states. Rather, for the most part the "buck has been passed" to nonstate actors and the cyber underground. Table 9.2 shows data of cyber attacks between the two dyadic rivalries from the past ten years. The attacks were minimal by cyber standards, as only DDoS and website defacements were employed. The Russian government denied any involvement in these attacks, instead passing the blame to Russian patriots sympathetic to the cause. Russia has the ability to inflict more damage on Georgian cyberspace; however, it chose not to. Georgia retaliated by flooding certain government sites with DDoS attacks, but the damage was minimal and temporary at best. Therefore, the full use of cyber warfare tactics is yet to be part of the Russian or Georgian

TABLE 9.2
Cyber Attacks between Russia and Georgia

Date	Direction	Title	Type	Damage
8/2/2004	Russia>Georgia	Massive Keystroke Logging Attack	Malware (keystroke logging)	Massive information theft
8/12/2008	Russia>Georgia	Russian Invasion Cyber Attacks	DDoS, website defacements, malware (logic bombs)	Disruption and defacement of government websites, erasure of data in military sites
8/12/2008	Georgia>Russia	Retaliation for Russian Cyber Attacks	DDoS	Disruption of various public and private Russian sites

arsenal, even in times of physical conflict. Most damage was done by Russian and Georgian guns, not cyber attacks.

The cyber attacks that accompanied this five-day war were merely disruptions in Georgian and Russian Internet service as well as defacements of various government websites. What came out of the war was the recognition by Russia and its Commonwealth of Independent States allies of Abkhazia and South Ossetia as independent states, denouncement of Russian actions by the West, and increased tensions between the rivals. The effects of the cyber attacks on the rivalry escalation were minimal at best.[38]

Israel and Iran

The rivalry between Israel and the Islamic Republic of Iran began in the aftermath of the Iranian Revolution of 1979, when religious fundamentalists took control of Tehran and have been in control ever since. Israel became the sworn enemy of Iran, and the rivalry has been escalating because of the Iranian regime change.[39] Iran has been the most vocal supporter of the Palestinian state and has vowed to see the Zionist state wiped off the face of the Earth. Iran remained rather benign in the 1980s when it came to front-line attacks (physical or rhetorical) on the Israeli–Palestinian peace process. However, beginning in the 1990s the state began to more directly undermine the Israeli–Palestinian peace process and to fund anti-Israeli terrorist groups such as Hamas and Hezbollah.[40] Terrorist attacks on Israel funded by Iranian money are too numerous to discuss in this chapter. Espionage and assassinations have been the catalyst for Iranian animosity against Israel. In this new era of supposed cyberwarfare, espionage, and terror, it has been found that this may be the new realm where the Israeli–Iranian rivalry escalates. The animosities of these two states could see unconstrained and unrelenting cyberwar.

Only in the past two years have the cyber tactics between the rivals of Iran and Israel escalated. Earlier, these attacks had been limited to DDoS attacks and website defacements in reaction to certain foreign policy choices. The first three events in table 9.3 represent only minor incursions in each others' cyberspace. "Electronic Jihad" and "Cyber Jihad" were joint efforts by the Iranian government and various anti-Zionist terrorist groups such as Hezbollah. These were reactions to Israeli policies toward the disputed Palestinian territories of Gaza and the West Bank. Tensions increased on both sides because of these events; however, the role of cyber attacks in the heightened tensions remains to be seen. Many issues exist between the rivals; therefore, any action taken by either side could possibly escalate to conflict.

Retaliation against the Iranian government's 2006 sponsorship of an online contest that poked fun at the existence of the Holocaust was one of the first cyber attacks in which Israel directly targeted Iran. Israeli hackers flooded the website until it was for all intents and purposes shut down. The contest never declared a winner, but Israel was relentless in its attack on Iran. The Iranian government denied sponsoring the online event, but sources point to Iranian president Mahmoud Ahmadinejad as the mastermind behind the idea.

TABLE 9.3

Cyber Attacks between Israel and Iran

Date	Direction	Title	Type	Damage
9/1/2000	Iran>Israel	Electronic Jihad	DDoS	Disruption of service, lost time and money
8/1/2001	Iran>Israel	Cyber Jihad	DDoS	Disruption of service, lost time and money
2/7/2006	Israel>Iran	Iran Holocaust Cartoon Contest	DDoS, website defacements	Disruption of web-based cartoon contest in Iran
10/27/2006	Iran>Israel	Israeli-Lebanon Conflict	DDoS	Disruption of service, lost time and money
12/17/2008	Iran>Israel	Operation Cast Lead Retaliation	DDoS, website defacements	Disruption of Israeli government sites
7/7/2009	Israel>Iran	Nuclear Facilities Virus	Malware (virus)	Disruption of communications, theft of secret information
9/30/2010	Israel>Iran	Stuxnet	Malware (worm)	Disruption of Iranian nuclear facilities, destruction of centrifuges

Cyber attacks began to heat up between the rivals in 2008 with the Israeli invasion of Lebanon in response to short-range missile attacks by the terrorist group in northern Israel. Again, as with the Russia–Georgia dyad, cyberwarfare was a supplement to physical attack, not the primary weapon that caused the most damage. The DDoS attack was a joint effort by Iran and other pro-Palestinian governments as well as nonstate actors such as Hezbollah and Hamas. Defacing of government websites and flooding of important Israeli commercial websites until they shut down was the damage done. The tables would be turned on Iran in 2009 and 2010, when some of the most sophisticated malware released on a state's infrastructure manifested itself.

Because of Iran's nuclear ambitions, Israel has stepped up its cyberwar against its rival. Only in 2009 did Israel begin using malware against Iran. The Nuclear Facilities Virus was malware intended to steal information from top-secret government sites as well as disrupt communication between parties working in Iran's nuclear program. Iran has pointed the finger at Israel and the United States and has denounced the attack in typical Iranian anti-Zionist fashion. Both governments have denied that the attack originated in their cyberspace. Nevertheless, tensions have increased within the rivalry.

The most recent worm released on Iran's network in 2010, Stuxnet, is becoming known as the most ambitious and most damaging piece of malware released into a state's infrastructure. Recent evidence has shown that the worm was developed in Israel, but where it was released has still not been pinpointed.[41] This worm has destroyed Iranian centrifuges and has severely disrupted the progress made by Iranian nuclear scientists. The genius behind the worm is that it only became malicious when specific targets, the Iranian centrifuges, were activated. It told the centrifuges to spin out of control, effectively destroying them. Furthermore, the worm sent code to the Iranian facilities' control panels to indicate that everything was operating smoothly while the centrifuges were destroying themselves. Reports estimate that the Stuxnet attack has set back Iran's nuclear program by at least three years.[42]

Iran has yet to retaliate, but maybe Stuxnet is the beginning of a new age of more malicious and more destructive cyberwar. Iran has vowed to beef up its cybersecurity as well as its cyber-offensive capabilities as a result of the Stuxnet attack. However, Iran does not have the domestic manpower to mount such sophisticated attacks as Stuxnet, and how this new "beefing up" of Iranian cyber capabilities may provoke Israel or the United States remains to be seen.[43] Furthermore, the assassinations of Iranian scientists and the threat of airstrikes seem to more effective at getting Iran's attention than this most recent malicious Stuxnet worm.

Assessment of Case Examinations

Why have these very vocal and much-hated rivals failed to take credit for these minimal attacks that one would assume they would be proud to take credit for? Several reasons come to mind, which have implications for the future of cyberwarfare between rivals and the international community in general.

Cyber Constraints

Perhaps a reason for the relevant lack of serious malware attacks between rivals is fear of retaliation from the other side. If a state within a rivalry openly and blatantly attacks its adversary's infrastructure or secret government databases, that state may perceive the attack as it would a physical attack such as an airstrike or infantry invasion. Attacks like these are considered acts of war, and it is likely that these states are not quite ready or willing to escalate the rivalry to this point. Israel may have the malware available to completely destroy Iran's nuclear program, but the repercussions of this action may escalate to all-out war between the countries, which could very well escalate to include major powers such as the United States and China. Therefore, cyberwarfare may not have escalated to more harmful attacks in the same way nuclear deterrence allowed for peace between major powers during the Cold War. Neither adversary wanted to act first and be blamed for causing World War III.

Cyber Norms and a Normal Relations Range

The rules and norms in the realm of cyberspace have yet to be determined, but it does seem clear that rivals operate as rivals should. They are able to manage their tensions in such a way as to forestall violence for long periods. The rules of the game in cyberspace have yet to be determined, and states have yet to employ blatant widespread damage via the Web out of fear of the unknown or disturbing the balance of harmony during a rivalry. Surprisingly, Russia has pushed for treaties among the international community that would set up norms of cyberwar among states. The European Union has also promoted this idea. However, the United States and China are major powers that are skeptical about signing on to such agreements.[44] These skeptics are the roadblocks to more talks about an agreed-upon mode of behavior by adversaries in cyberspace.

Plausible Deniability

States with cyber capabilities also have the advantage of being able to deny any involvement in cyber attacks originating within their borders. Because cyber attacks are difficult to trace, and even more difficult to trace to a government, states that may have sponsored or coordinated a cyber attack against its rival will have the advantage of plausibly denying any involvement in a malicious breach of security. For example, the website defacements and DDoS attacks perpetrated by Russia and Georgia during the 2008 wars were blamed on the patriotic nonstate actors sympathetic to each side's cause. Cyber-attack denial by states actively involved in a physical war is puzzling, especially since the purpose of war is to get the other side's government to capitulate to demands. Either the Russians and Georgians were tell-ing the truth, or the cyber constraints and lack of cyber norms discussed earlier played a part. Russia perhaps feared retaliation by the United States, and Georgia perhaps feared escalated Russian attacks.

As of this writing, the Stuxnet worm, it appears, is the work of a joint Israeli–American effort. Although diplomats and representatives from both governments are officially denying involvement in the development and deployment of the worm, they do so with what can be interpreted as a metaphorical "wink" in that they were unofficially involved.[45] They state their pleasure with the fact that Iran's nuclear program has been set back because of the worm but will not cross the line in bla-tantly admitting their involvement. Thus far, it has been rare that a government has openly admitted to committing acts of cyberwar.

Lack of "Shock Value"

The September 11, 2001, attacks were a spectacle that changed the course of Ameri-can foreign policy and put the world on high alert ever since. Visuals of the burning Twin Towers and Pentagon are ingrained in the mind of every American old enough to remember. These physical attacks propagated by terrorists have had lasting "shock value" that has changed the behaviors of major states. Cyber attacks, on the other hand, may not have the shock value that a conventional physical attack may demon-strate. Therefore, in order to get rivals to capitulate to a state's demands, an airstrike, artillery strike, or all-out invasion may get the desired outcomes that rivals are look-ing for. Cyber attacks, although potentially lethal, do not have the same "punch" as a physical attack. Russia's cyber attack in 2008 was accompanied by a major military campaign, and Georgia quickly surrendered because of the bullets, not the botnets. Furthermore, Israel still has not ruled out extensive airstrikes on Iran's nuclear facili-ties, even though the Stuxnet worm that Israel has been accused of releasing has set back the Islamic Republic's nuclear ambitions.

The attacks in cyberspace between the rivalries of Russia and Georgia and Iran and Israel have been limited, constrained, and denied. These covert methods of attack are equivalent to a twenty-first-century version of a very ancient form of for-eign policy—spying. Gathering information from and sabotaging valuable infrastruc-ture of enemies has been part of human history since the advent of warfare. Thus far, this form of spying has yet to be normalized, and because of this, the true nature of states' cyber capabilities has yet to be realized. Rivals tend to not use cyber opera-tions very often, and when they do, these operations do not exasperate tensions beyond a normal relations range. Escalation of malicious attacks are very possible and may be apparent in the very near future; however, constraints, lack of norms, deniability, and lack of shock value have allowed for damaging yet limited cyberwar-fare among rivals.

Assessment

This chapter is a preliminary evaluation meant to theoretically and empirically trace out the impact of cyber strategies on modern interstate relationships. Future work will go forward with quantifying the specific cyber capabilities of each state engaged in current rivalries. We can only know the true impact of a policy by studying its actual use in current foreign policy. It does little good to trump up a factor as a "game changer" before its true impact is even measured.

Seymour Hersh makes an interesting point in his contention that the danger expounded by cyberwar theorists results from a confusion between cyber espionage and cyberwar.[46] We have a similar finding in this chapter; rivals tend to use cyber tactics. However, these tactics are not widespread, nor do these tactics escalate tensions within a rivalry dyad.

This finding is surprising based on the increased attention cyber combat gathers in the realm of national security. Perhaps the danger stated by various authors is overstated, extreme, or—even worse—arises out of self-interest in the need to perpetuate a national security state. The fear caused by cyber tactics is much greater than the actual danger such actions have posed in real life. Fear is the basis for rivalry, and as long as enemies fear the other side, any tactic that could inflict damage is frightening.

The Future of Cyberwar and Rivalry

The shadow of the future plays heavily on the issue of cyberwar. At this point, no one knows the limits in terms of targets during an all-out cyberwar, but our initial hypothesis that states with cyber capabilities and engaged in a rivalry will use all means necessary to counter said rival has been falsified at this point. The remaining question concerns the future. Will we continue to see low-level use of cyber technologies to target rival states?

The danger lies in Stuxnet becoming a harbinger of the future. If the goal of Stuxnet was to hamper the industrial capabilities of a target state, the United States is the most vulnerable to retaliation on this point. By opening up Pandora's Box in the context of Iran, Israel and the United States are now opening themselves to all sorts of attacks because they went beyond the normal taboos of cyber operations in rivalry to this point. A *New York Times* article on Stuxnet makes the point that the worm likely harmed Iran's nuclear production capabilities as much as a direct strike by Israel would have.[47] Does this mean that Iran will seek to retaliate and escalate the conflict?

All too often rivalries are seen as innocuous, just part of the foreign policy project for all states. The fear for us is that some of these managed types of rivalries might increase in hostility due to the actions on the cyber battlefield. To this point we have seen little evidence of unrestricted cyber warfare against a rival, and we hope this trend continues. The future is very much dependent on how rival states react to actual conflict events launched by their enemies. On that point, the entire history of rivalry studies suggests that we have much to worry about because rivals tend to overreact to threats posed by enemies.

Notes

1. Dennis C. Blair, "Annual Threat Assessment of the US Intelligence Community for the Senate Select Committee on Intelligence," February 2, 2010, www.dni.gov/testimonies/2010 0202_testimony.pdf.

2. Mary Kaldor, *New and Old Wars: Organized Violence in a Global Era* (Stanford, CA: Stanford University Press, 1999). Dissent to this perspective is offered by many who use data to analyze war and foreign policy. See Errol Henderson and J. Singer, "'New Wars' and Rumors of 'New Wars,'" *International Interactions* 28, no. 2 (2002): 165–90.

3. Paul Diehl and Gary Goertz, *War and Peace in International Rivalry* (Ann Arbor: University of Michigan Press, 2000); and William R. Thompson, "Identifying Rivals and Rivalries in World Politics," *International Studies Quarterly* 45 no. 4 (2001): 557–86.

4. John Vasquez, *The War Puzzle* (Cambridge: Cambridge University Press, 1993).

5. Diehl and Goertz, *War and Peace in International Rivalry*; and Brandon Valeriano, "Becoming Rivals: The Process of Rivalry Development," in *What Do We Know about War?*, 2nd ed., ed. J. A. Vasquez (Lanham, MD: Rowman & Littlefield, 2012).

6. Stuart Bremer, "Who Fights Whom, When, Where, and Why?" in *What Do We Know about War?* ed. J. A. Vasquez, 23–36 (Lanham, MD: Rowman & Littlefield, 2000).

7. Martin C. Libicki, *Conquest in Cyberspace* (Cambridge: Cambridge University Press, 2007).

8. Richard A. Clarke and Robert K. Knake, *Cyber War: The Next Threat to National Security and What to Do about It* (New York: HarperCollins, 2010).

9. Seymour Hersh, "The Online Threat: Should We Be Worried about Cyber War?" *New Yorker*, November 2010.

10. William J. Lynn III, "Defending a New Domain," *Foreign Affairs* 89 no. 5 (2010): 97–108.

11. Vasquez, *War Puzzle*.

12. Valeriano, "Becoming Rivals."

13. Diehl and Goertz, *War and Peace in International Rivalry*.

14. Thompson, "Identifying Rivals."

15. Diehl and Goertz, *War and Peace in International Rivalry*.

16. On why rivals fight, see Michael P. Colaresi, Karen A. Rasler, and William R. Thompson, *Strategic Rivalries in World Politics: Position, Space and Conflict Escalation* (Cambridge: Cambridge University Press, 2007). On how rivalries start, see Valeriano, "Becoming Rivals."

17. Susan Sample, "Arms Races and Dispute Escalation: Resolving the Debate," *Journal of Peace Research* 34, no. 1 (1997): 7–22; Susan G. Sample, "Military Buildups: Arming and War," in *What Do We Know About War?* ed. J. A. Vasquez, 167–96 (Lanham, MD: Rowman & Littlefield, 2000).

18. Edward Azar, "Conflict Escalation and Conflict Reduction in an International Crisis: Suez, 1956," *Journal of Conflict Resolution* 16 (1972): 183–201.

19. Clarke and Knake, *Cyber War*.

20. Other countries include France, Ukraine, India, Pakistan, Belarus, Great Britain, and Germany.

21. Thompson, "Identifying Rivals."

22. Clarke and Knake, *Cyber War.*

23. Ibid.

24. Fareed Zakaria, *The Post-American World* (New York: W. W. Norton), 2008; and Daniel Drezner, "Bad Debts: Assessing China's Financial Influence in Great Power Politics," *International Security* 34 (Fall 2009): 7–45.

25. Jeffrey Carr, *Inside Cyber Warfare* (Sebastopol, CA: O'Reilly Media, 2010).

26. Ibid.

27. Ibid.

28. Ibid.

29. Ibid.

30. Clarke and Knake, *Cyber War.*

31. James P. Klein, Gary Goertz, and Paul F. Diehl. "The New Rivalry Dataset: Procedures and Patterns," *Journal of Peace Research* 43 no. 3 (2006): 331–48. Rivalry between the United States and China is not found in either dataset, so this dyad cannot be used for this study.

32. To locate and disseminate cyber attacks used with the Russian–Georgian and Israeli–Iranian rivalries, qualitative content analysis is used. Using the search engine Google News, we sifted through news stories reporting the instances of cyber attacks between the states. The keywords of "Iran Israel Cyber" and "Russia Georgia Cyber" were input, and the results are reported in the following.

33. Jim Nichol, "Russia-Georgia Conflict in South Ossetia: Context and Implications for US Interests" *Congressional Research Service Report for Congress*, October 24, 2008.

34. Ibid.

35. Gary King, "Ten Million International Dyadic Events" (2006). Accessed 1/20/2010, available at http://dvn.iq.harvard.edu/dvn/dv/king/faces/study/StudyPage.xhtml?studyId=505&studyListingIndex=0_ee2717d5514905203fbf4ce96055.

36. Shamil Midkhatovich Yenikeyoff, "The Georgia-Russia Standoff and the Future of Caspian and Central Asian Energy Supplies," *Middle East Economic Survey* 51, no. 36 (2008): 1–4.

37. Nichol, "Russia-Georgia Conflict."

38. Ibid., 17–19.

39. Trita Parsi, *Treacherous Alliance: The Secret Dealings of Israel, Iran, and the United States* (New Haven, CT: Yale University Press, 2007).

40. John P. Miglietta, *American Alliance Policy in the Middle East, 1945–1992: Iran, Israel, and Saudi Arabia* (Lanham, MD: Lexington Books, 2002).

41. William J. Broad, John Markoff, and David E. Sanger. "Israeli Test on Worm Called Crucial in Iran Nuclear Delay," *New York Times*, January 15, 2011.

42. Ibid.

43. Josh Lederman, "Iran Seeks to Boost Corps of Web Watchers," *Associated Press*, January 19, 2011, www.foxnews.com/world/2011/01/19/iran-seeks-boost-corps-web-watchers/.

44. Clarke and Knake, *Cyber War.*

45. Broad, Markoff, and Sanger, "Israeli Test on Worm."

46. Seymour Hersh, "The Online Threat," *New Yorker*, November 2010.

47. Broad, Markoff, and Sanger, "Israeli Test on Worm."

CHAPTER 10

Competing Transatlantic Visions of Cybersecurity

James Joyner

Introduction

THE UNITED STATES, UNITED KINGDOM, AND CONTINENTAL EUROPE have very different approaches to cybersecurity. The United States and United Kingdom conceive of cyber primarily as a national security problem to be handled by the military—which in turn sees the Internet as a fifth domain of war to be dominated. The remainder of the European Union, by contrast, sees cyber threats mostly as a nuisance for commerce and individual privacy that should be dealt with by civilian authorities in conjunction with private enterprise.

Further, while the United States can have a single policy, albeit one implemented by many different federal departments, the European Union is made up of twenty-seven nation-states with their own laws, ideas, and philosophical differences over how to approach cyber issues. Finally, there is NATO, where a unified transatlantic cyber vision must be reconciled and arranged in a coherent manner among twenty-eight allies through a cumbersome bureaucratic process. To make sense of these conflicting visions, this chapter reviews cyber attacks against NATO members, attempts to outline the challenges of developing a transatlantic vision for cyber policy, and highlights some of the fundamental differences among NATO members.

Thinking about Cyberwar

It is useful to remember that although the Internet is so ensconced in most of our lives that it is hard to imagine living without it, the first modern Web browser did not debut until 1993 and broadband access has only become widespread over the last decade. Consequently, senior government and military leaders did not grow up with the Internet and are slowly having to adapt to emerging cyber realities. Franklin Kramer, who served as assistant secretary of defense under President Bill Clinton, draws a comparison with fire, noting that the Great Fire of London nearly destroyed the city in 1666 "because an advance in living conditions—wooden houses for many—was not matched by security measures. There were no fire fighting technologies, no fire fighting processes, and no resources devoted to fire fighting." This remained true more than two centuries later with the Great Chicago Fire. Despite our slow learning curve, "in the modern world, while fire may strike, it is not the city-devouring scourge that it once was." Through government regulation that established building codes and through volunteer and government-run fire departments, a protective-response was developed over centuries.[1]

Former Deputy Secretary of Defense William J. Lynn III prefers a more martial analogy: "The first military aircraft was bought, I think, in 1908, somewhere around there. So we're in about 1928," he said. "We've kind of seen some . . . biplanes shoot at each other over France," he added. "But we haven't really seen kind of what a true cyberconflict is going to look like."[2]

Currently, European policymakers tend to see cybersecurity more along fire-prevention lines rather than as biplanes over France. And framing very much matters when thinking about cyber issues. As Kramer observes, "Ask the wrong question, and you generally will get the wrong answer. And cyber—and what to do about cyber conflict—is an arena where there is generally no agreement on what is the question, certainly no agreement on what are the answers, and evolving so fast that questions are transmuted and affect and change the validity of answers that have been given." He argues that the lack of agreement over the nature of the problem, lack of coherent regulation and authority mechanisms, and conflict between connectivity and security together make cyber a "wicked problem" not easily susceptible to resolution.[3]

Lynn frames the issue in military and security terms but fully realizes that the reality is quite blurred and that no bright lines exist in this new domain. "I mean, clearly if you take down significant portions of our economy we would probably consider that an attack. But an intrusion stealing data, on the other hand, probably isn't an attack. And there are [an] enormous number of steps in between those two."[4]

Today, one of the challenges facing Pentagon strategists is "deciding at what threshold do you consider something an attack," Lynn said. "I think the policy community both inside and outside the government is wrestling with that, and I don't think we've wrestled it to the ground yet." In other words, it is difficult to know whether the house is on fire or biplanes are shooting at each other.[5]

Equally tricky, defense officials say, is how to pinpoint who is doing the attacking. And this raises further complications that go to the heart of the Pentagon's mission. "If you don't know who to attribute an attack to, you can't retaliate against that attack," noted Lynn in a discussion at the Council on Foreign Relations. As a result, "you can't deter through punishment, you can't deter by retaliating against the attack." He lamented the complexities that make cyberwar so different from, say, "nuclear missiles, which of course come with a return address."[6]

Cyber Attacks against NATO States

The cyber threat is not theoretical or the stuff of science fiction. Over the last several years several NATO members and partners, including the United States, have been targeted with cyber attacks, many of them severe.

Estonia

What many believe to be the "first known case of one state targeting another by cyber-warfare" began on April 27, 2007, when a massive denial-of-service attack was launched against Estonia over a petty dispute involving a statue. The attack crippled "websites of government ministries, political parties, newspapers, banks, and companies."[7] It has been dubbed Web War One.[8] Nick Gvosdev explores the attack in detail in chapter 11 of this volume, but it is worth noting here that the attack resonated within transatlantic national security circles.

The German newspaper *Deutsche Welle* noted that "Estonia is particularly vulnerable to cyber attacks because it is one of the most wired countries in the world. Nearly everyone in Estonia conducts banking and other daily activities on line. So when the cyber attack occurred, it nearly shut Estonia down."[9] Then-EU Information Society and Media commissioner Viviane Reding called the attacks "a wakeup call," exclaiming that "if people do not understand the urgency now, they never will." But her planned action was to incorporate a response into an EU-wide law on identity theft over the Internet.[10] However, NATO did establish a Cyber Center of Excellence in Tallinn, which will be discussed later in the chapter.

Georgia

While not a NATO member, Georgia is a NATO partner, and the April 2008 Bucharest Summit declared that it "will become a member" at some unspecified time in the future, a promise reiterated at the November 2010 Lisbon Summit.[11] Weeks before the August 2008 Russian land invasion and air attack, Georgia was subject to an extensive, coordinated cyber attack. American experts estimated that the "attacks against Georgia's Internet infrastructure began as early as July 20, with coordinated barrages of millions of requests—known as distributed denial of service, or DDOS, attacks—that overloaded and effectively shut down Georgian servers."[12] The pressure was intensified during the early days of the war, effectively shutting down critical communications in Georgia.

Writing as the attacks were under way, security consultant Dancho Danchev believed it "smells like a three letter intelligence agency's propaganda arm has managed to somehow supply the creative for the defacement of Georgia President's official web site, thereby forgetting a simple rule of engagement in such a conflict—risk forwarding the responsibility of the attack to each and every Russian or Russian supporter that ever attacked Georgian sites using publicly obtainable DDOS attack tools in a coordinated fashion."[13] Bill Woodcock, the research director at Packet Clearing House, a California-based nonprofit group that tracks Internet security trends, notes that the attacks represented a landmark: the first use of a cyber attack in conjunction with an armed military invasion.[14]

The nature of cyber attacks is such that, two and a half years later, there is no definitive answer on who caused the attack. They certainly emanated from Russia, but the precise role of Moscow's military and intelligence services remains unclear. Given that the cyber attacks preceded and accompanied conventional military attacks, there appears to be a link to the Russian government. A March 2009 report by Greylogic "concluded Russia's Foreign Military Intelligence agency (the GRU) and Federal Security Service (the FSB), rather than patriotic hackers, were likely to have played a key role in coordinating and organizing the attacks." They add, "The available evidence supports a strong likelihood of GRU/FSB planning and direction at a high level while relying on Nashi intermediaries and the phenomenon of crowd-sourcing to obfuscate their involvement and implement their strategy."[15]

United States

In a 2010 essay for *Foreign Affairs*, Lynn revealed that

> in 2008, the US Department of Defense suffered a significant compromise of its classified military computer networks. It began when an infected flash drive was inserted into a US military laptop at a base in the Middle East. The flash drive's malicious computer code, placed there by a foreign intelligence agency, uploaded itself onto a network run by the US Central Command. That code spread undetected on both classified and unclassified systems, establishing what amounted to a digital beachhead, from which data could be transferred to servers under foreign control.[16]

The upshot is that "adversaries have acquired thousands of files from US networks and from the networks of US allies and industry partners, including weapons blueprints, operational plans, and surveillance data."[17]

Lynn classified this attack as "the most significant breach of US military computers ever" and stated that it "served as an important wake-up call."[18] He acknowledged that "to that point, we did not think our classified networks could be penetrated."[19] The result of this new awareness was Operation Buckshot Yankee, a fourteen-month program that rid US systems of the agent.btz worm and "helped lead to a major reorganization of the armed forces' information defenses, including the creation of the military's new Cyber Command."[20]

United Kingdom

In a speech at the 2011 Munich Security Conference, British foreign secretary William Hague revealed that a series of cyber attacks on his country took place the previous year. He noted that "in late December a spoofed email purporting to be from the White House was sent to a large number of international recipients who were directed to click on a link that then downloaded a variant of ZEUS. The UK Government was targeted in this attack and a large number of emails bypassed some of our filters."[21]

Additionally, sometime in 2010 "the national security interests of the UK were targeted in a deliberate attack on our defense industry. A malicious file posing as a report on a nuclear Trident missile was sent to a defense contractor by someone masquerading as an employee of another defense contractor. Good protective security meant that the email was detected and blocked, but its purpose was undoubtedly to steal information relating to our most sensitive defense projects."[22]

Finally, in February 2011, "three of my staff were sent an email, apparently from a British colleague outside the FCO, working on their region. The email claimed to be about a forthcoming visit to the region and looked quite innocent. In fact it was from a hostile state intelligence agency and contained computer code embedded in the attached document that would have attacked their machine. Luckily, our systems identified it and stopped it from ever reaching my staff."[23] Still, the prevalence and sophistication of these attacks are a principal reason why cybersecurity and cybercrime were listed as two of the top five priorities in the UK's National Security Strategy.[24]

Given the interconnectivity of the Internet, Hague argued that more comprehensive international collaboration is vital, noting that, while "cyber security is on the agendas of some 30 multilateral organizations, from the UN to the OSCE and the G8," the problem is that "much of this debate is fragmented and lacks focus." He continued, "We believe there is a need for a more comprehensive, structured dialogue to begin to build consensus among like-minded countries and to lay the basis for agreement on a set of standards on how countries should act in cyberspace."[25]

US–European Attitudinal Differences

Readers will have already discerned a pattern: The United States and the United Kingdom take cyber security very seriously and view it primarily through the lens of national security. The EU and most Western European members of NATO see it primarily as a national infrastructure problem. In the run-up to the November 2010 Lisbon NATO Summit, Pentagon officials were pressing very firmly to incorporate a concept of "active cyber defense" into the revised NATO Strategic Concept. Lynn argued that "the Cold War concepts of shared warning apply in the 21st century to cyber security. Just as our air defenses, our missile defenses have been linked so too do our cyber defenses need to be linked as well." But this notion was firmly rejected by the Europeans, with the French particularly adamant.[26]

USCYBERCOM

A July 2010 *Economist* story proclaimed: "After land, sea, air and space, warfare has entered the fifth domain: cyberspace."[27] It noted that President Obama had declared the digital infrastructure a "strategic national asset" and had appointed Howard Schmidt, the former head of security at Microsoft, as the first cybersecurity tsar. Peter Coates notes that the air force had actually anticipated this move in December 2005, declaring cyber a fifth domain when it changed its mission statement to "To fly and fight in air, space, and cyberspace." In November of the following year, it redesignated the 8th Air Force to become Air Force Cyberspace Command.[28]

In May 2010 the Defense Department launched a new subunified command, United States Cyber Command, with Gen. Keith Alexander dual-hatted as its chief while continuing on as director of the National Security Agency. CYBERCOM is charged with the responsibility to "direct the operations and defense of specified Department of Defense information networks and prepare to, and when directed, conduct full spectrum military cyberspace operations in order to enable actions in all domains, ensure US/Allied freedom of action in cyberspace and deny the same to our adversaries."[29]

As the scale of cyberwarfare's threat to US national security and the US economy has come into view, the Pentagon has built layered and robust defenses around military networks and inaugurated the new US Cyber Command to integrate cyber-defense operations across the military. The Pentagon is now working with the Department of Homeland Security to protect government networks and critical infrastructure and with the United States' closest allies to expand these defenses internationally. An enormous amount of foundational work remains, but the US government has begun putting in place various initiatives to defend the United States in the digital age.[30] Even with stepped-up vigilance and resources, Lynn admits, "adversaries have acquired thousands of files from US networks and from the networks of US allies and industry partners, including weapons blueprints, operational plans, and surveillance data."[31]

The cyber policy of the United States is rapidly evolving, with major developments under way as this book was going to press. The White House issued a new *International Strategy for Cyberspace* in May 2011. While not by any means moving away from a defense-oriented posture—indeed, it generated breathless commentary by declaring the right to meet cyber attacks with a kinetic response—it sought to bring commercial, individual, diplomatic, and other interests into the equation. This was followed by a new Department of Defense cyber strategy in July 2011, which built on Lynn's *Foreign Affairs* essay.

European Network and Information Security Agency (ENISA)

While CYBERCOM is the most powerful and well-funded US cyber agency, the lead EU cyber agency is ENISA, the European Network and Information Security Agency. Whereas CYBERCOM is run by a general with an intelligence background, ENISA is run by a physics professor with long experience in the IT sector, including the "energy industry, insurance company engineering, aviation, defense, and space industry."[32] The agency's mission is to "develop a culture of Network and Information Security for the benefit of citizens, consumers, business and public sector organizations in the European Union."[33]

In December 2010 ENISA released a report identifying what it sees as the top security risks and opportunities of smartphone use and gives security advice for businesses, consumers and governments. The agency considers spyware, poor data cleansing when recycling phones, accidental data leakage, and unauthorized premium-rate phone calls and SMSs as the top risks.[34] New regulations are proposed that would see the perpetrators of cyber attacks and the producers of related and malicious software prosecuted, and criminal sanctions increased to a maximum two-year sentence. European countries would also be obliged to respond quickly to requests for help when cyber attacks are perpetrated, and new pan-European criminal offences will be created for the "illegal interception of information systems." Home affairs Commissioner Cecilia Malmström added that criminalizing the creation and selling of malicious software and improving European police cooperation would help Europe "step up our efforts against cybercrime."

ENISA's new mandate will let the agency organize pan-European cybersecurity exercises, public–private network resilience partnerships, and risk assessment and awareness campaigns. ENISA's funding will also be boosted, and its management board will get a "stronger supervisory role." ENISA's mandate is also to be extended by five years to 2017. The new directive will also supersede a 2005 council framework decision on cybercrime because that previous regulation did not focus sufficiently on evolving threats—in particular, large-scale simultaneous attacks against information systems, such as Stuxnet, and the increasing criminal use of botnets. Stuxnet was recently used to attack Iran's nuclear power infrastructure, and a single botnet, Rustock, is estimated to be responsible for two-fifths of the world's spam.[35]

Additionally, EU states are constrained by Directive 95/46/EC, better known as the Data Protection Directive, which provides enormous protection for "any information relating to an identified or identifiable natural person." Compare this to the USA Patriot Act, which gives enormous leeway to US law enforcement and intelligence agencies to access electronic data held by US companies in order to investigate and deter terrorist activities. In June 2011 Gordon Frazer, managing director of Microsoft UK, set off a firestorm when he declared that European customer data stored on cloud computing services by companies with a US presence cannot be guaranteed the protections afforded under the Data Protection Directive, setting off a demand from some EU lawmakers to resolve this issue.[36]

Germany

In late February 2011 Germany's outgoing minister of the interior, Thomas de Maizière, unveiled the country's Nationale Cyber-Sicherheitsstrategie (National Cyber Security Strategy).[37] To American eyes, the fact that it was the interior ministry, not the defense ministry, issuing the strategy is striking. It was no accident: this is by no means a defense document.

The document's introduction notes that "in Germany all players of social and economic life use the possibilities provided by cyberspace. As part of an increasingly interconnected world, the state, critical infrastructures, businesses and citizens in Germany depend on the reliable functioning of information and communication technology and the Internet." Among the threats listed: "Malfunctioning IT products and components, the break-down of information infrastructures or serious cyber attacks may have a considerable negative impact on the performance of technology, businesses and the administration and hence on Germany's social lifelines." Contrast this with Lynn's analogy of biplanes over France, and his pondering "at what threshold do you consider something an attack?"

German security scholar Thomas Rid laments that the strategy is "coming a bit late" and that Germany's thinking lags that of the United States and the United Kingdom. Beyond that, he notes that the two agencies created to manage cyber issues are woefully understaffed and tasked with myriad responsibilities related tangentially at best to cyber security. And, according to a cyber "kodex" established in the new strategy, "German interests in data security . . . would be pursued in international organizations such as the UN, the OSCE, the European Council, the OECD, and NATO—in that order."[38]

United Kingdom as Outlier

As is frequently the case on matters of international security, the United Kingdom is much more in line with its American cousin than its neighbors on the Continent. In an October 12, 2010, speech at London's International Institute for Strategic Studies, Iain Lobban, director of GCHQ (the UK's National Security Agency analogue, responsible for signals intelligence) noted that his country combines the intelligence and information assurance missions in a single agency, an arrangement "shared by only a few other countries, most notably the US. It gives us a richer view of vulnerabilities and threats than those who consider them purely from the point of view of defense."[39]

He confessed to constant barrages of spam, worms, "theft of intellectual property on a massive scale, some of it not just sensitive to the commercial enterprises in question but of national security concern too," and all manner of other attacks that have caused "significant disruption to Government systems." Consequently, his government was looking to significantly increase its investment in the cyber realm even at a time when the global recession was forcing significant austerity in other departments, including in more traditional military assets.[40]

Thomas Rid notes the sheer breadth of Lobban's focus: "*Cyber* encompasses, for instance, more and more online government services (read: steadily increasing vulnerability); critical national infrastructure, publicly or privately run; online crime in all its facets; espionage (both industrial and governmental), and such things as the "proper norms of behavior for responsible states."[41]

The implications are vast, as Lobban hints and Rid explicates: "partnerships of a new kind are needed to deal with cyber threats and risks. International partnerships, with like-minded countries that need to establish and maintain appropriate norms of behavior in crisis situations—and intersectoral partnerships, between government agencies and industry, especially the high-tech sector."[42]

In his Munich Security Conference speech, Hague noted that "we rely on computer networks for the water in our taps, the electricity in our kitchens, the 'sat navs' in our cars, the running of trains, the storing of our medical records, the availability of food in our supermarkets and the flow of money into high street cash machines." Further, "Many government services are now delivered via the internet, as is education in many classrooms. In the UK, 70 percent of younger internet users bank online and two thirds of all adults shop on the internet."[43]

Given the new awareness of vulnerabilities and the degree of dependence, then, the United Kingdom's new National Security Strategy "ranks cyber attack and cyber crime in our top five highest priority risks." This is not lip service. At the same time that the British military is suffering such severe cutbacks that the Royal Navy is reduced to sharing a single aircraft carrier with France, the current budget "provided £650 million of new funding for a national cyber-security program, which will improve our capabilities in cyber-space and pull together government efforts." As part of that effort, Hague said, "We have established a new Ministerial Group on cyber security which I chair. And we have boosted the UK's cyber capabilities with the establishment of a new Defense Cyber Operations Group, incorporating cyber security into the mainstream of our defense planning and operation."[44]

NATO Responses

After months of study and debate the 2010 NATO Summit in Lisbon issued a new strategic concept on November 19, 2010. In it, cyber issues were officially recognized for the first time as a core alliance mission. Recognizing that "cyber attacks are becoming more frequent, more organized and more costly in the damage that they inflict," NATO pledged to "develop further our ability to prevent, detect, defend against and recover from cyber-attacks, including by using the NATO planning process to enhance and coordinate national cyber-defense capabilities, bringing all NATO bodies under centralized cyber protection, and better integrating NATO cyber awareness, warning and response with member nations."[45]

This was followed in June 2011 by a revised NATO policy on cyber defense and a parallel cyber defense action plan. Combined, they "offer a coordinated approach to cyber defense across the Alliance with a focus on preventing cyber threats and building resilience." Additionally, "all NATO structures will be brought under centralized protection."[46]

What practical actions will flow from these policy statements remains unclear, especially in an era of radically declining budgets. But they give an overview of what it terms "NATO's principle cyber defense activities."[47]

Coordinating and Advising on Cyber Defense

The cyber-defense policy is implemented by NATO's political, military, and technical authorities, as well as by individual allies. A main aspect of the policy was the establishment of a NATO Cyber Defence Management Authority (CDMA) with the sole responsibility for coordinating cyber defense throughout the Alliance. The NATO CDMA is managed by the Cyber Defence Management Board, which comprises the leaders of the political, military, operational, and technical staffs in NATO with responsibilities for cyber defense. It constitutes the main consultation body for the North Atlantic Council on cyber defense. NATO CDMA is currently operating under the auspices of the Emerging Security Challenges Division (i.e., chairmanship and its Cyber Defence Coordination and Support Centre) in NATO headquarters and provides advice to member states on all main aspects of cyber defense.

Assisting Individual Allies

Prior to the cyber attacks on Estonia in 2007, NATO's cyber-defense efforts were primarily concentrated on protecting the communication systems owned and operated by the Alliance. As a result of the attacks, which were directed against public services and carried out throughout the Internet, NATO's focus has been broadened to the cybersecurity of individual allies. This implies that NATO has developed mechanisms for assisting those allies who seek NATO support for the protection of their communication systems, including through the dispatch of Rapid Reinforcement Teams. However, the allies themselves continue to bear the main responsibility for the safety and security of their communication systems.

Research and Training

The Cooperative Cyber Defence Centre of Excellence in Tallinn, which was accredited as a NATO center of excellence in 2008, conducts research and training on cyber warfare and includes a staff of thirty, including specialists from the sponsoring countries (Estonia, Germany, Italy, Latvia, Lithuania, Slovakia, and Spain). Three additional allies, Hungary, Turkey, and the United States, are in the process of joining the Centre.

Cooperating with Partners

NATO is developing practical cooperation on cyber defense in accordance with the Council Guidelines for Cooperation on Cyber Defence with Partners and International Organisations (approved in August 2008), and the Framework for Cooperation on Cyber Defence between NATO and Partner countries (approved in April 2009). In line with existing policy, NATO is prepared, without reducing its ability to defend itself, to extend to partner countries and international organizations its experience and, potentially, its capabilities to defend against cyber attacks. However, cooperation on cyber defense should be a two-way street: NATO should also profit from consultations and exchanges with other actors and should be able to receive assistance in case of need. By making use of existing cooperation and partnership tools, NATO may tailor cooperation to the needs and interests of individual partners or international organizations, and may match it with available resources.

Conclusion

It will likely be years before the practical issues of implementation are sorted out through the NATO bureaucracy. Again, the United States and the United Kingdom are the most aggressive members pushing for the issue to be dealt with through military channels in NATO. Most of the others see little for the alliance to do here, seeing it predominately as a civil matter. One mechanism through which NATO has been exploring the issue is through the Cooperative Cyber Defence Centre of Excellence in Tallinn, Estonia. It was established in May 2008 in the wake of the cyber attacks on Estonia, discussed earlier in the chapter.

Ilmar Tamm, the center's director, explains that "our main goal here is to conduct post-incident analysis and research trying to identify what was the root cause, what was the potential motivation and what could be the potential threats and trends for the future." He notes, however, that "the center is not an operational center. So we are not here 24 hours a day seven days a week monitoring the networks and doing network defense as such." Therefore, "incident handling and such type of operations are still carried out by national institutions, by certain NATO institutions if NATO networks are involved and of course the private sector is doing their own work on their networks."[48]

It is notable, too, that the center's team does not include representatives from NATO's three most powerful members—the United States, United Kingdom, or France—but currently includes Estonia, Latvia, Lithuania, Germany, Hungary, Italy, the Slovak Republic, and Spain as sponsoring nations.[49] As of March 2011, active efforts were under way to resolve this issue. Lynn was routinely meeting with key European leaders, including NATO Secretary General Anders Fogh Rasmussen, to discuss "ways to strengthen cybersecurity and to follow through on the Lisbon Summit declaration to develop and implement a NATO cyber policy and implementation plan with real capabilities." The goal was clear: "bringing these nations together under this NATO common vision and having them leverage each others' expertise and experiences and drawing a common vision based on the threat to better secure NATO's networks."[50]

At the same time, US officials are clearly frustrated with the slow pace of movement on the issue. "I think the discussion for NATO at this point, the threshold step is we need to be able to protect our own military networks, and frankly we're not there yet," Lynn told journalists after meetings with European Union and NATO officials as well as the private sector.[51] Thomas Rid offers a pessimistic role for the prospects of that changing any time soon: "Don't bet on NATO." He argues that "some in the Alliance seem to see cyberspace as a life-saving opportunity. Anders Fogh Rasmussen, the Alliance's secretary general, reportedly pushes the envelope on cyber-defense within the Atlantic Alliance." But Rid contends that competition, secrecy, budget constraints, and other factors will keep it from congealing.[52]

Predicting the future is beyond the scope of this chapter and beyond my ability. But, if there is to be meaningful transatlantic cooperation on cyber—and there simply must be—NATO is the only game in town. Not only has it been the premier transatlantic institution of the postwar period but it is the only venue where the United States and United Kingdom, who will dominate the issue through sheer commitment to it and who see it through a military lens, can readily achieve wider consensus.

Notes

1. Franklin D. Kramer, "Cyber Conflict: Challenging the Future," speech at Black Hat Federal Briefings, January 18, 2011, http://acus.org/news/franklin-kramer-us-should-aim-cyber-resilience.

2. Quoted in Anna Multrine, "Pentagon: The Global Cyberwar Is Just Beginning," *Christian Science Monitor*, October 5, 2010, www.csmonitor.com/USA/Military/2010/1005/Pentagon-The-global-cyberwar-is-just-beginning.

3. Kramer, "Cyber Conflict."

4. Quoted in Multrine, "Pentagon."

5. Ibid.

6. Ibid.

7. Ian Traynor, "Russia Accused of Unleashing Cyberwar to Disable Estonia," *Guardian*, May 17, 2007, www.guardian.co.uk/world/2007/may/17/topstories3.russia.

8. "War in the Fifth Domain," *Economist*, July 1, 2010, www.economist.com/node/16478792.

9. Andy Valvur, "Estonian NATO Cyber Center Keeps an Eye on the Internet," *Deutsche Welle*, July 7, 2009, www.dw-world.de/dw/article/0,,4462466,00.html.

10. Quoted in "Attack on Estonia Puts Cyber Security on EU Agenda," *Reuters*, June 30, 2007, www.reuters.com/article/2007/06/30/us-eu-digital-idUSL3044463420070630.

11. "Bucharest Summit Declaration," April 3, 2008, *NATO*, www.nato.int/cps/en/natolive/official_texts_8443.htm; and "Lisbon Summit Declaration," November 20, 2010, *NATO*, www.nato.int/cps/en/natolive/official_texts_68828.htm.

12. John Markoff, "Before the Gunfire, Cyberattacks," *New York Times*, August 12, 2008, www.nytimes.com/2008/08/13/technology/13cyber.html?_r=1.

13. Dancho Danchev, "Coordinated Russia vs Georgia Cyber Attack in Progress," *ZDNet*, August 11, 2008, www.zdnet.com/blog/security/coordinated-russia-vs-georgia-cyber-attack-in-progress/1670.

14. Travis Wentworth, "You've Got Malice: Russian Nationalists Wages Cyber War against Georgia. Fighting Back Is Virtually Impossible," *Newsweek*, August 23, 2008, www.thedailybeast.com/newsweek/2008/08/22/you-ve-got-malice.html.

15. John Leyden, "Russian Spy Agencies Linked to Georgian Cyber-Attacks," *Register*, March 23, 2009, www.theregister.co.uk/2009/03/23/georgia_russia_cyberwar_analysis/.

16. William J. Lynn III, "Defending a New Domain: The Pentagon's Cyberstrategy," *Foreign Affairs*, September/October 2010.

17. Ibid.

18. Ibid.

19. Quoted in Multrine, "Pentagon."

20. Noah Shachtman, "Insiders Doubt 2008 Pentagon Hack Was Foreign Spy Attack," *Wired*'s *Danger Room*, August 25, 2010, www.wired.com/dangerroom/2010/08/insiders-doubt-2008-pentagon-hack-was-foreign-spy-attack/.

21. William Hague, "Security and Freedom in the Cyber Age: Seeking the Rules of the Road," Munich Security Conference speech, February 4, 2011, www.fco.gov.uk/en/news/latest-news/?view=Speech&id=545383882.

22. Ibid.

23. Ibid.

24. Nick Heath, "Hague Details Cyber Attacks on Whitehall," *Silicon.com*, February 7, 2011, www.silicon.com/technology/security/2011/02/04/hague-details-cyber-attacks-on-whitehall-39746929/.

25. Hague, "Security and Freedom in the Cyber Age."

26. Valentina Pop, "US Call for NATO Cyber-Strike Capacity Causes Division," *EUObserver* .com, http://euobserver.com/9/30962.

27. "Cyberwar: War in the Fifth Domain: Are the Mouse and Keyboard the New Weapons of Conflict?" July 1, 2010, www.economist.com/node/16478792.

28. Peter Coates, "The Fifth Battle Domain: Cyberspace" *News Weekly*, July 21, 2007, www .newsweekly.com.au/articles/2007jul21_cover.html.

29. US Department of Defence, "US Cyber Command Fact Sheet," May 25, 2010, www.de fense.gov/home/features/2010/0410_cybersec/docs/CYberFactSheet%20UPDATED%20replaces %20May%2021%20Fact%20Sheet.pdf

30. Lynn, "Defending a New Domain."

31. Ibid.

32. "New Executive Director at ENISA: Helmbrecht at the Helm," *ENISA*, www.enisa.euro pa.eu/media/press-releases/new-executive-director-at-eu-2018cyber-security2019-agency-enisa-helmbrecht-at-the-helm.

33. "About ENISA," *ENISA*, www.enisa.europa.eu/about-enisa.

34. "Europe's Cyber Security Agency Issues Report on Smartphone Risks and Opportuni-ties," *Security Week*, December 10, 2010, www.securityweek.com/europes-cyber-security-agency-issues-report-smartphone-risks-opportunities.

35. David Meyer, "Europe to Get Stronger Cybersecurity Laws," *ZDNet*, September 30, 2010, www.zdnet.co.uk/news/security-threats/2010/09/30/europe-to-get-stronger-cybersecurity-laws-40090356/.

36. Zack Whittaker, "Microsoft Admits Patriot Act Can Access EU-based Cloud Data," *ZDNet*, June 28, 2011, www.zdnet.com/blog/igeneration/microsoft-admits-patriot-act-can-access-eu-based-cloud-data/11225; and Jennifer Baker, "EU Upset by Microsoft Warning about US Access to EU Cloud," *IT World*, www.itworld.com/government/179977/eu-upset-microsoft-warning-about-us-access-eu-cloud?page=0,1.

37. "Cyber Security Strategy for Germany" (English translation), *Bundesministerium des Innern*, March 14, 2011, www.bmi.bund.de/SharedDocs/Downloads/DE/Themen/OED_Verwal tung/Informationsgesellschaft/cyber_eng.pdf.

38. Thomas Rid, "Germany's Cyber Security Strategy," *Kings of War*, March 8, 2011, http:// kingsofwar.org.uk/2011/03/germanys-cyber-security-strategy.

39. "Director GCHQ, Iain Lobban, Makes Cyber Speech at the IISS," GCHQ press release, October 12, 2010, www.gchq.gov.uk/Press/Pages/IISS-CyberSpeech.aspx.

40. Ibid.

41. Thomas Rid, "Cyber, Not Cypher," *Kings of War*, October 17, 2010, http://kingsofwar.org .uk/2010/10/cyber-not-cypher/.

42. Ibid.

43. Hague, "Security and Freedom in the Cyber Age."

44. Ibid.

45. "Active Engagement, Modern Defence," *NATO*, November 19, 2010, www.nato.int/cps/ en/natolive/official_texts_68580.htm.

46. "NATO Defence Ministers Adopt New Cyber Defense Policy," *NATO*, June 8, 2011, at www.nato.int/cps/en/natolive/news_75195.htm.

47. "Defending against Cyber Attacks," *NATO*, www.nato.int/cps/en/natolive/topics_ 49193.htm.

48. "Estonian NATO Cyber Center Keeps and Eye on the Internet," *Deutsche Welle*, July 7, 2009, www.dw-world.de/dw/article/0,,4462466,00.html.

49. "Cyber Defense," *NATO Cooperative Cyber Defence Centre of Excellence*, www.ccdcoe.org/ 2.html.

50. Jim Garamone, "Lynn Arrives in Brussels for Cybersecurity Talks," *Armed Forces Press Service*, www.defense.gov/news/newsarticle.aspx?id = 62541.

51. "NATO Networks Vulnerable to Cyber Threat," AFP, January 25, 2011, www.google .com/hostednews/afp/article/ALeqM5hPI87Zn7uY0TyKhDpX8n6-fzSvGA?docId = CNG.148a6c 382024ebbebe64021de441dac9.991.

52. Rid, "Cyber, Not Cypher."

CHAPTER 11

The Bear Goes Digital

Russia and Its Cyber Capabilities

Nikolas K. Gvosdev

IN SPITE OF ITS SOVIET PAST, contemporary Russia does not have the reputation of being in the vanguard of the most technologically advanced countries in the world. In 2009 President Dmitry Medvedev lamented the fact that Russia was "significantly behind other countries in developing advanced technologies, particularly in the field of supercomputers."[1] In the area of cyberwarfare, however, Russia is proving to be a trailblazer. Russian "hacktivists" convincingly demonstrated their skill in attacking and disabling the computer and communications infrastructure of Estonia in 2007 in a series of incidents that have been described as the world's first cyberwar.[2] The cyber attacks directed against Georgia in 2008 were more significant because this time they took place in apparent coordination with an ongoing conventional military operation.[3] Western military and governmental institutions report regular cyber probes emanating from Russian sources, with a particularly serious attack having occurred against the US Department of Defense in late 2008.[4]

The use of cyber attacks is indicative of a shift in the thinking and approach of the Kremlin national security establishment over the last three decades, from a Soviet-era reliance on overwhelming conventional military superiority as the prime factor for affecting the "balance of forces" on the world stage to a greater appreciation of the nonmilitary tools of national power—of achieving Russian aims "if not by tanks, then by banks."[5] In addition to a greater appreciation of how control of energy supplies as well as other economic and financial instruments can be wielded as tools of national power, there is a growing appreciation for what can be achieved in cyberspace—a theme sounded directly by Medvedev. Speaking to student cadets in September 2010 in Orenburg, the Russian president bluntly stated, "The computer today is now no less important of a weapon than an automatic weapon or a tank, but, to be serious, is actually much more important, because practically all government processes, including control over the Armed Forces, now occurs with the help of computers."[6]

Russia and the Digital Age

The popular perception of post-Soviet Russia as a digital and cyber backwater—despite an educational system known to produce large numbers of graduates well-versed in math and science—is a legacy of the Soviet system and its fear of the free flow of information. During the Soviet period, the government was very suspicious of technologies that might break down the carefully constructed compartmentalization of information that existed in the country. There was no room in the Soviet system for breakthroughs such as those that produced the personal computer and the Internet in the United States. Soviet scientific leaders acknowledged the importance of computing technologies in the modernization of the economy but warned that any large-scale introduction of computers needed to be very carefully managed and controlled.[7] Through to the very end of the USSR, the state continued to impose stringent controls on the dissemination of computers.[8] In 1985, at the start of perestroika, the USSR had a grand total of fifty thousand personal computers (in contrast to the thirty million in the United States). Even with General Secretary Mikhail Gorbachev's reforms, by the time the USSR collapsed, there were still only four hundred thousand personal computers in use.[9] The impact of these Soviet restrictions is still felt today; citing the situation in the aircraft industry, Medvedev complained, "Everything . . . is done on Whatman's drawing paper like in the 1920s and 30s using the old approaches. It's obvious that here only a digital approach can have a breakthrough effect, lead to dramatic improvements in quality, and reduce the cost of the product."[10]

Comparing the Internet usage of the United States and Russia demonstrates the persistence of this gap. The International Telecommunications Union data presents a stark contrast: while there are 75.9 Internet users for every 100 Americans, that number drops to 31.9 per 100 in the case of the Russian Federation.[11] However, this aggregate statistic masks some important trends. In some regions of Russia—beginning with the capital, Moscow—Internet usage parallels the trends observed in other parts of the developed world. In addition, if the penetration of the personal computing and Internet revolutions among lower-income and less-developed segments of Russia has lagged, there remains an active, vibrant digital community composed of younger Russians with higher levels of education and income.[12] There are very clear "islands" of high Internet usage—not only in places like Moscow and St. Petersburg but also in key regional economic, academic, and political centers, such as Novosibirsk and the oil- and gas-producing region of Khanty-Mansiysk.[13]

Moreover, while Russia may have been a late entrant to the cyber revolution, Russian society and the state are both attempting to rapidly close the gap. Under presidents Vladimir Putin and Dmitry Medvedev, the Russian government has been working to increase connectivity as well as the number of Russians with Internet access. By the start of 2012 the number of Russian Internet users had jumped to 55 percent of the population, and Internet usage was increasing among non-elite segments of the population.[14]

Yet, while the Internet links Russians to a larger, global "information superhighway," a striking feature of the "RUNET" (so-called because of the domain address ".ru" for Russian sites) is its distinctiveness—a largely self-contained world where "Russians tend to communicate with Russians in Russian about Russia-related topics. . . . The Russian blogosphere is, for the most part, an inwardly-focused social network."[15] A distinctive online Russian language—usually referred to as *olbanskii iazyk* or *iazyk padonkov*—has also emerged among habitual users of the Internet. Yelena Novosyolova notes that the digital subculture, particularly among Russian hackers, "has a language that is unique in terms of its remoteness from everyday Russian."[16]

The emergence of a distinctive Russian Internet vernacular is also a reminder of the extent to which Russia, although a latecomer to the digital age, is rapidly indigenizing these technologies and capabilities. Some 95 percent of all Internet pages in Russia are hosted on the ".ru" (or its Cyrillic-companion ".РФ" zones—and in recent years there has been an explosion of usage. One million domains were registered as of 2007, but this number was doubled as of March 2009. And while Russian users can access and use the services of any company, there is a clear trend for using homegrown providers: there is an overwhelming preference for using the Yandex search engine; the webmail provider Mail.ru; and Russian social networking and blogging sites such as *V kontakte* and *Odnoklassniki* rather than using local affiliates of the "Western" brand names like Google.[17] In turn, Russian-owned and -operated providers have pulled in users from across the entire Russosphere;[18] as of October 2010, Yandex and *V kontakte* are the twenty-fifth and thirty-seventh, respectively, most trafficked Internet sites in the world.[19] As Russia enters the digital age, Moscow cannot turn the clock back to avoid the challenges posed by working and operating in cyberspace—particularly as the Russian state itself rapidly incorporates digital technologies into its own operations.

Thinking about Cyberwar

Cyberwarfare is usually subsumed, in Russian thinking, under the broader designation of "information warfare" (*informatsionniya voyna* or *informatsionnoye protivoborstbo*). Theorists of the Russian General Staff define "information warfare" as the "disruption of the key enemy military, industrial and administrative facilities and systems, as well as bring information-psychological pressure to bear on the adversary's military-political leadership, troops and population, something to be achieved primarily through the use of state-of-the-art information technologies and assets."[20]

Traditional Soviet military doctrine recognized the importance of paralyzing and disabling an enemy's command-and-control systems and infrastructure, and of interfering with its ability to obtain and process information. But such efforts were usually understood to be supplemental to a larger, kinetic operation. Moreover, the emphasis was on destroying or sabotaging physical establishments (e.g., blowing up electrical power transmission lines rather than on using computer networks to deliver such blows.[21] In turn, Russian defense analysts now conclude that the Soviet failure to appreciate the threats and challenges posed by "information warfare" was a critical factor "to its defeat in the Cold War and dissolution."[22]

The breakup of the USSR also exposed Russia to a new set of cyber-based vulnerabilities. As Timothy L. Thomas noted, "The problem of computer viruses became particularly acute for Russian software security specialists when the USSR ceased to be one gigantic 'information space' and the republics broke away as independent entities. All weapons or command posts shared similar if not identical software programs. After the breakup, the possibility of a virus attacking all such systems increased."[23]

The Russian experience during the First Chechen War (1994–96)—particularly the use by the Chechens of computer and communications technologies to conduct military strikes and information operations—further alerted the Russian national security community to the dangers posed by these new technologies to the Russian Federation—as well as ways in which a weakened and diminished Russia might be able to use such tools itself. By the mid-1990s, officers attached to the Russian General Staff were focusing more attention on information warfare, with some noting: "The goal is for one side to gain and hold an information advantage over the other. This is achieved by exerting a specific information/psychological and information/technical influence on a nation's decisionmaking system, on the nation's populace and on its information resource structures, as well as by defeating the enemy's control system and his information resource structures with the help of additional means, such as nuclear assets, weapons and electronic assets."[24]

Some, like professor V. I. Tsymbal, were arguing about the "the possible catastrophic consequences of the use of strategic information warfare means by an enemy, whether on economic or state command and control systems, or on the combat potential of the armed forces," and were openly stating that in the event of such an attack on Russia, even the use of nuclear weapons might have to be considered.[25]

Gen. Viktor Samsonov, chief of the Russian General Staff, summarized the shift in thinking in a December 1996 address: "The high effectiveness of 'information warfare' systems in combination with highly accurate weapons and 'non-military means of influence' makes it possible to disorganize the system of state administration, hit strategically important installations and groupings of forces, and affect the mentality and moral spirit of the population. In other words, the effect of using these means is comparable with the damage resulting from the effect of weapons of mass destruction."[26]

And as another Russian officer writing on this subject in the 1990s noted, cyberwar was a way to pursue the Clausewitzian directive of "politics by other means" but without resorting to open (and potentially destructive) conflict. "There is no need to declare war against one's enemies and to actually unleash more or less large military operations using traditional means of armed struggle. This makes plans for 'hidden war' considerably more workable and erodes the boundaries of organized violence, which is becoming more acceptable."[27]

Many of these concerns about information warfare were incorporated into the Doctrine of the Information Security of the Russian Federation, issued during the first year of Vladimir Putin's presidency.[28] This document opened with recognition of "the growing role of the information sphere which represents a combination of information, the information infrastructure, the agents that gather, form, disseminate and use information as well as the system of regulating the social relations arising from this. . . . The national security of the Russian Federation depends to a substantial degree on ensuring information security, a dependence that will increase with technological progress."[29]

Section 2 of this doctrine specifically addressed cyber threats, among them

> the introduction in the hardware and software products of components performing functions not stipulated in the documentation covering these products; the development and dissemination of programs that disrupt the normal functioning of information and telecommunications systems, including the systems of information protection; the break-up, damage, radio-electronic suppression or destruction of the means and system of information processing and telecommunications; tampering with password and key systems protecting computerized systems of information processing and transmission; the compromising of keys and means of cryptographic protection of information . . .

and identified both state and nonstate actors as sources of these kinds of threats (Section 3). The fourth section set priorities for the Russian government, noting that "work to counteract these threats in an effective and comprehensive manner is not coordinated well enough and is poorly financed."

The information security doctrine was an explicit effort to define the Russian Internet as a national security concern and to raise awareness about cyberwarfare and cybersecurity issues. Many of the themes contained in the information security doctrine have now been incorporated into Russia's military doctrine as well. The latest iteration of that strategy, approved on February 5, 2010, sees the "intensification of the role of information warfare" as a major characteristic of contemporary conflict (12d) and calls for "the prior implementation of measures of information warfare in order to achieve political objectives without the utilization of military force" (13d). It further commits the Russian government to equip the military with "forces and resources for information warfare" (41c) and calls for further development of "information management systems" and their integration with command-and-control systems (41g).[30]

In practical terms, Aleksandr Krikunov and Alekandsr Korolev argue that this means:

> Information weapons comparable with the weapons of mass destruction (WMD) in terms of effects do not require specialized production facilities or complex infrastructure for their using. The means of software/hardware information warfare methods are computer viruses, logic bombs and instrument bugs, as well as special information and telecommunications

system penetration aids. These information warfare assets and methods combine a relatively low production cost and high wartime and peacetime effectiveness.

... The uniqueness of information weapons lies in the fact that any country, while developing its civil information infrastructure, creates a material basis for the military use of information technology against it. The higher scientific and technical potentials of the country, the more targets it offers, e.g., telecommunications, spacecraft, command, control, communications, computers and intelligence (C4I) systems, computerized power plant and oil and gas pipeline control systems, etc.[31]

Government statements are important for indicating the interest of the state, but what steps are being taken to translate theory into action?

The Kremlin's Cyber Initiatives

The 2000 Information Security Doctrine pointed to the "massive introduction of foreign information technologies in the activities of individuals, society and the state as well as wide-scale use of open information and telecommunications systems and the integration of the domestic information systems and international information systems" as the main drivers of the information warfare threat against the Russian Federation (section 4). Not surprisingly, therefore, gaining Russian control over the RUNET and other communications platforms has been a major priority of the Kremlin.

By the late 1990s the Russian Federal Security Service (Federal'naia Sluzhba Bezopasnosti, or FSB), required Russian Internet service providers (ISP) "to install hardware that allowed FSB to monitor Internet usage and e-mail messages of the provider's customers. ... Upon its introduction in 1999, SORM2[32] ... required all ISPs to route their incoming and outgoing data through FSB computers. Those providers who did not cooperate were forced out off line by FSB, which also at the time controlled the government's ISP licensing procedure."[33]

One of the first steps was to require foreign software, computer, and ISPs to share source codes and algorithms with the Russian government. Since 2002 Microsoft has been required, under an agreement reached with the state, to "allow state bodies to study the source code and develop cryptography for the Microsoft products through the Science-Technical Centre 'Atlas,' a government body controlled by the Ministry of Communications and Press. . . . . Employees of Atlas and the FSB will be able to share conclusions about Microsoft products."[34]

To ensure that the FSB can access all telecommunications and computer networks operating in Russia, amendments to the laws regulating these systems now require

that intercepted communications which have additional encryption be turned over in decoded form. This includes Research In Motion and all other foreign-owned companies who sell services in the RF through a Russian vendor, which, in RIM's case, is Mobile

TeleSystems. . . . It also requires remote access from a console installed in FSB headquarters which reports the names of the sender and receiver of the targeted phone call, e-mail, or SMS message, the message itself, and the geo-location of the sender as well as access to the customer database and billing records.[35]

Sergei Goncharov, who heads the "veterans' association" for former members of the elite anti-terrorist unit "Alfa," asserts that as a result of these capabilities, "The FSB and the MVD (Ministry of Internal Affairs) have special technical subunits that track all operationally important information on the Internet in an on-line mode. This is now one of the most effective ways to keep track of extremist groups." Russian Federation FSB official data states that ten terrorist acts were prevented in Russia in 2010; Goncharov says that "information regarding preparations for several of them were intercepted on the Net."[36]

While the FSB has the ability to monitor Russia's cyber environment—in theory—the sheer size of the data flow presents problems of its own. Therefore, a second prong of the Kremlin's strategy has been to cultivate and sponsor the individuals and companies that create and sustain Russia's digital environment. Today Kremlin-friendly business interests own the majority of Russia's popular social networking sites and websites, meaning that the RUNET is increasingly falling into "safe" hands, from the point of view of the government. Among the business leaders tapped for this strategy has been Alisher Usmanov, who owns a 50 percent stake in SUP, the Russian Internet firm that controls the country's most popular blogging platform, LiveJournal (having purchased it from the US company Six Apart), and who is the "angel" behind Digital Sky Technologies, which not only has the controlling interest in *V kontakte*, *Mail.ru*, and *Odnoklassniki* but is also acquiring stakes in Western Internet properties, among them Facebook. The state-controlled energy behemoth Gazprom, through its Gazprom-Media subsidiary, is also gobbling up Internet firms, as are other business figures who are part of the new political-economic elite of the country, including Mikhail Prokhorov and Vladimir Potanin.[37] This has raised the possibility that these companies would be prepared to "cede their business interests to government priorities" should the Russian government express concerns about possible threats to its position or stability emanating from the Russian Internet.[38] Synergies between the security services and the business sector in Russia also produce interlocking networks; for instance, the vice president for corporate security of a leading Russian mobile communications provider, Mobile TeleSystems, is Pavel D. Belik, a former FSB officer. In turn, the close ties between Russia's cyber entrepreneurs and the government have raised concerns among some Western analysts. Yuri Milner, the CEO of Digital Sky Technologies (who sits on the presidential commission tasked with overseeing Russia's economic modernization) has been asked to look at ways that "illegal content" could be purged from RUNET sites—a legitimate effort certainly to deal with copyright violations, but this has also raised concerns that these efforts might also be extended to cover other activities as well, such as opposition political views.[39] Others have raised concerns as to whether the acquisition of Western technology firms by Russian interests will facilitate technology transfers that may boost the cyber capabilities of the Russian state.[40]

Since the firms that deal with cyberspace in Russia—which hold a large portion of the "market share" of Russian users—are, for the most part, in hands friendly to the Kremlin, it means that these companies have been very useful as a training ground for Internet-savvy media managers that could then go and join the Kremlin's own projects. "However, direct state support to various online ventures is only the most visible layer of ways in which the Kremlin tries to manipulate cyberspace. In what could be a textbook example of classical economics, the Kremlin's most successful new media projects have so far been started and run by for-profit companies that had strong connections to the Kremlin. Those companies usually attract bright web developers, pay well, and actually adjust themselves to the needs of the market."[41]

And to the extent that the Russian government can encourage the continued "walling off" of Russian cyberspace, it may produce what some term a "cyber-ghetto"—the "isolation of the Russian segment of the Internet from the international Internet space," as Ilya Ponomarev, a member of the Duma's Committee on Information Technology and Communications, concluded.[42]

Cyber Mercenaries?

A final step taken by the Russian government has been to reach out to the sources of cyber threats—the hacker community—to enlist their services on behalf of the Russian state. The techniques pioneered by Russian hackers during the 1990s—first motivated by the "simple, anonymous thrill of exposing chinks in American software," then graduating upward to seeing cybercrime as a lucrative, profitable enterprise—can easily be adapted to meet the "aim of accessing or disabling the computers, Web sites and security systems of governments opposed to Russian interests."[43] Russian hackers, therefore, fit the bill for the right type of "information warfare" specialists because it is possible to disguise their activities "as banal computer hooliganism" rather than as a direct, state-sponsored attack.[44]

But Russia's hackers were not going to accept the role of automatons carrying out the directives of the state. They enjoy a certain degree of immunity, which is based on the lack of resources on the part of the government, particularly law enforcement, to severely crack down on their activities. As Alex Rodriguez notes: "The huge amount of money cyber-crime generates has created a vast underworld market that so far has proved to be virtually impregnable by Russian police. Viruses and other types of so-called 'malware' are bought and sold for as much as $15,000 . . . . Rogue Internet service providers charge cyber-criminals $1,000 a month for police-proof server access."[45] But what has appeared to happen is the evolution of a bargain that has been struck between the state and Russia's class of computer-savvy operators; one that no one openly admits to but for which there is compelling circumstantial evidence.

The first tenet is that Russia's hackers are to voluntarily refrain from targeting the state and its key interests. Western law enforcement agencies have often complained that, in dealing with their Russian counterparts, the "sense here [is] that

Russian hackers afflict the West far more than Russia, so why bother with them."[46] The infamous Russian Business Network facilitated cybercrime around the world by providing services for hire—at one point being held responsible for up to 70 percent of the world's "spam" cluttering e-mail inboxes around the globe[47]—yet an analysis of its activities concluded that "criminals using the Russian Business Network tend to target non-Russian companies and consumers rather than Russians."[48] In addition, some Western experts point to law enforcement actions taken against Russian hackers only after they targeted Russian institutions.[49]

In return, the Russian government seems to be prepared to turn a blind eye. Some of this is due to lack of resources and a perception that Russia faces far more serious security challenges than going after those who use computer networks to steal funds and create problems for Western institutions. But there has been no sustained campaign taken against cybercrime either. After all, as one analysis concluded, "cyber-criminals [need] time to work on their products without having to worry about getting their doors kicked down. But in Russia, that almost certainly needs some sort of political protection."[50] This may be changing, as indicated by police actions against the alleged Russian spam king, Igor Gusev, in the fall of 2010.[51]

Hackers who have been arrested because they went after Russian interests or because their crimes attracted too much attention to be safely ignored do not always need to fear imprisonment. Instead, there have been consistent reports that "the FSB even started offering jobs instead of sentences to hackers caught committing cybercrimes"[52]—a claim also made by former KGB Colonel Oleg Gordievsky.[53] Moreover, some of the cyber instruments developed by criminal groups have espionage applications; "software worms" used to steal funds can be adapted to steal secrets and information.[54]

The word is also out that the Russian security services can be an attractive patron to those with the skill-set needed to bolster Russia's own cyber defenses and to conduct cyber operations. Over the last ten years, there have been signs that there are "organized groups of hackers tied to the FSB."[55] In more recent years the Kremlin's open desire to beef up and expand the country's information operations capabilities has demonstrated to "other aspiring Internet technologists that they could be very well compensated—both financially and politically—for their service to the country."[56]

Of particular importance has been the role of the youth movement НаШИ (Nashi), an organization created in 2005—building on the previous pro-Putin group "Walking Together"—and set up to help forestall the emergence of youth movements that backed the so-called colored revolutions in other former Soviet states. Nashi, created by Vasily Yakemenko (who was later appointed to head the State Committee for Youth), strongly supports the current system of governance in Russia and takes a stridently nationalist-patriotic approach to viewing Russia's place in the world. Nashi has served as an intermediary between the state and the hacker community and has developed its own network of hacktivists to target those inside and outside of Russia that they view as opponents of the country's modernization and return to great power status.[57]

Nashi's ability to fuse youthful rebelliousness and Russian nationalism provides a basis for effective hacktivism that also has plausible deniability for the government. Evgeny Morozov's account as to how he too became a "digital soldier" in the Kremlin's "army of ones and zeroes" during the Georgia–Russia conflict in 2008—simply by following a few steps outlined on different blog sites in the RUNET—led him to the following conclusion:

> In less than an hour, I had become an Internet soldier. I didn't receive any calls from Kremlin operatives; nor did I have to buy a Web server or modify my computer in any significant way. If what I was doing was cyberwarfare, I have some concerns about the number of child soldiers who may just find it too fun and accessible to resist. My experiment also might shed some light on why the recent cyberwar has been so hard to pin down and why no group in particular has claimed responsibility. Paranoid that the Kremlin's hand is everywhere, we risk underestimating the great patriotic rage of many ordinary Russians, who, having been fed too much government propaganda in the last few days, are convinced that they need to crash Georgian Web sites. Many Russians undoubtedly went online to learn how to make mischief, as I did. Within an hour, they, too, could become cyberwarriors.[58]

While the Russian military and security services are setting up official cyber units, problems with making these capabilities "official" means that the Russian approach, at present, seems to focus on reaching out to "skilled hackers who have some type of handshake arrangement or some other compensation with the state entity but also at the same time create plausible deniability" for such operations, turning to "non-state actors to run their cyber campaigns."[59]

Significantly, despite extensive research (such as the work done by the Grey Goose project or the US Cyber Consequences Unit), there was no public "smoking gun" tying the Russian state to the cyber attacks that were launched against Estonia in 2007 and Georgia in 2008.[60] NATO's own report on the Estonia case could not conclusively demonstrate Russian government involvement and focused blame primarily on the state's unwillingness to prevent such attacks from happening.[61] Roland Heickerö's own extensive survey of the available information also came to the conclusion that there was "no conclusive evidence of Russian government involvement in either case."[62] This led him to observe that this could "set the standard for future cyber conflicts . . . for an actor to use nationalist hackers, thus gaining deniability together with the ability to enjoy the strategic benefits of their actions, but not sharing the risks. Moreover, the cyber weapon could be used in order to put psychological pressure on opponents to act in a favourable way."[63]

The Balance Sheet

Cyber probes launched against Western military and defense networks from Russia (as well as from other locations) are ongoing, leading NATO's secretary-general, Anders Fogh Rasmussen, to categorize cyber attacks as a "new form of permanent, low-level warfare."[64] Yet many of these attacks, while harassing and annoying, have not compromised security. Russian criminal groups continue their efforts to relieve international banks and corporations of their funds and to steal personal data in order to commit fraud, but cybercrime has become an acknowledged fact of life in the digital age. (The March 2011 theft of thousands of documents from the Pentagon, however, may be a worrying exception, if, as some analysts believe, Russian organized crime hackers backed by the intelligence services were responsible.[65])

There are no unified conclusions as to the long-lasting impact of the cyber attacks on Estonia and Georgia—which have been covered in great detail in a number of sources[66]—and smaller, less publicized incidents involving Ukraine, Lithuania, Poland, Kazakhstan, and Kyrgyzstan. Despite all of the hype about superweapons in cyberspace, the conclusion drawn from most experts is that we have witnessed "relatively unsophisticated types of attacks" that were nonetheless "carried out in a very sophisticated manner."[67] Yet in Estonia, one of the world's most networked countries, denial-of-service attacks did paralyze both governmental and commercial activities, leading to millions of euros in immediate losses, and some have estimated losses that resulted from the effective shutdown of the country's network at 750 million euros.[68] Estonia was able to bring its network back on line and to find more effective ways to block the attacks, which they then shared with Georgia in 2008.

The cyber attacks on Georgia took place as a conventional military operation was under way, and most experts conclude that the cyber campaign "reduced the ability of the Georgian government to counter" the Russian incursion, particularly by affecting the government's ability to communicate with its citizens. Some of the worrying features of this attack, however, included the fact that hackers had already "developed a detailed campaign plan" and appeared to be ready to go into action, indicating that their efforts "probably coordinated their operations with the Russian military even if no conclusive evidence exists of such collaboration."[69]

But unanswered questions remain. Was this campaign secretly authorized by the Russian state, or was it an effort on the part of cybercriminals "to advertise their contribution to the war to gain the gratitude (and ideally protection) of Russian government and military leaders"?[70] Did the disabling of key institutions—such as media and mass communications sites—using cyber attacks mean that the Russian military did not have to use conventional weapons to bring them off-line? And finally, could the cyber attackers have done more damage, beyond shutting services down? Were these attacks sophisticated enough to override safety controls at power plants or energy pipelines that could in turn have produced catastrophic accidents? Fears about possible cyber-caused sabotage, along with actual threats of damage posed by the conventional military campaign, did cause international oil companies to reroute energy shipments away from pipelines transiting Georgia[71]—but whether Russian hackers could have shut the line down by remote control is not entirely clear.

Russia's ability to wield the cyber weapon is also constrained by the fact that Russia itself remains vulnerable to cyber attack and disruption. There are no guarantees that the current modus vivendi will endure, that the nationalist hackers of today will not at some point turn against the Russian state itself, or that the current "bargain" might not be altered as rising prosperity in Russia makes Russian domestic targets much more inviting to cybercriminals. There are also risks with entrusting a nation's cyberwar capabilities to the hands of independent actors; while it produces plausible deniability for the government, it also increases the risk of matters getting out of control. Russia also cannot assume that it will be "left alone" by the rising numbers of skilled hackers in India or China. Finally, the Russian government does not have the financial resources to match the major investment being made by both the United States and China in cyber and information warfare capabilities.[72]

Not surprisingly, the Russian government has called for an international treaty to regulate cyberwarfare. Elements of the Russian proposal, unveiled in March 2009 by Vladislav P. Sherstyuk, the deputy secretary of the Security Council, would "ban a country from secretly embedding malicious codes or circuitry that could be later activated from afar in the event of war" and would prohibit "deception operations in cyberspace." Other facets include greater state-to-state regulation of the Internet. However, the United States has tended to oppose sweeping treaties, in part seeing such mechanisms as a way to strengthen the ability of undemocratic regimes to censor the Internet and block the free flow of information and instead favoring greater law-enforcement cooperation to crack down on cybercrime.[73]

Whether it would be possible to find workable treaty language and an effective enforcement mechanism remains to be seen. But in the meantime, a resurgent Russia has shown it can deploy an effective volunteer cyber army on its behalf. A former ultranationalist member of the Russian Duma, Nikolai Kuryanovich, summed it up as follows: "In the very near future many conflicts will not take place on the open field of battle, but rather in spaces on the Internet, fought with the aid of information soldiers, that is hackers. This means that a small force of hackers is stronger than the multi-thousand force of the current armed forces."[74] Russia's national security establishment, looking for more cost-effective ways to project power in the international arena, appears inclined to agree.

Notes

1. Deborah Gage, "Russia Lags in Supercomputers, Medvedev Warns," *Information Week*, July 30, 2009, www.informationweek.com/news/hardware/supercomputers/showArticle .jhtml?articleID=218900059.

2. See, for instance, Charles Cooper, "Coming Attractions for History's First Cyberwar," *CNET News*, July 15, 2007, http://news.cnet.com/Coming-attractions-for-historys-first-cyber war/2010-7349_3-6191184.html.

3. Richard Weitz, "Russia Refines Cyber Warfare Strategies," *World Politics Review*, August 25, 2009, www.worldpoliticsreview.com/articles/4218/global-insights-russia-refines-cyber-war fare-strategies.

4. Julian E. Barnes, "Pentagon Computer Networks Attacked," *Los Angeles Times*, November 28, 2008, http://articles.latimes.com/2008/nov/28/nation/na-cyberattack28.

5. Andrei P. Tsygankov, "If Not by Tanks, Then by Banks? The Role of Soft Power in Putin's Foreign Policy," *Europe-Asia Studies* 58, no. 7 (November 2006): 1079–99.

6. "Speech at opening of the first Presidential Cadet Academy," September 1, 2010, http://eng.kremlin.ru/transcripts/865.

7. A. Ershov, "EVM v Klasse," *Pravda*, February 6, 1985, 3.

8. Loren Graham, "Science and the Soviet Social Order," Working Paper no. 6, Program in Science, Technology and Society, Massachusetts Institute of Technology, 1990, 16.

9. Joseph S. Nye, "Gorbachev and the End of the Cold War." *New Straits Times*, April 5, 2006, http://belfercenter.ksg.harvard.edu/publication/1531/gorbachev_and_the_end_of_the_cold_war.html.

10. Dmitry Medvedev, "Opening Address at Security Council Meeting on Supercomputers," July 28, 2009, Kremlin website, http://archive.kremlin.ru/eng/speeches/2009/07/28/2014_type82913_220247.shtml.

11. World Bank data, http://data.worldbank.org/indicator/IT.NET.USER.P2.

12. "Number of Internet Users in Russia Increased by over 20% in 2009," *Interfax*, January 15, 2010, *School of Russian and Asian Studies* website, www.sras.org/russian_Internet_usage_increases.

13. "Razvitie Interneta v raznikh sub'yektakh Rossiiskoi Federatsii," Report issued by the Fond Obshchestvennoe Mnenie (Public Opinion Foundation), January 10, 2007, http://rumetrika.rambler.ru/review/0/3031?article=3031.

14. "Russian Opinion Poll Highlights Growing Popularity of Social Networking Sites," *Interfax*, February 13, 2012, www.cdi.org/russia/johnson/russia-social-networking-popularity-401.cfm.

15. Eugene Gorny, "Understanding the Real Impact of Russian Blogs," *Russian Analytical Digest*, 69, no. 9 (December 14, 2009), 8.

16. Yelena Novosyolova, "Children of Decadence," *Rossiiskaya Gazeta*, October 24, 2003, 6; an English version is available in *Current Digest of the Post-Soviet Press*, 42, no. 55 (November 19, 2003): 14, http://dlib.eastview.com/browse/doc/19933832.

17. "Russian Opinion Poll"; and "Russian Internet: 15 Years Online," *Russia Today*, April 15, 2009, http://rt.com/news/sci-tech/russian-internet-15-years-online.

18. The Russosphere refers to countries and regions where the Russian language is used and is the primary medium for communication and discourse. Beyond the Russian Federation, the Russosphere is said to encompass many of the former Soviet republics and large Russian-speaking communities in the diaspora, notably in Israel. For a discussion of the Russosphere, and of the broader question of "network commonwealths," see James C. Bennett's summary of a roundtable event, "The Uses of the Network Commonwealth," held at the *National Interest* magazine, Washington DC, April 29, 2004, http://explorersfoundation.org/archive/anglo sphere_tni-apr04.pdf.

19. Based on information as calculated by Alexa, a web information service (www.alexa.com), accessed on October 20, 2010.

20. Quoted in Roland Heickerö, *Emerging Cyber Threats and Russian Views on Information Warfare and Information Operations* (Stockholm: FOI, Swedish Defence Research Agency, 2010), 17.

21. Soviet diplomat Arkady N. Shevchenko, for instance, relates the discussion among KGB officers stationed in New York about ways to cripple US infrastructure, but they were focused

on the physical destruction of assets rather than using technological means of sabotaging these systems. See his *Breaking with Moscow* (New York: Random House, 1987), 408.

22. Aleksandr Krikunov and Aleksandr Korolev, "Features of Information Warfare of the Future," *Voennyii Diplomat* 1 (2009): 100. This debate has intensified with repeated claims made that the CIA allowed the Soviet Union to obtain software shot through with malicious code for its energy projects. This software "that was to run the pumps, turbines, and valves was programmed to go haywire, after a decent interval, to reset pump speeds and valve settings to produce pressures far beyond those acceptable to pipeline joints and welds." This corrupted software is said to be responsible for a major explosion in June 1982 that severely disrupted Soviet efforts to be able to sell natural gas to Western Europe, a key source of income. The claim was advanced by Thomas Reed, a former Reagan administration national security official; see Eric J. Byres, "Cyber Security and the Pipeline Control System," *Pipeline and Gas Journal* 236, no. 2 (February 2009), www.pipelineandgasjournal.com/cyber-security-and-the-pipeline-control-system. The Russian side denies this occurred and says that a small explosion that occurred on the line in 1982 was easily repaired. However, there are indications that feeding the Soviets "tainted software" was part of the CIA campaign to blunt Soviet economic measures.

23. Timothy L. Thomas, "Russian Views on Information Based Warfare," *Airpower Journal*, Special Issue (1996), www.airpower.au.af.mil/airchronicles/apj/apj96/spec96/thomas.html.

24. These two anonymous staff officers are quoted by Thomas, in ibid.

25. Tsymbal delivered this pronouncement in a famous paper ("Kontseptsiya 'informatsion-noi voiny" [Conceptions of Information Warfare]), delivered at the Russian Academy of Civil Service, Moscow, September 14, 1995.

26. Samsonov's speech, delivered December 23, 1996, is quoted in Heickerö, *Emerging Cyber Threats*, 16.

27. Sergei Modestov, "Na Nevudimom FrontyeAktivizatsiya Boyevykh Deystviy," *Delovoi Mir*, February 24, 1994, 7.

28. This document was issued on September 9, 2000. An English translation is found at www.medialaw.ru/e_pages/laws/project/d2–4.htm.

29. Ibid., I.1.

30. An English version of the doctrine can be read at the School of Russian and Asian Studies website, www.sras.org/military_doctrine_russian_federation_2010.

31. Krikunov and Korolev, "Features of Information Warfare," 95.

32. SORM is the Russian acronym for System for Operational-Investigative Activities.

33. Marcus Alexander, "The Internet in Putin's Russia: Reinventing a Technology of Author-itarianism," Paper presented at the Annual Conference of the Political Studies Association, University of Leicester (UK), April 15–17, 2003, 10, www.psa.ac.uk/journals/pdf/5/2003/Mar cus%20Alexander.pdf. Technically, the FSB requires a warrant prior to reading a person's e-mail or tracking their Internet usage.

34. Tom Espiner, "Microsoft Opens Source Code to Russian Secret Service," *ZDNet UK*, July 8, 2010, www.zdnet.co.uk/news/security/2010/07/08/microsoft-opens-source-code-to-russian-secret-service-40089481/.

35. Jeffrey Carr, "Russia's FSB Receives Decrypted BlackBerry Messages from Mobile Tele-Systems," *Forbes: The Firewall*, August 16, 2010, http://blogs.forbes.com/firewall/2010/08/16/russias-fsb-receives-decrypted-blackberry-messages-from-mobile-telesystems/.

36. Goncharov's comments appeared in the May 14, 2010, issue of *Trud*'; they were quoted in "FSB and MVD Are Aggressively Mining Runet with a Facebook Algorithm," *Greylogic*, June

2, 2010, http://greylogic.us/2010/06/02/fsb-and-mvd-are-aggressively-mining-runet-with-a-facebook-algorithm/.

37. See the Open Source Center's report, "Kremlin Allies' Expanding Control of Runet Provokes Only Limited Opposition," February 28, 2010, 1–2, www.fas.org/irp/dni/osc/run et.pdf.

38. Ibid, 1.

39. Carr, "Russia's FSB"; and Evgeny Morozov, "Does Silicon Valley's New Favorite Russian Moonlight as Kremlin's Censorship Czar?" *Net.Effect*, May 25, 2010, http://neteffect.foreignpolicy .com/posts/2010/05/25/does_silicon_valleys_new_favorite_russian_moonlight_as_kremlins_ censorship_czar. On the larger concerns about Russian owners of cyber services acting at the behest of the state, see Benjamin Bidder and Matthias Schepp, "Will Russia's Bloggers Survive Censorship Push?" *Der Spiegel*, September 1, 2010, www.spiegel.de/international/world/0,1518, 714848-2,00.html.

40. This is a definite concern raised by, among others, Jeffrey Carr, who sees the prospects for this occurring with many of the new Russian corporate acquisitions. Carr writes: "A Face-book algorithm has found its way onto the Russian Internet in the service of the Ministry of the Interior—compliments of Milner, Usmanov, et al. Not only does Russian Security Services have insider access to the world's largest social networks, it's turning a profit as well. Plausible deniability, self-funding intelligence operations, and technology transfer from foreign R&D labs characterize the three key strategies of what I've termed 'Ultra Low Intensity Asymmetric Warfare.'" Jeffrey Carr, "The War That We Don't Recognize Is the War We Lose," *The Firewall*, July 13, 2010, http://blogs.forbes.com/firewall/2010/07/13/the-war-that-we-dont-recognize-is-the-war-we-lose/.

41. Evgeny Morozov, "The Kremlin's Quest for Pravda 2.0," *Net.Effect*, May 9, 2009, http:// neteffect.foreignpolicy.com/posts/2009/05/09/kremlins_quest_for_pravda_20.

42. Quoted in Open Source Center, "Kremlin Allies' Expanding Control," 7.

43. Alex Rodriguez, "Russia's Hackers Pose Growing Global Threat," *Physorg.com*, December 30, 2008, www.physorg.com/news149839691.html.

44. Modestov, "Na Nevudimom FrontyeAktivizatsiya Boyevykh Deystviy," 7.

45. Rodriguez, "Russia's Hackers."

46. Clifford J. Levy, "What's Russian for 'Hacker?'" *New York Times*, October 20, 2007, at www.nytimes.com/2007/10/20/world/europe/20iht-21levy.7975205.html.

47. "The Evil (Cyber) Empire: Inside the World of Russian Hackers," *Newsweek*, December 30, 2009, www.newsweek.com/2009/12/29/the-evil-cyber-empire.html.

48. Brian Krebs, "Shadowy Russian Firm Seen as Conduit for Cybercrime," *Washington Post*, October 13, 2007, www.washingtonpost.com/wp-dyn/content/article/2007/10/12/AR2007 101202461.html?sid = ST2007101202661.

49. Kara Flook, "Russia and the Cyber Threat," *AEI Critical Threats*, May 13, 2009, www.criti calthreats.org/russia/russia-and-cyber-threat.

50. Peter Warren, "Hunt for Russia's Web Criminals," *Guardian*, November 15, 2007, www .guardian.co.uk/technology/2007/nov/15/news.crime.

51. Gusev's peddling of illegal medicines drew the interest of Russian authorities, especially after China also had begun to crack down on this trade, which may indicate that the Kremlin was responding to both negative international press about Gusev's practices but also com-plaints from a growing number of online Russian consumers. See Sayan Guha, "Russian Busi-nessman Charged with Trading Illegal Medicine Online," *BSR Russia*, November 9, 2010,

www.bsr-russia.com/en/healthcare-a-pharmaceuticals/item/1120-russian-businessman-charged-with-trading-illegal-medicine-online.html.

52. "Russian Internet politics," *BBC News*, March 5, 2001, http://news.bbc.co.uk/2/hi/europe/1198603.stm.

53. Brian Krebs, "Report: Russian Hacker Forums Fueled Georgia Cyber Attacks," *Washington Post*, October 16, 2008, http://voices.washingtonpost.com/securityfix/2008/10/report_russian_hacker_forums_f.html?nav = rss_blog6.

54. Gregory Feifer, "Russia's Silicon Valley Dreams May Threaten Cybersecurity," *Radio Free Europe/Radio Liberty*, November 14, 2010, www.rferl.org/content/Russias_Silicon_Valley_Dreams_May_Threaten_Cybersecurity/2219756.html.

55. John Varoli, "Hackers Gatecrashing Russia's Internet Party," *St. Petersburg Times*, October 6, 2000, www.sptimes.ru/index.php?action_id = 100&story_id = 12804.

56. Morozov, "Kremlin's Quest."

57. Carr, "War That We Don't Recognize." Konstantin Goloskokov, a Nashi activist and a Duma staff member working for Sergei Markov, has claimed that he and other friends in Nashi undertook actions like the denial-of-service attacks directed against Estonia in 2007, on their own initiative and without the sponsorship or direction of the Russian state. See "NATO Hacker Claims It Was a Protest," *PCMag.com*, March 13, 2009, www.pcmag.com/article2/0,2817,2343035,00.asp.

58. Evgeny Morozov, "An Army of Ones and Zeroes: How I Became a Soldier in the Georgia-Russia Cyberwar," *Slate*, August 14, 2008, www.slate.com/id/2197514/.

59. Cyberwar is recognized as one of the threats for which the official military must be prepared; see the comments of the first deputy chief of the General Staff, Lt. Gen. Aleksandr Burutin, in *Voennyi Parad*, 3 (May–June 2008), 14. How well the military is doing in this regard, however, is the subject of a more critical news report. See Dmitry Litovkin, "Order to Deploy Cell Phones," *Izvestiia*, January 12, 2010, 1, 4. See also Michael W. Cheek, "What Is Cyberwar Anyway? A Conversation with Jeff Carr, Author of Inside Cyber Warfare," *The New New Internet*, March 2, 2010, www.thenewnewInternet.com/2010/03/02/what-is-cyberwar-anyway-a-conversation-with-jeff-carr-author-of-inside-cyber-warfare/2/.

60. The US Cyber Consequences Unit report, spearheaded by John Bumgarner and Scott Borg, concludes that the "cyber attacks against Georgian targets were carried out by civilians with little or no direct involvement of the Russian government or military." "Overview by the US-CCU of the Cyber Campaign against Georgia in August of 2008," A US-CCU Special Report, August 2009, www.registan.net/wp-content/uploads/2009/08/US-CCU-Georgia-Cyber-Campaign-Overview.pdf, 2.

61. "Evil (Cyber) Empire."

62. Heickerö, *Emerging Cyber Threats*, 5.

63. Ibid, 47.

64. Siobhan Gorman and Stephen Fidler, "Cyber Attacks Test Pentagon, Allies and Foes," *Wall Street Journal*, September 25, 2010, http://online.wsj.com/article/SB10001424052748703793804575511961264943300.html.

65. Robert Windrem, "US Intelligence Agencies Getting Better at Classifying Cyber-Attacks," *MSNBC*, July 15, 2011, http://openchannel.msnbc.msn.com/_news/2011/07/15/7092451-us-intelligence-agencies-getting-better-at-classifying-cyber-attacks.

66. See Heickerö, *Emerging Cyber Threats*, 39–47.

67. "Overview by the US-CCU," 4.

68. Anna Dunin, "Intel Brief: Russia Online and on the Attack," *ISN*, October 28, 2009, www.isn.ethz.ch/isn/Current-Affairs/Security-Watch/Detail/?lng = en&id = 108943.

69. Weitz, "Russia Refines Cyber Warfare Strategies."

70. Ibid.

71. "Overview by the US-CCU," 7–8.

72. Heickerö, *Emerging Cyber Threats*, 50.

73. John Markoff and Andrew E. Kramer, "US and Russia Differ on a Treaty for Cyberspace," *New York Times*, June 27, 2009, www.nytimes.com/2009/06/28/world/28cyber.html?pagewanted =1&_r=1.

74. Quoted in Krebs, "Russian Hacker Forums."

CHAPTER 12

China in Cyberspace

Nigel Inkster

As with much else about China, the speed and intensity with which the country has developed Internet usage has taken the world by surprise. The Internet first came to China in 1994 in a project linking some three hundred physicists. By 1998, two years after Internet accessibility became available to the general population, China had just over two million users. By the end of 2010 this number had risen to 420 million, 346 million of whom had broadband connectivity.[1]

With such high Internet penetration, there are an estimated 50 million bloggers and an estimated 800 million microbloggers via cell phones, which have become a pervasive medium of communication. Between 1997 and 2009 the Chinese state spent RMB 4.3 trillion ($630 billion) on Internet infrastructure construction.[2] The rapid evolution of China's Internet culture makes any attempt to chronicle it vulnerable to equally rapid obsolescence. But underlying this evolution are some more persistent themes: the struggle by China's leadership to maintain control of information flows while trying to accommodate public pressure for greater transparency and accountability. Further, China has an uneasy relationship with the United States, which perceives Chinese behavior in the cyber domain as aggressive. US concern for China is matched by China's concern over perceived US efforts to maintain dominance in the cyber domain. Both perceptions constitute one of a number of issues that continue to dog this important relationship.

The Evolution of China's Internet

If China's leaders were nervous about the implications of unrestricted access to information for its population, this did not inhibit the Communist Party from enthusiastically promoting the Internet as an indispensible adjunct to achieving China's overriding strategic goal of economic modernization. There was from the outset an awareness of the risks of unfiltered access, but it is likely that ignorance among China's leadership of how the Internet operated led them to underestimate these risks. In the mid-1980s Jiang Zemin, then minister for the electronics industry—and one of the few members of the Chinese leadership who understood how modern computers worked—talked about the importance for China of developing modern IT capabilities on the basis that such capacities constituted "the strategic high ground in international competition. . . . The discrepancy between China's level and the world's advanced level is so great that we have to do our utmost to catch up."[3]

The benefits to China's modernization program of developing Internet connectivity have been considerable. The Internet shrank the enormous distances and geographic barriers that had proven such a challenge for China's development in the past. Internet connectivity proved particularly important in rural communities, enabling farmers to access up-to-date information about production techniques and market conditions, and promoting better standards of health care. Unsurprisingly, Internet access has been a major feature of China's education system. A recent study by the Chinese Academy of Social Sciences (CASS) revealed that 40 percent of middle schools, 70 percent of high schools, and 60 percent of vocational schools are now connected to the Internet.[4] A June 2010 white paper produced by China's State Council Information Office, the state entity primarily responsible for the Internet, made it clear that rapid nationwide expansion of the Internet and mobile telephone penetration is a strategic priority for China and critical for China's long-term global competitiveness.[5]

China's indigenous information and communication technology (ICT) industries have already established themselves as a major component of China's economic growth. Although accurate figures are hard to come by, it is estimated that China's overall ICT industry has grown at between two and three times the speed of China's overall gross domestic product, with the software industry alone accounting for RMB 584.2 billion—US$ 86 billion in 2008.[6] Lenovo has become the fourth-largest manufacturer of PCs on the planet.

The advent of IT and Internet connectivity has brought particular benefits to a country whose language up until that point had seemed like enough of a barrier to raise questions about whether a romanized written language should take the place of traditional Chinese characters. Before the era of PCs and laptops, Chinese documents could only be produced using typewriters that were effectively mini printing presses, requiring extensive specialist training. The advent of software programs that permit word processing and texting in Chinese characters has been little short of revolutionary and indeed arguably plays to the strengths of a language that is both much terser than most Indo-European languages, enabling more information to be conveyed in less space, and that can be read without needing to know how it is pronounced. The most successful Chinese word processing systems have in fact been developed by Western companies such as Microsoft; these systems require the user to be able to type in pinyin, the official standard form of romanization for Chinese characters, with the computer offering a menu of characters corresponding to the romanized text. Because Chinese is a language with many homophones, these menus can be long, although predictive software minimizes the time spent scrolling through lists of options. Type in the romanized word "shi" and Microsoft's word processing system offers a menu of 209 options. But type in "shiqing"—the Chinese for "matter, affair"—and the menu will offer 事情 as the most likely combination.

One factor influencing the way China's Internet developed is the fact that many Chinese, although familiar with pinyin, were not especially comfortable using it. Another is the fact that popularization of the Internet has been driven primarily by its role as a provider of entertainment, in particular online gaming, downloading of music and films, and social networking. Online gaming, an industry whose turnover in 2009 was estimated at RMB 25.8 billion (US$3.8 billion) has evolved to the point where in June 2009 the Chinese government was obliged to outlaw the use of virtual currency to purchase real-world goods in order to limit the impact on China's actual currency.[7] There have been cases of individuals who were prosecuted and imprisoned for perpetrating crimes such as extortion and robbery of virtual currency.[8] Even the People's Liberation Army (PLA) has had to bite the bullet to the point of permitting serving military to engage in online gaming, making a virtue of necessity by highlighting the contribution of such activity to the development of strategic thinking.

Internet Censorship

These two factors have substantially influenced the nature of most indigenous Chinese search engines whose portals consist of a huge amount of prepackaged information organized by different categories—news, business, real estate, entertainment—such that most users need use only mouse clicks to navigate their way around the sites rather than undertake free-text searches. To Western eyes, these portals appear very "busy" if not downright gaudy, and navigating around them is a relatively passive experience somewhat akin to supermarket shopping. From the perspective of the state, the way most Chinese Internet portals are arranged confers one significant benefit, namely, that it greatly facilitates the work of China's Internet censors whose activities have grown considerably in both scope and effectiveness from the days when then–US president Bill Clinton likened China's attempts at Internet censorship to "nailing Jell-O to the wall."[9] From the outset, the introduction of the Internet in China was subject to state control. The Ministry of Public Security was given an explicit responsibility for policing the Internet, and specific online offences were identified. These included defaming government agencies, engaging in "splittism," and betraying state secrets. The approach used by China's authorities has been a mixture of regulations, such as requiring all those opening an Internet account to register with the police (a requirement that had lapsed but is now about to be reintroduced); direct intervention, such as blocking access to websites including those of foreign news media; and an expectation of self-censorship. The latter included holding Internet service providers responsible for all content transmitted on their services, which subsequently translated into an obligation to take responsibility for removing content that violated state norms. The same obligation imposed on all those who operated Internet cafes—until recently, the primary point of Internet access for many Chinese—the responsibility for all activity taking place on their premises.

As with most aspects of Chinese legislation, the rules—often drafted in a vague, catch-all fashion—have been applied in an arbitrary and opaque manner, often observed in the breach until a particular episode leads to them being applied in a more systematic and draconian fashion. But, overall, it has been possible to observe a gradual but steady tightening of controls, combined with increasing technical and political sophistication on the part of China's Internet censors. The number of such censors is impossible to quantify because Internet censorship takes place at multiple levels. Much of the day-to-day activity is undertaken at a provincial and local level with the Ministry of Public Security—that is, the police—taking a frontline role. Technology has rendered this task much easier.

A *Financial Times* report cites a Beijing-based IT manager as saying that although police forces still undertake basic keyword searches, the police are increasingly taking delivery of modern data-mining technologies that enable one operative to undertake the work previously done by ten.[10] In late December 2010 Wang Chen, the head of the State Council Information Office and Deputy Head of the Communist Party's Propaganda Department, announced that within the past year, 350 million pieces of harmful information had been deleted from China's Internet and 60,000 pornographic websites shut down.[11] Pornography has often been cited as the justification for much of China's Internet-monitoring activity, but crackdowns on online pornography tend to be of relatively short duration. In practice, pornography—much of it indigenous—abounds on the Chinese Internet and is not hard to find. Indeed explicit advertisements offering remedies for various forms of sexual dysfunction—male enlargements are especially popular—are prominently displayed on the most innocuous websites.

A much greater preoccupation of China's censors has been dealing with the challenge posed by China's so-called Netizen community acting in its capacity as a de facto civil society of the kind not formally acknowledged or encouraged in the non-cyber domain. The Internet—increasingly in the form of microblogging and social networking sites—has been used extensively to publicize a range of grievances, typically involving high-handed behavior by corrupt and until recently unaccountable provincial officials. A case in point is that of Li Qifan, son of the deputy head of the Baoding Public Security Bureau, Li Gang. On October 16, 2010, Li Quifan, driving while drunk through the campus of Baoding University, struck two female students, killing one and seriously injuring the other. After initially failing to stop, he was eventually forced to a halt by students and university security guards; he allegedly called out, "Sue me if you dare; my father is Li Gang." The online furor, when it appeared that no action would be taken against the perpetrator, resulted in Li Quifan being arrested and his father, Li Gang, being compelled to appear on local TV bowing and tearfully asking for forgiveness—although ultimately the case with the families of the two students was settled out of court. "My father is Li Gang—woba shi Li Gang" has now entered the vernacular as a catch-phrase used ironically whenever someone seeks to evade responsibility for an action, however trivial, epitomizing popular resentment at the behavior of the so-called *guan er dai*—the spoilt, arrogant, and unaccountable offspring of China's officialdom.[12] A similar case the previous year involved a hotel employee in Hubei, Deng Yujiao, who stabbed to death a senior government official who she claimed had tried to rape her. Netizen pressure resulted in the original murder charge against Deng being replaced by one of intentional assault. Although found guilty, Deng was not sentenced on the grounds of diminished responsibility.[13]

Although primarily focused on domestic issues, China's Netizen community has shown itself to be equally vocal on the subject of foreign policy. This reflects the effect of the so-called Patriotic Education Programme designed in the 1990s to inculcate in young Chinese a sense of nationalism and historical grievance in order to draw attention away from the violent suppression of student demonstrators in Tiananmen Square on June 4, 1989. Episodes such as the 2001 collision between a US EP-3 surveillance aircraft and a People's Liberation Army Air Force fighter off the coast of Hainan; then–UN secretary-general Kofi Annan's March 2005 statement that Japan should be considered for a permanent UN Security Council seat; and protests in favor of the Free Tibet movement in the run-up to the 2008 Beijing Olympics all led to manifestations of online anger against those seen as having caused offense to China. This extended to efforts by patriotic hacker groups— so-called hacktivists—to deface websites of those seen as having offended China. Internet-based activism has projected itself on more than one occasion into the real world. During the anti-Japanese protests, there were numerous rallies and episodes of attacks on Japanese diplomatic premises. And 2008 saw a nationwide boycott of the Carrefour supermarket chain in protest at perceived French government support for the Dalai Lama.

The Chinese government has tried to walk a delicate path between deriving political benefit from such outbursts of patriotic fervor and ensuring that they did not spill over into uncontrolled expressions of grievance against the regime. In 2005 this balance came close to being lost when anti-Japanese protests turned into protests against the Chinese government's perceived weakness vis-à-vis Japan. Typical of the views being expressed at the time was a blog that read, "How can China stand firm when its state leaders are all impotent? If China gives approval this time, the state leaders have no right to sit in their current positions—let them go home and embrace their children."[14] The same is broadly true of their approach to expressions of discontent about the kind of domestic issues outlined earlier. Monitoring the blogosphere gives China's leaders a means of keeping a finger on the pulse of public opinion, a valuable capacity in a state whose central government takes it for granted that provincial and local officials will seek to keep the truth from them. Campaigns in the blogosphere against corrupt officials offer Beijing a useful way to enforce discipline in a government and party hierarchy plagued by corruption, and a way to gain a degree of credit when malefactors are brought to justice.

Indeed, it can be argued that the Chinese government has developed over time a sophisticated strategy for managing China's blogosphere is a way that gives the impression of both tolerating a degree of free speech and being responsive to the concerns of the citizenry while at the same time subtly directing the discourse in ways favorable to the government. In her testimony to the US–China Economic and Security Review Commission in 2010, Rebecca MacKinnon, then visiting fellow at Princeton University's Center for Information Technology Policy, characterized this behavior as "networked authoritarianism." Elaborating on this concept, she said:

> This new form of Internet-age authoritarianism embraces the reality that people cannot be prevented from accessing and creating a broad range of Internet content. Networked authoritarianism accepts a lot more give-and-take between government and citizens than a pre-Internet authoritarian regime. The regime uses the Internet not only to extend its control but also to enhance its legitimacy. While one party remains in control, a wide range of conversations about the country's problems rage on websites and social networking services. . . . As a result, people with Internet or mobile access have a much greater sense of freedom—and may even feel that they can influence government behavior—in ways that weren't possible under classic authoritarianism. It also makes people a lot less likely to join a protest movement calling for radical political change. Meanwhile, the government exercises targeted censorship, focusing on activities that pose the greatest threat to the regime's power. It also devotes considerable resources to seeding and manipulating the nation's online discourse about domestic and international events.[15]

In China, this manipulation is achieved through a combination of covert and overt techniques. The covert techniques, which have been refined over a longer period, involve planting people in the blogosphere who can take part in debates on hot issues and either seek to nudge discussion in ways favorable to the government or intervene more directly to challenge views that risk becoming overly heterodox. And once any given discussion is judged to have outlived its usefulness, it will be summarily shut down as happened with the Li Gang case cited earlier. The more overt route, and also the more recent, is epitomized by initiatives such as the inauguration, in 2010, of a new online bulletin board "Direct Line to Zhongnanhai—zhitong zhongnanhai" (a reference to the central Beijing compound occupied by China's top leadership) that supposedly enables citizens to connect directly with their leaders.[16] At a more humble level, some five hundred police forces have sought to burnish their image with the public by opening microblogs, a case in point being the *Safe Beijing* blog, which reportedly has more than three hundred thousand followers.[17]

While China's government aspires to exercise control of the Internet, China's Netizen community has until relatively recently not shown signs of being cowed. Indeed, there are signs of a vibrant online counterculture of oblique opposition to censorship that appears to be tolerated to some degree. A good example of this counterculture, and particularly the language to which it has given rise, is an article that appeared in the *Chongqing Evening News* in March 2010 reflecting on Google's impending departure from China:

> The Ancient Dove [Chinese *guge* (古鸽)—a pun on the Chinese name for Google, also pronounced *guge* but written 谷歌] is a species of the dove family which, within China's borders, is rapidly moving towards extinction.

This bird originated in North America with biologists estimating its birthplace as being in the vicinity of Mountain View, Santa Clara County, California. For a period around the turn of the twentieth century it expanded across the planet but after 23 March 2010, this bird began a large-scale migration towards a port off China's southern coast following which it can no longer be found in China proper.

The best assessment of environmental experts is that the strange behaviour of this bird may be related to recent extremes in climate around the world and in particular to the emergence in China in recent years of ecological, environmental, climatic and geological damage. In the face of difficulties the bird shows none of the resilience of the "grass mud horse" [in Chinese, *caonima* (草泥马), depicted as a small alpaca-like animal that has achieved iconic status as a symbol of opposition to Internet censorship. The name is a homophone of a phrase written 肏你妈, which means f—ck your mother] and simply migrates away, a cause of much sadness to animal lovers. . . .

Initial research suggests that the departure of the Ancient Dove could result in another ferocious species of bird emerging with sharp claws and looking remarkably like the Ancient Dove but with a very different temperament. The Baidu bird [the characters used are 百毒, meaning "one hundred poisons," rather than the name of the search engine, which is written 百度], this fabled indigenous species, has proliferated drastically and the Chinese people have been left with no option but to resort to this most ferocious of mythical birds which is full of venom and animosity [a possible reference to the enthusiasm with which Baidu polices and censors the content of its search engine], can only make its call in Chinese and only eats money, as a substitute for the functions previously provided by the Ancient Dove. . . . The latter on the other hand consumes all kinds of printed matter, can independently evaluate it, and has complex capacities for cataloguing it. The natural enemy of the Ancient Dove is the river crab [in Chinese, "*hexie*" 河蟹, a homonym for 和谐 meaning "harmonize," which is a euphemism employed by the censors to describe what is done to offending websites and now by extension used to mean "censors"].

Not surprisingly, this article disappeared from China's search engines within days of publication, a reflection of the sensitivity of the whole Google saga for China's leadership. But the terms "*caonima*" and "*hexie*" have become an integral part of the lexicography of China's Netizen community.

But irrespective of whether the more vocal elements of China's Netizen community are acting with full freedom or, as Rebecca MacKinnon argues, they are actually living in a gilded cage, there is little evidence to suggest that many seek to challenge directly the Chinese Communist Party's right to govern. The "Three Represents" policy, which represents former president and Communist Party chairman Jiang Zemin's contribution to Marxist-Leninist theory, has sought to co-opt China's intellectual elite, entrepreneurs, and emerging middle classes by permitting them to become Party members. Many young Chinese, including those at China's elite educational establishments, see Party membership as both a status symbol and a way to enhance their career prospects. And while the Party continues to provide economic growth and opportunities, and more or less total freedom for those who do not seek to challenge its authority, there is little obvious appetite for political change. Educated young Chinese who wish to access banned sites are generally able to do so. But in practice few do so, and those who do illuminate themselves as targets of interest for China's intelligence services who can thus focus their efforts on those who threaten subversion.

China Challenges the West

While the Chinese government may be increasingly confident in its ability to manage the Internet within China, there nonetheless remains a strong concern for the extent to which the Internet, still seen as heavily dominated by the West, poses a threat to the Chinese political system. This concern relates both to the medium itself—hardware and software—and to content, and it reflects Beijing's overriding preoccupation with political stability and fears of subversion. A *PLA Daily* op-ed of August 6, 2009, headlined "Internet Subversion: The Security Threat That Cannot Be Ignored," put the case as follows:

⋄ The West enjoys total dominance over the Internet due to its ownership of the majority of hardware and software.
⋄ It seeks to use the Internet to spread subversion and promote its own world view.
⋄ The failed "colour revolution" in Moldova in 2009 was largely instigated via Twitter and Facebook.
⋄ The same was true of the period following Iran's 2009 election when foreign subversion from the Internet gave rise to widespread social unrest.
⋄ After achieving naval, air and space domination, the USA is attempting to achieve dominance in the cyber domain as evidenced by the establishment of the US Cyber Command.[18]

Similar points were made in a *People's Daily* editorial dated January 24, 2010. More recently, the April 29, 2010, edition of the military newspaper *Jun Bao* carried an article with the characteristically snappy headline: "Our Armed Forces Must Beware of Western Exploitation of the Internet to Engage in Brainwashing." This article states that the exponents of westernization were making use of issues such as human rights, democracy, and religion to brainwash China's youth. It enjoins China's Armed Forces to remain alert to the threat, keep a clear head, cultivate good practice on Internet use, avoid breaking the rules, and refrain from visiting vulgar (disu) websites or expressing political views online.

This concern has led China to align itself with Russia in arguing for international rules for the policing of cyberspace that take account of "information security"—that is, control of content—in contrast to the United States, which has argued for a system based on network security. At a conference in Dallas organized by the East-West Institute in May 2010, Liu Zhengrong, deputy director-general of the Internet Affairs Bureau of the State Council Information Office, called for international cooperation to safeguard cyberspace. In doing so, he emphasized China's view that "the Internet sovereignty of each country needs to be respected and different national and cultural conditions taken into account."[19]

China has also sought to challenge the California-based International Corporation for Domain Names and Numbers' monopoly on the assignment of Internet domain names through a system of thirteen root servers, a situation that offers the potential for China to be cut off from the outside world. The June 2010 white paper on the Internet states: "China holds that the role of the UN should be given full scope in international Internet administration. China supports the establishment of an authoritative and just international Internet administration organisation under the UN system through democratic procedures on a worldwide scale. . . . China maintains that all countries have equal rights in participating in the administration of the fundamental international resources of the Internet, and a multilateral and transparent system should be established . . . so as to allocate those resources in a rational way and to promote the balanced development of the global Internet industry."[20]

It has also led China to focus on the question of developing indigenous alternatives to Western software, dependence on which is seen as a major vulnerability. The perceived vulnerability derives not just from the use of Western software per se but rather from the fact that much of this software, because it is pirated, lacks the protection in the form of regular security updates that properly licensed software would offer. This makes Chinese systems vulnerable to both hacking operations and manipulation by cybercriminal groups who often route their activities through Chinese sites because they are comparatively easy to penetrate. In his best-selling book *Internet Wars*, Dong Niao, a young academic specializing in the cyber domain, refers to a period in 2009 when Microsoft introduced security patches that caused the screens of people using pirated Microsoft software to go blank for short periods, forcing them to buy licensed Microsoft updates. Dong likens this behavior to that of the nineteenth-century British merchants who introduced opium into China.[21] The announcement by China's State Intellectual Property Office on January 6, 2011, that central government offices would have until May and local government offices until October 2011 to ensure that only licensed software was installed in their IT systems may well have been motivated at least in part by a desire to minimize this vulnerability.[22] It is, however, also likely that China's growing enthusiasm for intellectual property rights may have as much to do with its own efforts to develop an indigenous software sector and the realization that this is just as vulnerable to piracy as anything produced in Silicon Valley.

China's efforts to develop indigenous software form part of a wider strategy enunciated by the State Council's 2006 Guidelines on Medium and Long-Term Programmes for Science and Development and reflect a wider awareness that, if China is to continue successfully to develop economically, it must move rapidly up the value chain. The guidelines characterize reliance on the technology of other states—in particular the United States and Japan—as a threat to China's national and economic security and argue that China should avoid purchasing any "core technologies in key fields that effect the lifeblood of the national economy and national security, including next-generation Internet technologies."[23]

In 2009 the Chinese government sought to introduce regulations that would require all companies that wished to be listed in a register of those eligible to bid for government procurement contracts to demonstrate that the products to be provided were the product of indigenous innovation and devoid of foreign intellectual property. And in April 2010 it was announced that all companies that wished to be on the government contractors register would be required to make available the encryption codes for all ICT products. Both initiatives have met resistance, primarily from foreign corporation alleging that they are both discriminatory and pose a threat to intellectual property rights (IPR). In response to this pressure the Chinese government has undertaken to revise the proposals, and China has declared its intention to join the World Trade Organization's (WTO) Agreement on Government Procurement. But negotiations on the latter have made slow progress, with China seeking numerous derogations, and an early conclusion seems unlikely.

Efforts within China to develop an indigenous Internet capability have been driven by the concepts of indigenous innovation (*zizhu chuangxin*), network sovereignty (*wangluo zhuchuan*), and state information security (*guojia xinxi anquan*). Early Chinese efforts to promote and internationalize indigenous standards, a case in point being that of the wireless encryption standard WAPI (WLAN Authentication and Privacy Infrastructure), fell afoul of a combination of international resistance orchestrated by the United States, technical weaknesses, and an inability by the Chinese government to mobilize behind the project Chinese IT companies such as Lenovo, whose business model was critically dependent on cooperation with foreign partners.[24] But efforts toward indigenization have persisted. Chinese programmers have sought to promote Linux as an alternative to Microsoft software, and much emphasis has been placed on the development of Internet protocol version 6 (IPv6), a 128 Internet address space as an alternative to the current IPv4, which uses only 32 bits as the basis of a China Next Generation Internet (CNGI) project originally conceived in 2003. Given that the Chinese system is less monolithic, and power centers more widely distributed than outsiders often suppose, the Chinese government may struggle to impose its vision on an indigenous IT industry motivated like their Western counterparts by the bottom line. But the crescendo of slogans to promote the concept of indigenous innovation since the start of 2011 suggests that the determination to do so is undiminished.

Cyber Exploitation and Cyberwarfare

For at least the past decade, western and other foreign governments have become increasingly preoccupied with an increasing range of hostile activity within the cyber domain that appears to have its origins in China. The nature of the Internet is such that attribution for such attacks can rarely if ever be demonstrated to evidential standards; identities can easily be disguised, attacks rerouted through multiple intermediate points to disguise their origins, and most of the techniques used in such attacks are common to hackers, organized criminal groups, and state institutions. This accounts for the careful formulation of the US Department of Defense in its August 2010 report to Congress, which states that "numerous computer systems around the world, including those owned by the US government, continued to be the target of intrusions that appear to have originated within the People's Republic of China. These intrusions focused on exfiltrating information, some of which could be of strategic or military utility. The accesses and skills required for these intrusions are similar to those necessary to conduct computer network attacks. It remains unclear if these intrusions were conducted by, or with the endorsement of, the People's Liberation Army or other elements of the People's Republic of China government. However, developing capabilities for cyberwarfare is consistent with authoritative People's Liberation Army military writings."[25]

The list of cyber exploitation activities apparently originating in China is long, and the targets are a mix of government departments and the private sector. In 2003 the US Defense Department began to register a series of intrusions of US government and contractor sites code-named Titan Rain.[26] During 2006–7 a number of Western governments including the United Kingdom, New Zealand, and Germany publicized the extent to which they too had suffered intrusions apparently originating from China. The director-general of the British Security Service took the unprecedented step of writing a letter to three hundred chief executives and security advisers or private-sector corporations alerting them to the threat of cyber exploitation from China.[27] In 2009 the Information Warfare Monitor Citizen Lab at the University of Toronto's Munk School released a report on the so-called Ghost Net attack against the computer systems of the Dalai Lama, which encompassed 1,200 computers in 103 countries.[28] And the genesis of Google's decision in 2010 to cease cooperation with China over censorship and to redirect users to their Hong Kong-based search engine was the discovery of a sophisticated hacking operation with the name Operation Aurora, the apparent purpose of which was to gain access to Google's source code and thereby to access the systems of other US corporations.[29]

Western intelligence services appear to identify the Chinese state as responsible for nefarious cyber activity. But that bald assertion does not adequately convey the reality of a complex spectrum of activity taking place with varying degrees of state sanction. Nor does it take full account of the degree to which in contemporary China a proliferation of powerbases and interest groups makes it increasingly difficult for the central government to keep pace or to exercise effective control. Formally speaking, China has two authorities responsible for cyber exploitation and cyber-security. These are the 3rd Department of the General Staff of the PLA (3/PLA), China's signals intelligence (SIGINT) agency; and the 4th Department of the General Staff of the PLA (4/PLA), which is responsible for electronic warfare. The latter is responsible for a new Information Safeguards Base—*xinxi baozhang jidi*—the establishment of which was made public in July 2010 and whose purpose was described as addressing cyber threats and safeguarding China's information security and informa-tion infrastructure.[30] Before looking further at the nature of cyber attacks against foreign targets imputed to China, it is worth examining what is known of Chinese strategic and military thinking on the subject of cyber exploitation and cyberwarfare.

China's Cyber Forces

China's military has long been alert to the military potential of the cyber domain. In the late 1990s two PLA Air Force officers, in a book titled *Unrestricted Warfare* (*chaoxianzhan*) identified the dependence of US military systems on ICT as an impor-tant asymmetric advantage that the PLA should seek to exploit.[31] That asymmetric advantage has since diminished as the PLA too has developed increasingly sophisti-cated capabilities to undertake local wars under informationized conditions. China's military doctrine effectively conflates cyberwarfare and electronic warfare (EW) in a concept termed integrated network electronic warfare (*wangdian yiti zhan*), the pur-pose of which has been described in an article in the *Liberation Army Daily* as follows: "In future hi-tech warfare, offensive operations will often necessitate pre-emptive destruction of the enemy's integrated battlefield command-and-control systems and warfare networks. . . . And to attack its state or military communications hubs, financial centres and C4ISER systems, so as to directly affect the enemy's strategic decision-making."[32]

In short, the PLA sees the Internet as an additional domain within which warfare can be conducted with the primary aim of shaping the battle space, though not necessarily as a substitute for conventional warfare. When it comes to cyber exploita-tion as manifested in the episodes referred to earlier, it is hard to determine to what degree the PLA, primarily in the form of 3/PLA, can be considered to have direct responsibility. Much of the activity attributed to the Chinese state appears to be carried out by hackers with multiple identities—members of university IT depart-ments, employees in the IT departments of state-owned enterprises, online gamers, criminals—who can also be co-opted as members of militias to which all Chinese males of military age in theory belong. And while it is highly probable that hacking groups are used by the PLA and other departments of the Chinese state as a deniable capability to engage in a range of deniable cyber exploitation activities, it is equally likely that such actors are encouraged to engage with external targets in preference to focusing their attentions on indigenous targets. At the lower end of the spectrum, such activity is often organized on a very informal basis, as evidenced by the testi-mony of an unidentified FBI officer on the White House website: "25 year-olds or 17 year-olds have 40 year-old fathers who happen to be working within (government) institutions. Very often the opportunistic exploitation of a particular low-tech approach is derived through that chain, completely informally, rather than through somebody sitting in committee and deciding let's build 500 botnets that we're going to use to attack the Tibetan community."[33]

Cyber exploitation attacks on the networks of foreign governments and private sector corporations can be seen as the most recent of a scientific and technical intelligence collection strategy dating back to the early days of the modernization process launched by Deng Xiaoping in the 1970s. This process, which became known in the 1980s under the generic title of the 863 Programme, involved a large-scale, indiscriminate collection of information relating to a range of Western technologies by a range of actors. In the early days much of this activity was random, haphazard, and widely duplicated, but lately it has become more focused and structured. Some of this collection effort is undertaken by China's intelligence services, but the majority is now directed by the factories and research institutes comprising China's military-industrial complex.[34] Cyber exploitation offers an effective, low-risk alternative to politically embarrassing HUMINT operations, exploiting what until relatively recently has been a remarkably naïve approach by Western governments and private-sector corporations alike to cyber security issues. Though this is not to condone such behavior, it is perhaps unsurprising that China, with its need to sustain a high tempo of economic growth to meet the expectation of the 20 million workers coming onto the jobs market each year and to lift another 400 million of its citizens out of poverty, has shown a single-minded determination to acquire the necessary technology and IPR by whatever possible means.

Conclusion

There can be no doubt that China has emerged as a major global cyber power in the same way that it has emerged as a major geopolitical, economic, and military power and that the evolution of the Internet has played a catalytic role in China's rapid rise to great power status. It has had a similarly catalytic role in determining the nature of societal trends in a society that had been deeply traumatized by events such as the Cultural Revolution. It would be realistic to assume that China's aspirations to develop an indigenous IT sector capable of rivaling that of the United States and other major Western states will be realized, probably sooner rather than later. It can also be expected that China will seek to exercise more influence on issues such as global Internet governance.

It remains to be seen whether ultimately China's influence on the Internet will be benign, malign, or a mixture of the two. Notwithstanding its public posture of advocating Internet freedom, it seems probable that the Chinese government, with a mindset favoring control of information, which long predates its adherence to Marxism-Leninism, will continue to exercise tight control on Internet content. And it may find this possible to achieve without resorting to the creation of what China's best-known blogger, Han Han, has described as the world's biggest intranet. How the Internet evolves in China will both reflect and be determined by the nature of the government's relations with its own people and its perception of external threat, particularly that coming from the United States. This latter Chinese concern perhaps gives western policymakers more leverage than they might imagine—if they are able to use it wisely.

Notes

1. China Internet National Information Centre, "Internet Statistics" June 30, 2010, www1 .cnnic.cn/en/index/0O/index.htm.

2. State Council Information Office, "White Paper: The Internet in China," June 8, 2010, http://news.xinhuanet.com/english2010/china/2010-06/08/c_13339232_2.htm.

3. Jiang Zemin, *On the Development of China's Information Technology Industry* (Oxford: Elsevier, Academic Press, 2009).

4. "Study Says China's Internet Access Matches That of Developed World," *China Post*, August 21, 2010, www.chinapost.com.tw/business/asia-china/2010/08/21/269517/Study-says.htm.

5. US–China Economic and Security Review Commission, "2010 Report to Congress" (Washington, DC: GPO, November 2010), www.uscc.gov/annual_report/2010/annual_report_ full_10.pdf, 225.

6. Tony Jin, "China's Software Industry to Cross 1t," *The China Perspective*, November 13, 2009, http://thechinaperspective.com/articles/china039ssoftwa-6590/.

7. "China Cracks Down on Virtual Currency, for Real." *Wall Street Journal*, June 29, 2009, http://blogs.wsj.com/chinarealtime/2009/06/29/china-cracks-down-on-virtual-currency-for- real/.

8. Xinhua News Agency,"Four People Sentenced for Virtual Property Theft," May 24, 2009, http://news.xinhuanet.com/english/2009–05/24/content_11427265.htm.

9. "Clinton Says Trade Deal and Internet Will Reform China," *Tech Law Journal*, March 9, 2000, www.techlawjournal.com/trade/20000309.htm.

10. Kathrin Hille, "How China Polices the Internet," *Financial Times*, July 17, 2009, www.ft .com/cms/s/2/e716cfc6-71a1-11de-a821-00144feabdc0.html#axzz1C3orwAcT.

11. Rebecca MacKinnon, "Inside China's Censorship Machine," *National Post*, January 27, 2012, www.vancouversun.com/story_print.html?id = 6061567&sponsor = true.

12. Kathrin Hille, "How Beijing Shapes and Monitors Public Opinion Online," *Financial Times*, November 17, 2010, www.ft.com/cms/s/0/2af0086a-f285-11df-a2f3-00144feab49a.html #axzz1C3orwAcT.

13. Duncan Hewitt, "The March of the Netizens," *Newsweek*, November 2, 2010, www.bbc .co.uk/news/world-asia-pacific-11576592.

14. John Chan, "Anti-Japan Protests Erupt in China," *World Socialist*, April 8, 2005, www .wsws.org/articles/2005/apr2005/chin-a08.shtml.

15. Quoted in US–China Economic and Security Review Commission, "2010 Report to Congress," 222–23.

16. Kathrin Hille, "Chinese Communist Party Opens Online Forum," *Financial Times*, September 14, 2010, www.ft.com/cms/s/0/b5f79600-bf9d-11df-b9de-00144feab49a.html#ax zz1C3 orwAcT.

17. BBC News, "Chinese Police Use Micro-Blogs to Connect with Public," January 4, 2010, www.bbc.co.uk/news/world-asia-pacific-12112008.

18. "Wangluo dianfu: Burong xiaoqu de anchuan weixie," August 6, 2009, www.chinanews .com.cn/cul/news/2009/08–06/1806701.shtml.

19. "Cybersecurity Meet Ends with Global Cooperation Call," *Myanmar Times* 26, no. 522 (2010), www.mmtimes.com/2010/info/522/tech02.html.

20. State Council White Paper, "The Internet in China," Sec. VI, http://news.xinhuanet .com/english2010/china/2010–06/08/c_13339232_8.htm.

21. Dong Niao, *Internet Wars* (Beijing: Jiuzhou Press, 2009), 257–58.

22. Wang Qian, "Government Offices to Purge Pirated Software," *China Daily*, January 7, 2011, www.chinadaily.com.cn/china/2011-01/07/content_11805864.htm.

23. Adam Segal, "China's Innovation Wall: Beijing's Push for Homegrown Technology," *Foreign Affairs*, September 28, 2010, www.foreignaffairs.com/articles/66753/adam-segal/chinas-innovation-wall.

24. Yuezhi Zhao, "China's Pursuits for Indigenous Innovations and Technologies Development: Hopes, Follies and Uncertainties," Simon Fraser University (2007), 13–17, www.all academic.com//meta/p_mla_apa_research_citation/2/3/1/2/1/pages231214/p231214-12.php.

25. US Department of Defense, August 2010 report to Congress on Military and Security Developments Involving the People's Republic of China, www.defense.gov/pubs/pdfs/2010_CMPR_Final.pdf, 7.

26. Nathan Thornburgh, "Inside the Chinese Hack Attack," *Time*, August 25, 2005, www.time.com/time/nation/article/0,8599,1098371,00.html.

27. Sophie Borland, "MI5 Warns Firms over China's Internet 'Spying,'" *Daily Telegraph*, April 12, 2008, www.telegraph.co.uk/news/worldnews/1571172/MI5-warns-firms-over-Chinas-internet-spying.html.

28. "Tracking GhostNet: Investigating a Cyber Espionage Network," *Information Warfare Monitor*, September 1, 2009, www.infowar-monitor.net/2009/09/tracking-ghostnet-investigating-a-cyber-espionage-network/.

29. Bill Gertz, "Cyber-attack on US Firms, Google Traced to Chinese," *Washington Times*, March 24, 2010, www.washingtontimes.com/news/2010/mar/24/cyber-attack-on-us-firms-google-traced-to-chinese/.

30. Peng Pu, "PLA Unveils Nation's First Cyber Center," *Global Times*, July 22, 2010, http://military.globaltimes.cn/china/2010-07/554647.html.

31. Liang Qiao and Wang Xiangsui, *Unrestricted Warfare* (Beijing: PLA Literature and Arts Publishing House, 1999).

32. "Xiandai xinxi duikang: wangluo yitizhan." *Jiefangjun Bao*, September 7, 2004, www.people.com.cn/GB/junshi/1078/2146063.html.

33. US China Economic and Security Review Commission 2009, "China's Propaganda and Influence Operations, Its Intelligence Activities That Target the United States, and the Resulting Impacts on US National Security," April 21, 2009, www.uscc.gov/hearings/2009hearings/transcripts/09_04_30_trans.pdf.

34. Ibid., 149.

CHARACTERISTICS OF CYBER POWER

- RELIANT ON THE ELECTROMAGNETIC SPECTRUM
- REQUIRES MAN-MADE OBJECTS TO EXIST
- CAN BE CONSTANTLY REPLICATED
- COST OF ENTRY IS CHEAP
- OFFENSE IS CURRENTLY DOMINANT
- CONSISTS OF 4 LAYERS & CONTROL OF 1 ≠ CONTROL OF OTHERS
    - -- INFRASTRUCTURE: HARDWARE, CABLES, SATELLITES
    - -- PHYSICAL: ELECTRONS, PHOTONS, FREQUENCIES
    - -- SYNTACTIC: FORMATION OF INFO & RULES THAT INSTRUCT & CONTROL
    - -- SEMATIC: CYBER-COGNITIVE NEXUS — INFO ITSELF

CHAPTER 13

Toward a Theory of Cyber Power

Strategic Purpose in Peace and War

John B. Sheldon

Previous chapters focused on the technical, tactical, and operational aspects of operating in the cyber domain. These are undoubtedly important topics, but this chapter focuses on the strategic purpose of cyber power for the ends of policy. Understanding the strategic purpose for cyber power is important if we are to make informed judgments about its operational and tactical use. This chapter seeks to address a conceptual gap and advance an argument that cyber power does indeed have strategic purpose relevant to achieving policy objectives. This purpose centers on the ability to manipulate the strategic environment through and from cyberspace in peace and war for the ends of policy while simultaneously disrupting, denying, and otherwise interfering with the ability of an adversary to do the same.

Cyberwar—An Unhelpful Term

Emphatically, this chapter has no use for the term "cyberwar" as it is commonly described in what passes for popular debate. Recently Adm. Mike McConnell, US Navy (ret.), argued that the United States is in the midst of a cyber "war" because of the thousands of "attacks" that take place daily against US government networks as well as the private networks upon which our economy and society depend. He argues, less controversially, that greater investments are needed in cyber defenses, as well as greater regulation of the open architectures on which we rely.[1] Yet, the thousands of daily attacks Admiral McConnell describes are actually composed of many incidents, very few—if any—of which could be described as war. These cyber incidences range from attempts by actors to enter our networks to conduct espionage, to criminal elements seeking to extort and steal, through to political activists wishing to protest government policies or corporate activities by vandalizing and disrupting legitimate cyber activity, and hackers looking to make a name for themselves among their peers.[2] All of these cyber activities are major problems for cybersecurity. They are even a serious threat to overall economic well-being and the security of information and networks. Yet as Clausewitz reminds us, "War is a clash between major interests, which is resolved by bloodshed," and "War is nothing but a duel on a larger scale. Countless duels go to make up war, but a picture of it as a whole can be formed by imagining a pair of wrestlers. Each tries through physical force to compel the other to do his will; his immediate aim is to throw his opponent in order to make him incapable of further resistance. War is thus an act of force to compel our enemy to do our will."[3] According to Clausewitz's description of war, cybercrime, espionage, and other such nefarious activities do not constitute war. Lawlessness certainly, violence perhaps—but war? Most certainly not. As Derek Reveron argues earlier in this volume, cyber attacks are disruptive and not yet destructive.

Thousands of cyber incidences every day in peacetime do not make a war, but we can think about the use of cyber power in war. The issue, therefore, is not cyberwar, but cyber *in* war. An understanding of the strategic meaning of cyber power within this context may be of immense value. Another context—the hostile use of cyber power for the ends of policy in what is otherwise peacetime—requires a more precise definition. In terms of cyber power, many of the same activities are being performed but are not necessarily being accompanied by the use of force in the other domains (with the possible exception of covert action by special operations forces or intelligence agencies). In such context, an incident is most definitely occurring, but it is not war. Such activities can be more accurately defined as covert cyber operations, although this term could withstand further refinement. Either way, the strategic purpose of cyber power still applies.

Strategy and Cyber Power

This chapter asserts that the strategic purpose of cyber power is the ability in peace and war to manipulate the strategic environment to one's advantage while simultaneously degrading the ability of the enemy to comprehend that same environment. With this assertion in mind, the question must then be asked: what is the relationship between cyber power and strategy? It is proper to attend to the technological, tactical, and operational implications, challenges, and opportunities of cyberspace.[4] However, this chapter concerns itself specifically with the use of cyber power—"The ability to use cyberspace to create advantages and influence events in all the operational environments and across the instruments of power"[5]—for achieving the policy objectives of the nation. Transforming the effects of cyber power into policy objectives is the art and science of strategy, which is defined here as "managing context for *continuing advantage according to policy*."[6] The definition provides the overall strategic impetus for the use of cyber power in peacetime and in war.

Cyber power is technically, tactically, and operationally distinct from the other instruments of military power, but it is not beyond strategy, nor does it subvert the enduring nature of war, which is unchanging throughout history. Yet while the nature of war is unchanging, its character changes constantly and continuously with changes in society: political actors, technology, geopolitics, and the emergence of new exploitable domains such as the sea, air, space, and, more recently, cyberspace.[7] A general understanding of strategy and, in particular, an understanding of the strategic meaning of cyber power can help senior commanders and policymakers comprehend the difference between enduring issues and unique, transient incidents in cyber power.

Cyber power is subservient to the needs of policy, and strategy is the process of translating those needs into action. Cyber operations take place in cyberspace and generate cyber power, but they do not serve their own ends; they serve the ends of policy. (The case studies about the Russia, China, and the European Union in this book are illustrative of this.) Strategy is the bridge between policy and the exploitation of the cyber instrument. The notion that cyber operations (along with land, sea, air, and space operations) must serve their own imperatives is astrategic. For example, the capability may exist through cyber means to shut down the power grids in foreign nations, disable their networks, or read every digital message they transmit and receive, but the needs of policy will often demand that the power be kept on, the networks remain unmolested, and the intelligence garnered from passively monitoring enemy e-mail stay unused. Such restraint may occur for many reasons, ranging from the very limited and nuanced objectives of policy, to restraint based on proportionality, to fear of unknown consequences from cyber actions. Additionally, one may not wish to "tip one's hand" by demonstrating a capability for a short-term goal that may only be used a few times before the enemy can devise a plausible defense.

It is important to understand that cyber power is one of many tools in a commander's strategic "toolbox." For example, given enough time, sufficient intelligence gathering, and precise targeting, cyber power may well be able to silently turn off an enemy's integrated air defense system (IADS). But what if time is of the essence? What if there is a perception that the intelligence available will not do the job? A cyber component commander may make assurances that the attack was successful, but can the commander really be sure? After all, it is entirely possible that enemies knew all along that their networks had been mapped and their vulnerable nodes identified, or they may have "turned" the human intelligence asset that initially provided access to the closed network. These are the kinds of things that will—and do—weigh on a commander's mind, and so the assurance that a cyber attack is successful may also be the enemy deceiving the commander into thinking that it was successful, only to turn the IADS back "on" as the first wave of the air campaign appears on the horizon.[8] Ultimately, cyber power may be able to deliver the required strategic effect, but the commander may want to rely on other forms of military power, or even other instruments of national power.

It is vital that commanders and senior officials develop a greater understanding not only of the strategic purpose of cyber power but also of its relationship to strategy. Education must play a key role, along with practice and experience. Hopefully, from the nexus of education, experimentation, and experience, a theory of cyber power can be developed that will sharpen the strategic judgments and understanding of future commanders and senior officials.

The Strategic Context of Cyber Power

Along with land, sea, air, and space power, cyber power is a strategic tool that can be used alone or in combination with other instruments of military and national power. Cyber power can be used in peacetime and war because it is stealthy and covert, it is relatively cheap, and its use favors the offense but is difficult to attribute to the perpetrator. Of course, it is these same attributes that render our own networks vulnerable to cyber attack by others, but with a more robust cybersecurity culture and a more realistic understanding of the limits of cyber power, we should consider that its value as an instrument to manipulate the strategic environment to one's advantage outweighs the risks.

The Cyber Realm Is Different

Cyberspace is the latest in a large collection of technologies in the history of information. In their own ways, the printing press, telegraph, telephone, radio, and television have each revolutionized society and, in turn, military affairs.[9] Cyberspace, however, is different from its technological predecessors because it is not only a means of communications but also the predominant form of creating, storing, modifying, and exploiting information.[10] The primary technological predecessors of cyberspace have always been the means of exchanging (transmitting and receiving) information; however, the creation, storage, modification, and exploitation of that information did not occur within those technologies.

Today, information and communication technologies (ICT) permeate every function and level of the US military.[11] An ICT can be anything from a personal computer or cell phone to supervisory control and data acquisition (SCADA) devices that monitor the functioning of utilities, infrastructure, facilities, and other complex hardware.[12] Their use is extensive, pervasive, and growing. Furthermore, most US military hardware is now digitized, making most platforms reliant on ICTs for their internal functioning and for their coordinated use in both peace and war. When ICTs communicate, or network, with each other, it can be said that cyberspace exists.[13] Furthermore, throughout the US economy and society, ICTs play a critical role in the everyday functioning of the country, and the same is true not only of other industrialized developed countries but also of emerging and developing countries.[14]

This expanding, deepening, and increasingly pervasive reliance on cyberspace is part of the mosaic of the shifting geopolitical and economic global environment that provides the strategic context for the use of cyber power. Admittedly, this strategic context is a challenging one for policymakers, commanders, and scholars to comprehend because fundamental power shifts are still under way and geopolitical alignments are in flux. However, the United States and its allies, while still the most important fulcrum of power in the international system, are not necessarily the sole focus of international affairs. As Philip Stephens of the *Financial Times* recently explicated:

> A multipolar world has been long predicted, but has always seemed to be perched safely on the horizon. Now it has rushed quite suddenly into the present. . . . The lazy way to describe the new geopolitical landscape is one of a contest between the west and the rest—between western liberal democracies and eastern market-economy autocracies. Neat as such divisions may seem, they miss the complexities. None are more determined, for example, than Russia and China to keep India from securing a permanent seat on the UN Security Council. Few are more worried than India by China's military build-up. . . . The rising nations prize state power over international rules, sovereignty over multilateralism. The transition to a new order is likely to see more rivalry and competition than co-operation. The facts of interdependence cannot be wished away but they will certainly be tested. It is going to be a bumpy ride.[15]

Compounding these rapid and dramatic changes is the fact that cyber power as a strategic tool has diffused widely among all actors—state and nonstate alike. The United States may continue to hold the preponderance of land, sea, air, and space power as well as cyber power, but other actors in the strategic environment are also cyber empowered and often wield their tools to some effect.[16]

The Character of Cyberspace and Cyber Power

It is necessary to describe the characteristics of both cyberspace and cyber power as a precursor to explaining the strategic purpose of cyber power or a theory of the same. Also, it is worth noting the difference between the two terms: "cyberspace" is the domain in which cyber operations take place; "cyber power" is the sum of strategic effects generated by cyber operations in and from cyberspace. These effects can be felt within cyberspace as well as within the other domains, and can be cognitively effective with individual human beings. With this in mind, this chapter will consider some of the main characteristics of cyberspace.

Cyberspace Relies on the Electromagnetic Spectrum

Cyberspace cannot exist without the capability to exploit the naturally existing electromagnetic spectrum (EMS). Without the EMS, not only would millions of ICTs be unable to communicate with each other, the ICTs would be unable to function. Integrated circuits and other microelectronic devices depend on electrons in order to function. Fiber-optic cables are nothing if they are unable to propagate light. Networks of ICTs also depend upon the myriad properties of the EMS for their essential connectivity via radio frequency and microwaves.[17]

Cyberspace Requires Man-Made Objects in Order to Exist

The fact that cyberspace requires man-made objects in order to exist makes cyberspace unique when compared to the other domains. Without integrated circuit boards, semiconductors and microchips, fiber optics, and other communications and information technologies, there would be no cyberspace capable of hosting the EMS. For example, space would still exist if humankind were not able to place satellites into Earth's orbit. Cyberspace would not exist if not for the ability of human beings to innovate and manufacture technologies capable of exploiting the properties of the EMS. Without them, the EMS would be nothing more than the luminiferous ether promulgated by the scientist Albert A. Michelson in the nineteenth century—in other words, although it can be said to exist, the velocity of the Earth's orbit around the Sun has no discernable effect on it.[18]

Cyberspace Can Be Constantly Replicated

As an entity, there is only one air, one sea, one space, and one land. In contrast, there can be as many cyberspaces as one can possibly generate. In reality, there is only one portion of the air, sea, and land that is important—the portion that is being fought over. The air over the United States is pretty much the same as that over any other place in the world; the only difference is that the air over the US is not contested. The same goes for the oceans. One could set off across the Atlantic tomorrow and have a pleasant passage to Europe—the same ocean that, several thousand miles away off the coast of Africa, is infested with pirates. Sovereignty applies in the physical domains.

With cyberspace, however, there can be many in existence at any time—some contested, some not. For the most part, nothing is final in cyberspace.[19] With air power, enemy aircraft can be destroyed until they are all gone, and there the matter ends. In cyberspace, a Jihadist website can be purposefully shut down, but the same Jihadists can start a new website within hours on a different server using a different domain name. Similarly, as Herb Lin reminds us in chapter 3 of this volume, networks can be quickly repaired and reconstituted thanks to the relatively inexpensive and readily available hardware required to set them up.[20]

The Cost of Entry into Cyberspace Is Relatively Cheap

The resources and expertise required to enter, exist in, and exploit cyberspace are modest compared to that required for exploiting the other domains. As Derek

Reveron points out in chapter 1, generating strategic effect in cyberspace does not require a budget of billions, manpower in the thousands, tracts of land, or large equipment reserves. Rather, modest financial outlays, a small group of motivated individuals, and access to networked computers that are accessible to a large portion of the world's population can provide entry to the cyber domain.[21] Deep computer expertise is an advantage but not always necessary. Modest computer science and programming knowledge can generate strategic effect in and from cyberspace. As Col. Stephen Korns points out, many cyber "weapons" are now commodified and can be easily purchased "off the shelf" at affordable prices, including denial-of-service software that can be downloaded to a personal computer and deployed against its target.[22] The commoditization of cyber capabilities is evidenced by the cyber attacks that took place against Estonia in April–May 2007 and against Georgia in August 2008, when individuals—the vast majority of whom were not experts in programming or computer science—downloaded readily available software to mount the denial-of-service attacks.[23] This is not to imply that deep cyber expertise cannot provide an advantage or that investment of billions of dollars into a cyber effort will not have a significant strategic return—far from it. Rather, the character of cyberspace is such that the number of actors able to operate in the domain—and potentially generate strategic effect—is exponential when compared to the other domains.

For the Time Being, the Offense rather than the Defense Is Dominant in Cyberspace

This is true for several reasons. First, network defenses rely on vulnerable protocols and open architectures, and the prevailing network defense philosophy emphasizes threat detection, not correcting vulnerabilities.[24] Second, attacks in cyberspace occur at great speed—to a human observer they may seem instantaneous—putting defenses under immense pressure since an attacker must be successful only once whereas the defender must be continuously successful.[25] Third, range is not an issue in cyberspace as it is in the other domains. Attacks can emerge from literally anywhere in the world.[26] Fourth, attributing attacks is mostly problematic, thus complicating any possible response.[27] Fifth, the overwhelming reliance on cyberspace in the military and throughout modern society presents any attacker with a target-rich environment, placing great strain on the ability to successfully defend the domain.[28]

Cyberspace Consists of Four Layers, and Control of One Layer Does Not Mean Control of the Others

Cyberspace consists of infrastructure, physical, syntactic, and semantic layers. The infrastructure layer consists of the hardware, cabling, satellites, facilities, and so on.[29] The physical layer consists of the myriad properties of the EMS—electrons, photons, frequencies, etc.—that animate the infrastructure layer.[30] The syntactic layer consists of the formatting of information and the rules that instruct and control the information systems that make up cyberspace.[31] The semantic layer consists of information useful and comprehensible to human users: it is essentially the cyber-cognitive nexus.[32] Controlling the infrastructure layer of cyberspace does not necessarily translate into control of the other layers. Similarly, semantic control does not require infrastructure control, as evidenced by the prevalence of cybercrime today, which exploits the semantic layer. While this proposition is generally true, there are exceptions that depend upon what one is attempting to do. If one is trying to destroy and disable a network, then attacking the infrastructure layer alone may be effective. If, on the other hand, one is trying to spoof an enemy commander into making certain decisions, then control of the infrastructure layer is largely irrelevant, but control of the semantic layer is everything.[33]

Cyberpower Is Everywhere

Land, sea, air, and space power are able to generate strategic effect on each of the other domains, but nothing generates strategic effect in all domains so absolutely and simultaneously as cyber power.[34] Given the cyber dependencies of the military, economy, and society in a growing number of countries, and given that cyberspace critically enables land, sea, air, and space power—as well as other instruments of power such as diplomacy, media, and commerce—cyber power is ubiquitous. Power in the other domains can return to base, or, in the case of satellites, be tasked to another target. Cyber power does not go back to its sender, nor is it expended.

Cyber Power Is Primarily Indirect

Unlike land, sea, and air power but in many ways like space power, cyber power is largely an indirect instrument, especially when used autonomously. It is indirect because the coercive ability of cyber power is limited, at least for the present. For example, the cyber attack against Estonia in the spring of 2007 was ostensibly in response to the Estonian government removing a Soviet war memorial from Tallinn to the suburbs, causing controversy among Estonia's ethnic Russian minority and in Russia itself. It is often forgotten that the cyber attacks occurred with violent protests in Estonia and a political warfare campaign allegedly perpetrated by the Russian government against Estonian interests. None of these—the protests, campaign, threats and diplomatic protests, and cyber attacks—swayed the Estonian government from its decision to move the memorial. This immovability is made more remarkable because Estonia is considered one of the most cyber-dependent countries in the world.

It can certainly be argued that the cyber attacks in Estonia were damaging, disruptive, and a nuisance, but they were not coercive.[35] It is even more evident that the cyber attacks during the short conflict between Russia and Georgia in August 2008 were likewise not coercive. Georgia, especially at the time, was not a particularly cyber-dependent country, and the Russian military campaign was relatively swift and decisive in achieving its objectives. The associated cyber attacks, which have never been publicly attributed to the Russian government but seemed impeccably timed to peak just as Russian forces crossed into South Ossetia and Abkhazia, certainly caused major disruptions to Georgian Internet services and other means of communication, but it is implausible to suggest that the Russian military campaign would have been less decisive had the cyber attacks not taken place or failed.[36]

The assertion that cyber power is an indirect instrument rests, of course, on the rarely observed use of meaningful cyber power in recent years. The nightmare scenarios of cyber power used to switch off power grids, disrupt air traffic control, or bring down Wall Street—all so beloved by Hollywood—have thankfully not yet occurred. This may change at some point, and in that case the assertion should be thoroughly revised. But coercion must be proven for this to happen. Shutting down a power grid via cyber power, for example, would undoubtedly have catastrophic consequences, but rather than an attacker coercing its victim to concede to demands, the attack may only invite an even more catastrophic response. Similarly, despite all the press about the damage caused by the Stuxnet worm, the worm has yet to coerce Iranian leaders into abandoning their nuclear program.[37] Until cyber power proves its coercive ability, it can be said that, at best, cyber power is an indirect instrument with the potential to be more.

Cyber Power Can Be Stealthy

One of the attractions of cyber power is the ability to wield it surreptitiously on a global scale without the action being attributed to the perpetrator. Malicious software can be planted in enemies' networks without their knowledge until the cyber weapon causes its intended damage. Databases can be raided for classified or proprietary information, and the owners of that information may not be the wiser as terabits of data are stolen. Similarly, private citizens can live in oblivion for months only to discover too late that cyber criminals have stolen their identities and maxed out all their credit cards. This ability to stealthily use cyber power, aided by the inherent difficulties of attributing the identity and motivation of most attackers, makes cyber power a very attractive instrument for governments and other actors.[38]

Manipulating the Strategic Environment through Cyber Power

The characteristics and attributes of cyber power are just some of those that can be ascribed to cyberspace, but they do not explain to the strategist what makes cyber power a unique instrument. This chapter emphasizes that the key strategic attribute of cyber power is the ability in peace and war to manipulate the strategic environment to one's advantage. This strategic utility of cyber power extends to all the other strategic mediums or domains, given their ubiquitous dependence upon cyberspace.

The currency of cyber power is information that can be disseminated in a variety of ways across, in, and to all the other mediums. The aim of the cyber strategist is to maximize to the greatest extent possible the various tools (or cyber "weapons") that can, among other things, disrupt and sabotage adversary cyber-dependent activities; deny adversary cyber-dependent communications; steal information that is valuable to the adversary; monitor and spy on adversary activities through cyberspace; and deceive cyber-dependent adversaries into making decisions that are favorable to the perpetrator through the manipulation of adversary information by cyber means.

While cyber power has yet to prove its worth as an independent coercive instrument, its capabilities provide real strategic value, as events of the past several years have demonstrated. The Stuxnet computer worm has disrupted and, as a result, delayed the Iranian nuclear program by sabotaging the computer operating system used to power its centrifuges.[39] The denial-of-service operation against Georgian cyberspace during the Russian invasion in 2008 contributed greatly to the inability of Georgian elites to communicate with each other and the outside world during the military campaign.[40] PFC Bradley Manning of the US Army apparently stole terabytes of classified US military reports and diplomatic cables on several CD-ROM discs (disguised as Lady Gaga compact discs, no less) and the ubiquitous flash drive, handing them over to Julian Assange's Wikileaks organization, which subsequently leaked the information to a global public via prominent newspapers across the world.[41] A number of Western governments allege that China is using cyberspace to conduct extensive espionage operations against political, governmental, industrial, and military targets throughout the West, with one official claiming that Chinese intelligence services have stolen enough classified and proprietary information to fill the Library of Congress.[42] Finally, millions of people, including members of Congress, government, and the military, are potential victims of various phishing scams that attempt to illicitly obtain sensitive user ID and password information in order to access proprietary databases.[43] Indeed, the pervasive nature of cyberspace—thanks in turn to the ubiquity of ICTs—has critical implications for military command, defined by Martin van Creveld as "a function that has to be exercised, more or less continuously, if the army is to exist and to operate."[44]

Because cyberspace shrinks organizational scope and can reach up, down, and across echelons and stovepipes, it offers military commanders the potential for greater control. Yet, as Martin van Creveld effectively points out, to use a communications technology solely for control of every tactical and operational activity is to abrogate effective command and stifle, if not strangle, tactical and operational performance.[45] Present-day cyber-enabled commanders would do well to emulate Helmuth von Moltke and his judicious use of the telegraph during the nineteenth century, rather than Field Marshal Douglas Haig's "telephonitis" during the catastrophic Battle of the Somme in World War I.[46]

The ubiquity of cyberspace may tempt many commanders to interfere at the lowest echelon and reach forward into tactical fights, yet the imperatives for effective command in the information age are the same as they were in the days of the Roman

Empire. These imperatives include the ability of the commander to grasp the strategic context of the time; bring internal and external coherence to the force under command; create a design for how the force is to be used; display the moral and intellectual courage to take action; possess nerve in the face of extreme pressure and uncertainty; create a persona to inspire those under command to obey orders in the face of mortal danger and to follow the commander who inspires them; possess a great intellect that is creative, bold, and curious; possess expertise in the practice of arms, without which there is no credibility; and, finally, identify those rare individuals who not only possess the capacity to carry out such imperatives but also epitomize them.[47]

Cyber power in the hands of a commander who is able to exercise all the imperatives of command will be a very powerful tool. As Van Creveld convincingly demonstrates, those commanders who shaped their command structure according to the mission to be accomplished, rather than the technology at their disposal, won. Those commanders who became slaves to the technology at their disposal—be it the telegraph, telephone, or wireless radio—have tended to exert control at the lowest echelons, thus strangling initiative and adaptability. Rather than leading their forces, they were cocooned by their favored means of communication.[48] Thus, in the wrong hands, cyber power will likely amplify the pathologies of poor senior commanders, stifle the ability of senior noncommissioned officers and subordinate commanders to lead and adapt, and render the entire structure of command reliant on the durability and survivability of what is, in essence, a collection of fragile and vulnerable communication links.

Profound implications arise out of these assertions. Future wars against cyber-savvy adversaries will have to be fought using command systems that anticipate having to fight in a degraded, if not denied, cyber environment. In other words, these systems must be structured in such a way that they can survive when information is not only unreliable but also scarce. Further, senior commanders will have to delegate tactical and operational authority to subordinate commanders and guide them through the use of mission orders that specify the minimum that must be achieved. And, finally, for a force to succeed in an information-deprived environment, a greater onus on unit cohesion, training, and education in the strategic arts becomes imperative.

Cyberspace is fragile and vulnerable to myriad methods of attack and disruption ranging from jamming of the EMS to the hacking of software, insertion of malware into operating systems, or denial-of-service attacks. This vulnerability, when considered with the ubiquity of cyberspace and the growing reliance upon it, means that cyber power is an offensive instrument. It is ideal for manipulating the strategic environment to advantage, and ultimately disrupting or denying the ability of an adversary—deprived of individuals steeped in the imperatives of command—to effectively command their instruments of national power. In future wars, in which cyber power will feature prominently, victory will favor the side able to effectively command forces deprived of information while simultaneously using cyber power to deceive, deny, demoralize, and disrupt enemies, thus compromising their ability to comprehend the strategic environment. Threats to cyberspace are myriad, and there are many sources of these threats. Even with better cyber defenses, especially in the United States, the effective use of cyber power will see networks disrupted and made unreliable for effective communications. That said, however, sufficient defensive measures should be instituted as quickly as possible to help facilitate offensive cyber operations.[49]

Toward a Theory of Cyber Power

It would be wrong to suggest that no attempt has been made to craft a theory of cyber power. Greg Rattray has done the field a great service with his excellent *Strategic Warfare in Cyberspace*, and Stuart H. Starr attempted to lay framework for a theory of cyberpower in a chapter he contributed to the valuable collection of essays *Cyberpower and National Security*.[50] These works have contributed greatly to the task of building a theory of cyber power, yet both have drawbacks. Rattray's work is arguably the superior of the two and offers the careful reader several strategic insights. However, his work also tends to overemphasize the technological and organizational dimensions at the expense of other pertinent elements and relies exclusively on the analogy of strategic air power.[51] Starr, on the other hand, usefully employs Harold Winton's taxonomy of what a theory should look like (more on this later) but then immediately digresses into the tactical and technical weeds and fails to relate cyber power to its political and strategic context.[52]

Under the rubric of the eternal logic of strategy, there should be a theory of cyber power that can aid the commander and cyber operator to maximize cyber power's usefulness as an instrument of policy. Land, sea, air, and space power each have a canon of military theory to support them, and these works are still taught in the staff and war colleges of the services around the world.[53] Likewise, a theory of cyber power is deemed useful because "it is based on the proposition that before one can intelligently develop and employ [cyber power], one should understand its essence."[54] Similarly, Adm. J. C. Wylie, US Navy, one of the finest strategic thinkers of the twentieth century, noted that "theory serves a useful purpose to the extent that it can collect and organize the experiences and ideas of other men, sort out which of them may have a valid transfer value to a new and different situation, and help the practitioner to enlarge his vision in an orderly, manageable and useful fashion—and then apply it to the reality with which he is faced."[55] A theory of cyber power, then, will be of practical use. But what should such a theory do? In broad terms, what should it look like? Harold Winton provides five criteria for developing military theory that can be applied to cyber power and that should be addressed in any attempt to craft a theory of cyber power.

◊ *Define the Field*[56]: This criterion would delineate what cyberspace and cyber power are and what they are not. Daniel T. Kuehl recently identified at least fourteen definitions of cyberspace, revealing that the study of the strategic application of cyber power is immature.[57] Reaching some kind of consensus on definitions of cyberspace and cyber power is ultimately important if a plausible theory of cyber power is to emerge.

◊ *Categorize into Constituent Parts*[58]: The next criterion of a theory of cyber power is to break down the field of study into its constituent parts. Imagine cyber power as a citrus fruit; cut it into slices and examine each one, then put them back together again to remake the whole. This involves identifying the component parts of what constitutes cyberspace—its infrastructure, physical, syntactic, and semantic layers—and the various tools (or weapons) that can be used to generate effects.

◊ *Explain*[59]: With cyber power defined and the workings of its constituent parts understood, the next criterion is to explain how cyber power functions. Ultimately, "theory without explanatory power is like salt without savor—it is worthy only of the dung heap."[60] Here a theory must explain how cyber power achieves its desired effects in the strategic environment, such as disruption, deception, denial, and so forth. Furthermore, a theory must attempt to identify the circumstances in which cyber power will be most effective.

◊ *Connect to Other Fields*[61]: A theory must then be able to connect cyber power to the wider universe. In what ways does cyber power interact with the other domains? In what ways is cyber power mitigated by friction, differences in cultures, economics, and so on? Such a description need not be exhaustive but should at least demonstrate the place of cyber power within the strategic cosmos.

◊ *Anticipate*[62]: A good theory of cyber power should be able to identify those aspects that are likely to remain timeless as society and technology change. Anticipation is not the same as prediction, which is impossible, but it should identify the larger influences of cyber power that are scalable in the future. For example, the maneuver warfare ably demonstrated in the First Gulf War of 1991 and the opening weeks of Operation Iraqi Freedom had its roots in a small coterie of Soviet Army officers in the 1920s and 1930s led by Marshal Mikhail Tukhachevskii and their concept of "deep operations."[63] At the time, the Soviets had neither the resources nor the technology to carry out the promise of the concept. But, more than sixty years later, the United States did carry it out—all because a coterie of American officers and strategic thinkers read and understood Tukhachevskii's works.[64] In other words, Tukhachevskii's theory of land power anticipated many of the great changes that were to come.

It should be noted that a theory of cyber power will have limitations. It will never be able to fully reflect reality and all the random and complex variables that occur daily. It is impossible for theory to capture such complexity, but it can educate the mind to cope with the complexity and act with purpose despite it.[65] Furthermore, elements such as technologies, actors, and the political context change at alarmingly rapid rates. Theory cannot be expected to capture such changes, but a good theory will recognize that change is inevitable. The best a cyber power theorist can expect is to get the big things mostly correct and to provide adequate tools to cope with the smaller things.

Conclusion

The technological and tactical story of cyber power has been an exciting (if not disquieting) one to date. Yet the strategic story has been slow to develop, in part because little effort has gone into identifying exactly what it is that cyber power strategically provides to its employer. This chapter contributes to this effort by asserting a strategic purpose for cyber power that should also contribute to a nascent theory of cyber power. Cyber power is a disruptive tool that can have strategic effect when used in conjunction with other instruments of power. In the hands of a commander versed in the timeless arts of command, it can create even greater strategic effect when used to push authority down the chain of command as disruption of cyber-based command systems is to be expected. When used by commanders to micromanage every tactical, operational, and administrative detail, cyber power becomes a dangerous tool that stifles initiative and renders such command systems even more vulnerable to disruption.

Notes

This chapter is based on a paper delivered to the "From Cybersecurity to Cyber War" workshop hosted by the EMC chair at the Naval War College, Newport, Rhode Island, on September 15-17, 2010, and a series of lectures delivered to the students of the Cyber 200 and Cyber 300 courses at the Center for Cyberspace Research, Air Force Institute of Technology, Wright-Patterson AFB, Ohio, in October and November of 2010. The author thanks Derek Reveron, Naval War College; Col. Harold J. Arata, USAF, and his exemplary team at the Center for Cyberspace Research; Drs. Harold R. Winton, Richard Muller, James W. Forsyth, Stephen Wright, and Stephen D. Chiabotti at the School of Advanced Air and Space Studies, Maxwell AFB, Alabama; and Lt. Col. William E. Young, USAF, currently at Air War College, Maxwell AFB, Alabama. All errors in this chapter are the author's alone.

1. See Mike McConnell, "Mike McConnell on How to Win the Cyber-War We're Losing," *Washington Post*, February 28, 2010, B01.

2. For a useful discussion about the difficulties of attributing what constitutes war, espionage, or criminality, as well as the identity and motivations of the perpetrators, see Susan W. Brenner, *Cyberthreats: The Emerging Fault Lines of the Nation State* (New York: Oxford University Press, 2009).

3. Carl von Clausewitz, *On War*, ed. and trans. Michael Howard and Peter Paret (Princeton, NJ: Princeton University Press, 1984), 149, 75.

4. This chapter uses Daniel T. Kuehl's definition of cyberspace: "A global domain within the information environment whose distinctive and unique character is framed by the use of electronics and the electromagnetic spectrum to create, store, modify, exchange, and exploit

information via interdependent and interconnected networks using information-communication technologies." Daniel T. Kuehl, "Cyberspace and Cyberpower," in *Cyberpower and National Security*, eds. Franklin D. Kramer, Stuart H. Starr, and Larry K. Wentz (Dulles, VA: Potomac Books, 2009), 28.

5. Ibid., 38.

6. Everett C. Dolman, *Pure Strategy: Power and Principle in the Space and Information Age* (London: Frank Cass, 2005), 6, emphasis in original text.

7. On the nature and character of war and cyber power, see David J. Lonsdale, *The Nature of War in the Information Age: Clausewitzian Future* (London: Frank Cass, 2004), 19–48; see also Lonsdale, "Clausewitz and Information Warfare," in *Clausewitz in the Twenty-First Century*, eds. Hew Strachan and Andreas Herberg-Rothe, 231–50 (Oxford: Oxford University Press, 2007).

8. See, for example, Richard A. Clarke and Robert K. Knake, *Cyber War: The Next Threat to National Security and What to Do about It* (New York: Ecco, 2010), 208.

9. See, for example, Elizabeth C. Hanson, *The Information Revolution and World Politics* (Lanham, MD: Rowman & Littlefield, 2008), 13–45.

10. See Daniel T. Kuehl's definition of cyberspace, Kuehl, "Cyberspace and Cyberpower," 28.

11. On the dissemination of ICTs throughout the military see, among others, John Arquilla and David Ronfeldt, "Cyberwar Is Coming!" *Comparative Strategy* 12, no. 2 (April–June 1993): 142–44; Gregory J. Rattray, *Strategic Warfare in Cyberspace* (Cambridge, MA: MIT Press, 2001), 312–14; and the collected essays in David S. Alberts and Daniel S. Papp, eds., *The Information Age: An Anthology on Its Impacts and Consequences*, Volume I, Part One: *The Information and Communication Revolution* (Washington, DC: National Defense University, June 1997).

12. On SCADA, see, for example, Robert A. Miller and Irving Lachow, "Strategic Fragility: Infrastructure Protection and National Security in the Information Age," *Defense Horizons*, no. 59 (January 2008), www.dtic.mil/dtic/tr/fulltext/u2/a476034.pdf.

13. See Capt. David R. Luber, USMC, and Col. David H. Wilkinson, USMC, "Defining Cyberspace for Military Operations: A New Battlespace," *Marine Corps Gazette* 93, no. 2 (February 2009): 40–46.

14. On the dissemination of ICTs throughout societies around the world, see Manuel Castells, *Communication Power* (New York: Oxford University Press, 2009), 54–136; Martin Campbell-Kelly and William Aspray, *Computer: History of the Information Machine*, 2nd ed. (Boulder, CO: Westview Press, 2004), 141–279; and Eric G. Swedin and David L. Ferro, *Computers: The Life Story of a Technology* (Baltimore, MD: Johns Hopkins University Press, 2005), 131–49.

15. Philip Stephens, "On the Way to a New Global Balance," *Financial Times* (London), December 16, 2010.

16. See Joseph S. Nye Jr., "The Future of American Power: Dominance and Decline in Perspective," *Foreign Affairs* 89, no. 6 (November/December 2010): 2–12, for a judicious view of America's prospect in a rapidly changing geostrategic context.

17. See Lonsdale, *Nature of War*, 179–200; Daniel T. Kuehl, "From Cyberspace to Cyberpower: Defining the Problem," in *Cyberpower and National Security*, eds. Franklin D. Kramer, Stuart H. Starr, and Larry K. Wentz (Dulles, VA: Potomac Books, 2009), 30; and Martin C. Libicki, *Conquest in Cyberspace: National Security and Information Warfare* (New York: Cambridge University Press, 2007), 5, 29.

18. See Albert A. Michelson, "The Relative Motion of the Earth and the Luminiferous Ether," *American Journal of Science* 22, nos. 127–32 (July–December 1881) 120–29; see also Gerald Holton, *Thematic Origins of Scientific Thought: Kepler to Einstein* (Cambridge, MA: Harvard

University Press, 1973), 261–352. My thanks to Dr. Stephen Chiabotti of the School of Advanced Air and Space Studies, Maxwell AFB, for relating this useful point to me.

19. See Libicki, *Conquest in Cyberspace*, 5–6.

20. See ibid., 84–85.

21. See also Col. Stephen W. Korns, USAF, "Cyber Operations: The New Balance," *JFQ*, no. 54 (3rd Quarter 2009): 97–98.

22. See ibid., 99–100.

23. See Clarke and Knake, *Cyber War*, 11–21.

24. For a critique of the lack of robust cyber defenses in the United States, see ibid., 103–49.

25. See Gregory J. Rattray, "An Environmental Approach to Understanding Cyberpower," in *Cyberpower and National Security*, eds. Franklin D. Kramer, Stuart H. Starr, and Larry K. Wentz (Dulles, VA: Potomac Books, 2009), 255–56.

26. See ibid.

27. See Brenner, *Cyberthreats*.

28. On US dependence on cyber, see Clarke and Knake, *Cyber War*, 170–75.

29. Libicki refers to the infrastructure layer as the physical layer; see his *Conquest in Cyberspace*, 8.

30. I have added the EMS physical layer to Libicki's taxonomy; see ibid, 8–10.

31. See ibid., 8–9.

32. See ibid., 9.

33. See ibid., 8–10.

34. Lonsdale makes a similar point in his *Nature of War*, 184–86.

35. See Stephen Blank, "Web War I: Is Europe's First Information War a New Kind of War?" *Comparative Strategy* 27, no. 3 (May 2008): 227–47.

36. See Stephen W. Korns and Joshua E. Kastenberg, "Georgia's Cyber Left Hook," *Parameters*, 38, no. 4 (Winter 2008–9): 60–76; US Cyber Consequences Unit, "Overview by the US-CCU of the Cyber Campaign against Georgia in August of 2008," A US-CCU Special Report, August 2009, www.registan.net/wp-content/uploads/2009/08/US-CCU-Georgia-Cyber-Campaign-Overview.pdf, accessed 3 January 2011; Stéphane Lefebvre and Roger N. McDermott, "Intelligence Aspects of the 2008 Conflict between Russia and Georgia," *Journal of Slavic Military Studies* 22, no. 1 (January 2009): 4–19; and Timothy L. Thomas, "The Bear Went through the Mountain: Russia Appraises Its Five-Day War in South Ossetia," *Journal of Slavic Military Studies* 22, no. 1 (January 2009): 31–67.

37. On Stuxnet, see, among others, Paul K. Kerr, John Rollins, and Catherine A. Theohary, *The Stuxnet Computer Worm: Harbinger of an Emerging Warfare Capability* (Washington, DC: Congressional Research Service, December 9, 2010); and David Albright, Paul Brannan, and Christina Walrond, *Did Stuxnet Take out 1,000 Centrifuges at the Natanz Enrichment Plant?* ISIS Report (Washington, DC: Institute for Science and International Security, December 22, 2010). See also Daniel Dombey, "US Fears Faster Iran Nuclear Arms Progress," *Financial Times* (London), December 29, 2010.

38. See, among others, Brenner, *Cyberthreats*; and Clarke and Knake, *Cyber War*, 197–200.

39. See Daniel Dombey, "US Says Cyberworm Aided Effort against Iran," *Financial Times* (London), December 10, 2010.

40. See Korns and Kastenberg, "Georgia's Cyber Left Hook," 60.

41. Among the surfeit of reports about WikiLeaks, one in particular offers a useful, albeit eminently debatable, long-term view: Neville Bolt, "The Leak before the Storm: What WikiLeaks Tells Us about Modern Communication," *RUSI Journal* 155, no. 4 (August–September 2010): 46–51.

42. See Clarke and Knake, *Cyber War*, 58–59.

43. On social engineering methods, such as "spear-phishing," see Jeffrey Carr, *Inside Cyber Warfare* (Sebastopol, CA: O'Reilly, 2010), 146–50.

44. Martin van Creveld, *Command in War* (Cambridge, MA: Harvard University Press, 1985), 5.

45. See ibid, 261–75.

46. On von Moltke's style of command see ibid, 103–47; see also Graf von Helmuth Moltke, *Moltke on the Art of War: Selected Writings*, ed. Daniel Hughes (Novato, CA: Presidio Press, 1995); Geoffrey Wawro, *The Austro-Prussian War: Austria's War with Prussia and Italy in 1866* (Cambridge: Cambridge University Press, 1996); and Wawro, *The Franco-Prussian War: The German Conquest of France in 1870–1871* (Cambridge: Cambridge University Press, 2003). On Haig's style of command, see van Creveld, *Command in War*, 155–68; Paddy Griffith, *The Great War on the Western Front: A Short History* (Barnsley, UK: Pen & Sword Military, 2008), 43–55; and David Stevenson, *1914–1918: The History of the First World War* (London: Allen Lane, 2004), 168–71.

47. See Lt. Col. Christopher Smith, Australian Army, *Network Centric Warfare, Command, and the Nature of War*, Study Paper No. 318 (Canberra, Australia: Land Warfare Studies Centre, February 2010), 49–56.

48. See Van Creveld, *Command in War*, 261–75.

49. There are various views and a lively debate regarding cyber defense in the United States. See, among others, Clarke and Knake, *Cyber War*, 151–78; Edward Skoudis, "Information Security Issues in Cyberspace," in *Cyberpower and National Security*, eds. Franklin D. Kramer, Stuart H. Starr, and Larry K. Wentz, 171–205 (Dulles, VA: Potomac Books, 2009); and John A. McCarthy, Chris Burrow, Maeve Dion, and Olivia Pacheco, "Cyberpower and Critical Infrastructure Protection: A Critical Assessment of Federal Efforts," in *Cyberpower and National Security*, eds. Franklin D. Kramer, Stuart H. Starr, and Larry K. Wentz, 543–56 (Dulles, VA: Potomac Books, 2009); Center for Strategic and International Studies, *Securing Cyberspace for the 44th Presidency: A Report of the CSIS Commission on Cybersecurity for the 44th Presidency* (Washington, DC: Center for Strategic and International Studies, December 2008); and White House, *Cyberspace Policy Review: Assuring a Trusted and Resilient Informational and Communications Infrastructure* (Washington, DC: White House, April 2009).

50. Rattray, *Strategic Warfare in Cyberspace*; and Stuart H. Starr, "Toward a Preliminary Theory of Cyberpower," in *Cyberpower and National Security*, eds. Franklin D. Kramer, Stuart H. Starr, and Larry K. Wentz, 43–88 (Dulles, VA: Potomac Books, 2009).

51. See Rattray's use of faulty strategic analogies, especially his chapters "Development of Strategic Airpower, 1919–1945: Challenges, Execution, and Lessons" (235–308) and "The United States and Strategic Information Warfare, 1991–1999: Confronting the Emergence of Another Form of Warfare" (309–459).

52. But Starr at least provides a starting point, and for that we are in his debt.

53. For land power, see, among others, Baron Antoine Henri de Jomini, *The Art of War* (London: Greenhill Books, 1996; first published in 1838), and Moltke, *Moltke on the Art of War*. For sea power, see A. T. Mahan, *The Influence of Sea Power upon History, 1660–1783* (Boston: Little, Brown, 1918; first published 1890), and Julian S. Corbett, *Some Principles of Maritime Strategy*, with an introduction and notes by Eric J. Grove (Annapolis, MD: Naval Institute Press, 1988; first published 1911). For air power, see, among others, Giulio Douhet, *The Command of the Air*, trans. Dino Ferrari (Washington, DC: Office of Air Force History, 1983; first English publication 1942); and William Mitchell, *Winged Defense: The Development of and Possibilities of*

224 · Toward a Theory of Cyber Power

Modern Air Power—Economic and Military (Port Washington, NY: Kennikat Press, 1971; first published 1925). For space power, see Everett C. Dolman, *Astropolitik: Classical Geopolitics in the Space Age* (London: Frank Cass, 2002); and John J. Klein, *Space Warfare: Strategy, Principles and Policy* (Abingdon, UK: Routledge, 2006).

54. Harold R. Winton, "On the Nature of Military Theory," unpublished manuscript (Maxwell AFB, AL: School of Advanced Air and Space Studies, 2006), 1.

55. J. C. Wylie, *Military Strategy: A General Theory of Power Control* (Annapolis, MD: Naval Institute Press, 1989; first published in 1967), 31.

56. Winton, "On the Nature of Military Theory," 2–3.

57. Kuehl, "From Cyberspace to Cyberpower," 26–27.

58. Winton, "On the Nature of Military Theory," 3.

59. Ibid. 4.

60. Ibid.

61. Ibid., 4–5.

62. Ibid., 5.

63. On Tukhachevskii and his milieu, see Condoleezza Rice, "The Making of Soviet Strategy," in *Makers of Modern Strategy: From Machiavelli to the Nuclear Age*, ed. Peter Paret, 651–76 (Oxford: Oxford University Press, 1986); on the evolution of this style of warfare to the Soviet-era Military Technical Revolution and to what became known as the Revolution in Military Affairs in the United States, see Dima Adamsky, *The Culture of Military Innovation: The Impact of Cultural Factors on the Revolution in Military Affairs in Russia, the US, and Israel* (Stanford, CA: Stanford Security Studies, 2010), esp. 24–92.

64. See Adamsky, *Culture of Military Innovation*, 72.

65. See Clausewitz, *On War*, 141.

CHAPTER 14

Conclusion

Derek S. Reveron

IN JUST A FEW SHORT YEARS, inexpensive computing and easy network access have broadened the scope of national security actors from states to groups and individuals. To appreciate the challenges associated with the new security landscape, this book has addressed various operational considerations associated with "weaponizing" the basic technology available in cyberspace. Further, the chapters place cyberspace in an international security context and have sought to understand national security and cyberspace, which is characterized by three components: the physical (servers, networks, and other hardware), the information (messages that can be coercive and noncoercive), and the cognitive (how audiences perceive the messages). When it comes to national security, the US government emphasizes protecting the physical (from attack), the information (from manipulation), and the cognitive (through information assurance). But by treating each component separately, national security fails to take advantage of the three components of cyberspace that are becoming a viable dimension with national security considerations. The chapters in this book represent an attempt to bring these components together to understand if we are moving from an era characterized by cybersecurity to one characterized by cyberwar and, if so, how this move is taking place. Government policy, military preparation, and international relations explain this movement.

At the onset, we must be reminded that science fiction underlies thinking about cyberspace, but operating in cyberspace is governed by physics and engineering. Unlike the other operating domains such as the seas or airspace, cyberspace was invented and lacks sovereign boundaries. For Patrick Jagoda, "one of the reasons that technological science fiction can appear futuristic has to do with a lack of knowledge, among the majority of computer users, about the machines and the networks on which they depend. This lack of digital literacy—the ability to read, write, and understand computer processes—represents a greater threat to cybersecurity than any single computer virus." We must appreciate that behavior in cyberspace is the best defense against cyber attacks. In chapter 2, Patrick Jagoda explores the ways that contemporary technologically charged literary works confront the psychology of hackers, the technical distribution of computer viruses, and the social effects of cyber attacks. Through fiction, national security actors can creatively explore the nature of decentralized network antagonisms and the future of cyberwarfare.

To give pause to our imaginations, Herb Lin in chapter 3 outlines the concept and technical limits to cyber attacks, which are directed against computers or networks. He notes that the range of possible direct targets for a cyber attack is quite broad. Attackers can target computer chips embedded in other devices, such as weapons systems, communications devices, generators, medical equipment, automobiles, elevators, and other devices and equipment with microprocessors. In general, these microprocessors provide some kind of real-time capability (e.g., a supervisory control and data acquisition system to control the operation of a generator or a floodgate, a chip in an automobile will control the flow of fuel, a chip in an automatic teller machine will control how cash is dispensed). Another target can be the computing systems controlling elements of the nation's critical infrastructure. A key dimension of a cyber attack is understanding the objective and where cyber attack fits in a larger campaign. It is unlikely that cyber attacks would take place outside of some greater context of state rivalry or espionage.

Steve Bucci highlights that not all people and governments in cyberspace are equally vulnerable, and groups with clear objectives are likely to employ cyber capabilities. He points out in chapter 4 that the majority of these cyber threats are aimed at the Western democracies or those countries linked to the global economy. To make sense of these threats, the chapter categorizes threats in cyberspace by offering a typology to consider both the most dangerous threat and the most likely threat. The analysis suggests that terrorism enabled by cybercriminals is the most likely major cyber threat. To fully understand the national security implications of this, the chapter traces the convergence of cybercriminals and terrorists, posits a strategy to contain the threats, and considers the necessary changes to protect US national security. For Bucci, it is simply a matter of time before groups with the technical know-how unite with groups with malicious intent to conduct cyber attacks for political purposes.

As policymakers grasp the implications of threats and actors in cyberspace, law must keep up. The evolution of weapons and war over centuries has produced international legal rules that attempt to govern when states use force in their international relations, what weapons can be developed and used in armed conflict, how combatants engage in conflict on the battlefield, and when individuals can be held accountable criminally for violating these rules. In chapter 5, David Fidler analyzes the implications of cyber conflict for the law of armed conflict and identified four problems that affect each set of rules—the problems of application, attribution, assessment, and accountability. These problems make the increasing likelihood of different kinds of cyber conflicts worrying from the perspective of implementing the law of armed conflict. When nonstate actors are included in the panoply of cyber actors, law is even more constrained to guide or regulate behavior. Determining how to balance cyber conflict with law requires examining previous challenges to these rules, including controversies surrounding domestic armed conflict, the war on terrorism, and the development and use of nonlethal weapons. This examination suggests that the legal aspects of cyberspace and national security will remain confused and increasingly controversial while states probe the tactical and strategic possibilities of different types of cyber conflicts. As nonstate actors fall outside international legal regimes, the challenges are even greater for governments to protect cyberspace for all users.

In recent years it has become increasingly apparent that critical infrastructure in the United States is highly vulnerable to cyber attack because of reliance on supervisory control and data acquisition (SCADA) control systems. Attacks on SCADA and other critical infrastructure are serious, but attacks have been too small to negatively impact critical infrastructure such as the power grid. The 2010 Stuxnet worm has changed this perception. Analysis of the worm suggests that a substantial resource base is required to effectively attack critical infrastructure, which enables deterrence as a defensive strategy among states. Unfortunately, as Richard Andres writes in chapter 6, several states are experimenting with well-resourced cyber militias. This support to militias represents a new dynamic that has the potential to significantly enhance states' willingness to attack each other and undermine deterrence. Further, the use of cyber militias poses a serious threat of uncontrolled escalation as semi-independent militias can act outside of state control.

With this in mind, it is important to recognize that cyber capabilities provide both powerful tools and weapons, but also represent sources of great potential vulnerability. As part of an overall strategy to protect the cyber environment, applying the lessons and tools of deterrence to the cyber domain merits attention as one component of a comprehensive security strategy. In chapter 7 Jeff Cooper notes that to deter the broad range of cyber threats requires moving beyond the common proposition that deterrence rests solely upon the threat of punitive retaliation. Not only is that proposition incorrect, but it too tightly binds deterrence to solving the twin problems of attribution and identity—both of which are very difficult in cyberspace. Through intolerance, deterrence is strengthened by implementing norms against unacceptable behaviors and creates a more mindful attitude towards using cyber systems. Through security cooperation, deterrence is enhanced by fostering collective action, which is necessary to protect cyber capabilities needed by individuals, groups, and societies. There may be a time when the international community establishes an international center to monitor and combat cyber threats, and to coordinate actions to protect computer systems and disrupt nonstate actors that operate in cyberspace. States would surrender some sovereignty to do this, but it may be reflective of the nonsovereign Internet.

As concerns about cyberspace have moved to the mainstream of national security thinking, long-time cyber thinkers such as Chris Demchak believe national strategy should emphasize resilience. This would account for unexpected outcomes across the deeply interconnected and complex critical systems of a modern society. She argues in chapter 8, "In a complex social system under threat, national-level agencies will have to engage in coordinating and guiding redundancy, slack, and continuous trial-and-error learning across critical internal national systems as much as identifying specific hostile foreign actors and attacking or negotiating with them across national borders."

Testing this idea in chapter 9, Brendan Valeriano and Ryan Maness affirm that society has moved to the point that technology has become a necessary aspect of daily life. Unfortunately, when goods and activities are critical to societal interactions, they become predatory targets too. Their chapter examines the concept of rivalry and repeated disputes through the lens of technology. Since most wars occur under a situation of long-standing, mutual animosity or rivalry, it is important to understand how these occur in cyberspace. To understand how rivalries evolve in the current era, it is important to investigate if cyberwarfare increases tensions in an enemy dyad. Valeriano and Maness ask, what are the consequences of technological attacks on infrastructure during international tensions? As a weapon, can cyber attacks increase hostility in a rivalry? All these questions are important policy concerns that must be addressed as rivalry and international competition shifts from the conventional battlefield to the technological one.

Cyberspace is global, but it is governed by national regulations and policies. While the United States has significant influence in cyberspace, it is not alone. As explored by James Joyner in chapter 10, cybersecurity and cyberwar are now coming into focus among the United States' European allies. While the US military is increasingly involved in cyberspace, Europeans rely on their ministries of trade and justice for protecting cyber infrastructure. The difference in perspective is complicating European–American cyber cooperation. The chapter offers a European perspective on cyber issues and illustrates the challenges of international cooperation to improve international security in cyberspace.

To meet these new cyber challenges, Nikolas K. Gvosdev discusses in chapter 11 how the Russian government is moving to take greater control of the tools of the digital age—by increasing the state's ability to supervise what happens throughout the broadband spectrum and to direct more of Russia's own computer and Internet usage into corporate channels owned outright by the state or by friendly business partners. It seeks to secure the Kremlin's interests by trying to isolate a specifically Russian subset of the Internet. To enable this, the Russian government has reached out to its prodigious hacker community to enlist a new generation of nationally minded "hacktivists" to provide the Kremlin with cyberwar capabilities—which have been demonstrated in recent years in sophisticated cyber attacks against Estonia (2007) and Georgia (2008). In the end the Russian approach is a calculated gamble: that its patriotic "computer class" will continue to spearhead new cyber campaigns abroad while helping to defend the digital Motherland at home—because a cash-strapped Russian government is in no position to compete with much better-funded US, European, and Chinese efforts in this area.

In addition to Russia garnering US attention, Nigel Inkster in chapter 12 examines how China's cyber capabilities are a source of anxiety for US national security. The overall impression today is that China, which now has over 500 million Internet users, has become a cyber superpower and increasingly incorporates cyber capabilities into its defense establishment. In response, governments and corporations have dealt with China's cyber activities by sanction, exposure, or counterattack, lending credence to fears of cyberwar. But while it is highly probable that the Chinese state is exploiting vulnerabilities in the cyber domain both to collect with minimal risk valuable scientific, technological, and commercial intelligence and to explore weaknesses in military and critical infrastructure systems, this is not a one-way street. Beijing too has considerable anxieties and vulnerabilities with regard to the Internet. Inkster explores the extent to which China exploits cyberspace, yet also shows that China is increasingly vulnerable to exploitation itself. Shared vulnerability with the United States might engender cooperation as it has with counterterrorism.

In an effort to bridge the theory and praxis of cyber power, John Sheldon argues in chapter 13 that governments will increasingly advance and defend their interests in cyberspace through cyber power. Sheldon defines cyber power as the total sum of strategic effect generated from cyberspace and impacts events on land, sea, air, space, and in cyberspace. Yet our understanding of both cyberspace and cyber power is impeded by a lack of understanding of the domain, rapid technological innovation and dissemination, and the wide range of actors in cyberspace. Policymakers and strategists lack a good understanding of the meta issues pertinent to cyberspace and cyber power and have no guide such as Alfred Thayer Mahan's *The Influence of Sea Power upon History* or Giulio Douhet's *The Command of the Air*. Toward that end this book and Sheldon's chapter advance a theory of cyber power that can aid policymakers and strategists to establish the first principles of cyberwar.

Fundamentally, cyber issues are now national security issues. While some want the Internet to remain as a commercial and social space, government now treats it as a sovereign space essential to national security and prosperity. This shift from information security to national security occurred over the last two decades as cyberspace emerged as an operating domain for militaries and as society became increasingly dependent on the microprocessor during daily life. As national security professionals catch up with the information technology industry to understand Internet architecture and challenges, this book considers several key questions. First, what is the nature of threats in cyberspace? As many contributors note, criminal organizations primarily inhabit the "dark side" of the Internet where nefarious activity is primarily motivated by profit through fraud, blackmail, or theft. While criminals dominate, the variety and number of malicious actors are increasing. These include intelligence agencies, which are shifting their activities to cyberspace as a means of penetrating a government network that is less risky than traditional espionage that relies on running human sources. Finally, militaries around the world are embracing cyberspace as a new operating domain and building cyber forces on par with air, sea, and land forces. These forces are most developed in the United States but China, Russia, Israel, and India are developing cyber capabilities to supplement traditional capabilities.

With the challenges in cyberspace largely known or at least discoverable, a second key question is, how are governments responding to challenges in cyberspace? Although cyber is largely dominated by information technology companies, when governments placed cyber on national security agendas, this set organizational change in motion within national security establishments. As several authors note, the US military created a cyber command, China deployed cyber units within its military, and other governments are experimenting with cyber militias. While these efforts are ongoing, not everyone agrees this is good or a logical path for governments to pursue. For example, Bruce Schneier sees the country going down a dangerous path since, "Cybersecurity isn't a military problem, or even a government problem—it's a universal problem."[1] This might become one area subject to militarization that should be preserved as a civilian space.

Finally, if cyber capabilities are developed as an offensive tool of warfare, what is the relationship between cyber capabilities and conventional capabilities? The question is not easily answerable since cyber capabilities are fundamentally different from traditional tools of warfare. While cyber attacks can destroy data and potentially destroy physical infrastructure by attacking SCADA systems, it is unlikely that cyber can exist as a sole source of coercion or can live up to classic definitions of war that encapsulate violence. Rather, cyber capabilities might be viewed as an extension of intelligence capabilities, but it will likely be at least a decade before doctrine and organizations settle.

Just because we can imagine cyberwar does not mean that it can be waged. The aim of cyber threats differs substantially from physical warfare; data loss is not the same as human loss. Defacing a website is not the functional equivalent of bombing a country's capital. Further, the potential for "blowback" is significant where a worm attack against an adversary propagates and infects friendly systems. To appreciate this, new work is required to operationalize cyber strategies. Today, much is borrowed from the nuclear deterrence literature to frame how cyber capabilities would be used; however, the potential for blowback points to the biological warfare literature. Just as bioweapons were too dangerous to use, cyber may follow suit. Near universality of the Windows operating system and the personal computer make preventing fratricidal cyber attacks a key planning consideration.

While these three questions underlie this book, the last two should guide future research. Given the infancy of the literature and unformed policies, continued cyber studies over the next decade will be essential. Unlike nuclear studies at the start of the Cold War, cyber studies will be more democratic, with the potential of the best ideas coming from outside of academia and the defense base. Cyber studies have a unique ability to bring together writers, gamers, engineers, academics, and national security professionals. This book is one contribution to this effort.

Note

1. Bruce Schneier, "Who Should Be in Charge of Cybersecurity?," *Wall Street Journal*, March 31, 2009.

CONTRIBUTORS

Richard Andres is a professor of national security strategy at the US National War College (NWC) and senior fellow at the Institute for National Strategic Studies. Andres's current work focuses on cyber conflict. Prior to joining NWC, Andres served in various positions in and out of government, including personal advisor to the secretary of the air force and special advisor to the commander of Air University. He has also served as a strategy consultant for the chief of staff of the air force, commandant of the marine corps, vice chairman of the Joint Chiefs of Staff, Office of the Secretary of Defense, the Office of Force Transformation, US Strategic Command, US Central Command, the Nuclear Posture Review, the Council on Foreign Relations, several large corporations, and various congressional offices. Andres has led groups writing security strategy documents for the White House, Office of the Secretary of Defense, and Combatant Commands. His publications appear in numerous military and academic journals. Andres was awarded the medal for Meritorious Civilian Service and has received numerous academic awards and fellowships. His PhD is from the University of California, Davis.

Steven P. Bucci is the senior fellow at the Heritage Foundation for all issues involving homeland security and defense. Bucci has more than thirty years of leadership experience and has held key leadership positions in the 82nd Airborne, the 5th and the 7th Special Forces. Bucci served as the deputy assistant secretary of defense, homeland defense, and defense support for civil authorities, overseeing policy issues involving the defense domains (air, land, and maritime), National Guard domestic operational issues, domestic counterterrorism, and Department of Defense responses to natural and man-made disasters, acting as the primary civilian oversight of US Northern Command. Bucci also helped lead the Department of Defense response to the growing cyber security threats facing the United States. He has published numerous articles on cyber security issues and is a regular cyber contributor to *Security Debrief*, a leading national security blog. He speaks at cyber-related conferences and is widely sought for his insights into cyber issues. He is an adjunct professor at George Mason University.

Jeffrey R. Cooper, technical fellow, is a Science Applications International Corporation (SAIC) vice president for technology and chief innovation officer for a major SAIC business unit. He received his undergraduate and graduate education at Johns

Hopkins University. In addition to a long-standing focus on strategic analysis and military transformation, his core interest is in using information to improve intelligence analysis, decision making, command and control, and operational effectiveness in order to enhance US national security. Cooper is a founding member of the Highlands Forum, an Office of the Secretary of Defense–sponsored program to identify cutting-edge technological developments that affect national security. He has served in several senior government positions, including White House staff and assistant to the secretary of energy. Cooper's recent work emphasizes cyber issues—cyber deterrence in particular—building on his vast experience with nuclear deterrence and strategic planning. In addition, for the past several years, his focus has been largely on intelligence matters, with particular emphasis on analytic failures and methods to improve all-source analysis capabilities. Cooper's research interests also include the implications of complex systems and complexity on analysis and decision making. He was a professional staff member of the Presidential Commission on Future Intelligence Capabilities (the Silberman-Robb Commission), chaired senior panels for the director of national intelligence's Quadrennial Intelligence Community Review, and has been actively involved in work on the revolution in intelligence affairs and intelligence transformation.

Chris Demchak has a PhD in political science from Berkeley with a focus on organization theory, security, and surprise in complex technical systems across nations, and also holds an MPA economic development (Princeton) and an MA in energy engineering (Berkeley). She has published numerous articles on societal security difficulties with large-scale information systems, security institutions, and new resilient organization models. Demchak has taught undergraduate- and graduate-level courses on comparative security and modernized organizations, the institutional history of war and the state, the emerging global information systems, and the worldwide diffusion of defense technologies to include the use of game-based simulations in security analysis. She has completed a co-edited book, *Designing Resilience* (with L. Comfort and A. Boin), and a forthcoming book, *Wars of Disruption and Resilience: Cybered Conflict, Power, and National Security*. At the Strategic Research Department of the US Naval War College, Demchak's research focus is the evolution in organizations, tools, social integrations, and range of choices emerging in westernized nations' cybersecurity/deterrence strategies, creations, or adaptations of institutions, and institutionalized organizational learning after experiences with cybered confrontations or attacks. Her current research project is an analysis of the establishment of national cyber commands as natural experiments in how three nations (the United States, the United Kingdom, and Germany) institutionally interpret and respond to the complexities of surprises from global cyberspace.

David P. Fidler is the James Louis Calamaras Professor of Law at the Indiana University Maurer School of Law where he teaches, among other things, cybersecurity law and policy: crime, terrorism, espionage, and war in cyberspace. Fidler is a fellow at the Indiana University Center for Applied Cybersecurity Research. He has also worked extensively on international legal issues relating to weapons of mass destruction (*Biosecurity in the Global Age: Biological Weapons, Public Health, and the Rule of Law*, Stanford University Press, 2008, with Lawrence O. Gostin). Fidler has also published widely on the international legal and policy issues created by the development of "nonlethal" weapons ("The Meaning of Moscow: 'Non-Lethal' Weapons and International Law in the Early 21st Century," *International Review of the Red Cross* 87, no. 859 [2005]: 525–52). In addition, Fidler has focused significant attention on the challenges of counterinsurgency (co-editor of the volume *India and Counterinsurgency: Lessons Learned*, Routledge, 2009, with Sumit Ganguly). His work on counterinsurgency has included participating in training undertaken by the Foreign Service Institute for civilian personnel being deployed to Afghanistan.

Nikolas K. Gvosdev is a professor of national security studies at the US Naval War College. He was the editor of *The National Interest* magazine and a senior fellow of Strategic Studies at The Nixon Center in Washington, DC. He is currently a senior editor at *The National Interest*. Gvosdev is a frequent commentator on US foreign policy and international relations, Russian and Eurasian affairs, developments in the Middle East, and the role of religion in politics. He received his doctorate from St. Antony's College, Oxford University, where he studied on a Rhodes Scholarship. He was also associate director of the J. M. Dawson Institute of Church-State Studies at Baylor University. Gvosdev is the author or editor of a number of books, including the coauthor of *The Receding Shadow of the Prophet: The Rise and Fall of Political Islam* (Praeger, 2004).

Nigel Inkster is the director of transnational threats and political risk at the London-based International Institute for Security Studies (IISS). He is responsible for the analysis of international political risk and development of programs on counterterrorism, international crime, proliferation of chemical, biological, radiological, and nuclear materials, cross-border conflict, and other transnational or global issues. Inkster is also responsible for the IISS Armed Conflict Database. Prior to joining IISS, he served in the British Secret Intelligence Service from 1975 to 2006. He was posted in Asia, Latin America, and Europe, and worked extensively on transnational issues. He is a Chinese speaker and graduated in Oriental Studies from St. John's College Oxford.

Patrick Jagoda is an assistant professor of English at the University of Chicago. He is also a coeditor of *Critical Inquiry*. He specializes in new media studies, twentieth-century American literature, and digital game theory and design. Jagoda's scholarship examines how contemporary American fiction, film, television, and digital media aestheticize global networks (including terrorist networks, economic systems, and computer webs). His publications appear in such journals as *Critical Inquiry, Social Text, Post45,* and *Neo-Victorian Studies*. Jagoda has also worked on projects that contribute to new media learning, digital storytelling, and transmedia game design. He is involved in the ongoing Game Changer Chicago initiative, a project that uses

234 · Contributors

digital storytelling and transmedia game production to promote participatory and systems-oriented forms of health learning aimed at adolescents. Jagoda received his PhD in English from Duke University and was a Mellon postdoctoral fellow at the University of Chicago.

James Joyner is the managing editor of the Atlantic Council since 2007. He has written the popular public policy weblog *Outside the Beltway*, which was named 2006 Blog of the Year by The George Washington University's Institute for Politics, Democracy, and the Internet. His previous work includes serving as managing editor of *Strategic Insights*, the professional journal of the Center for Contemporary Conflict at the Naval Postgraduate School; contract consulting to the Defense Information Systems Agency; acquisitions editor for international affairs at Brassey's (now Potomac Books); and political science professor at Troy University (Alabama), Bainbridge College (Georgia), and the University of Tennessee at Chattanooga. Joyner served in the US Army from 1988 to 1992 and is a combat veteran of Operation Desert Storm. He holds a PhD in national security affairs from the University of Alabama and BA and MA degrees in political science from Jacksonville State University.

Herbert Lin is chief scientist at the Computer Science and Telecommunications Board, National Research Council (NRC) of the National Academies, where he has been study director of major projects on public policy and information technology. These studies include a 1996 study on national cryptography policy ("Cryptography's Role in Securing the Information Society"), a 1991 study on the future of computer science ("Computing the Future"), a 1999 study of Defense Department systems for command, control, communications, computing, and intelligence ("Realizing the Potential of C4I: Fundamental Challenges"), a 2000 study on workforce issues in high technology ("Building a Workforce for the Information Economy"), a 2002 study on protecting kids from Internet pornography and sexual exploitation ("Youth, Pornography, and the Internet"), a 2004 study on aspects of the FBI's information technology modernization program ("A Review of the FBI's Trilogy IT Modernization Program"), a 2005 study on electronic voting ("Asking the Right Questions about Electronic Voting"), a 2005 study on computational biology ("Catalyzing Inquiry at the Interface of Computing and Biology"), a 2007 study on privacy and information technology ("Engaging Privacy and Information Technology in a Digital Age"), a 2007 study on cybersecurity research ("Toward a Safer and More Secure Cyberspace"), a 2009 study on health care informatics ("Computational Technology for Effective Health Care: Immediate Steps and Strategic Directions"), and a 2009 study on offensive information warfare ("Technology, Policy, Law, and Ethics Regarding US Acquisition and Use of Cyberattack Capabilities"). Prior to his NRC service, he was a professional staff member and staff scientist for the House Armed Services Committee (1986–90), where his portfolio included defense policy and arms control issues. He received his doctorate in physics from MIT.

Ryan Maness is continuing his graduate studies in international relations. Ongoing research includes cyberwar, post-Soviet space relations and interests, Russian domestic politics and its relation to foreign policy, American foreign policy, conflict–cooperation dynamics between states using events data, and regional security and energy politics. His dissertation focuses on conflict–cooperation dynamics between the United States and its enduring rivals using events data since the end of the Cold War. He earned his BA at the University of Illinois at Urbana-Champaign, and is a PhD candidate at the University of Illinois at Chicago.

Derek S. Reveron is a professor of national security affairs and the EMC Informationist Chair at the US Naval War College in Newport, Rhode Island. He specializes in strategy development, nonstate security challenges, intelligence, and US defense policy. He has authored or edited seven books. The latest are *Exporting Security: International Engagement, Security Cooperation, and the Changing Face of the US Military* (Georgetown University Press, 2010) and *Human Security in a Borderless World* (Westview Press, 2011). Reveron serves as an editorial board member of the *Naval War College Review*, and is a contributing editor to the *New Atlanticist*, the blog for the Atlantic Council of the United States. Before joining the Naval War College faculty, Reveron taught political science at the US Naval Academy. He received a diploma from the Naval War College, and an MA in political science and a PhD in public policy analysis from the University of Illinois at Chicago.

John B. Sheldon is professor for space and cyberspace strategy at the School of Advanced Air and Space Studies (SAASS) and interim director, National Space Studies Center, Maxwell AFB, Alabama. At SAASS he directs and teaches the Information, Intelligence, and Cyberpower course, and also teaches the Space and National Security course. Prior to his appointment in August 2006 at SAASS, Sheldon was director of the space security program at the UK-based Centre for Defence and International Security Studies, and was a founding coeditor of the space policy journal *Astropolitics*. Prior to his academic career, Sheldon served in the British Diplomatic Corps. He holds a BA (Hons.) in politics and international relations; an MA in security studies from the University of Hull, UK; and a PhD in political science and strategic studies from the University of Reading, UK.

Brandon Valeriano is an assistant professor of political science at University of Illinois at Chicago. He has previously taught at Vanderbilt and Texas State University. Valeriano's main research interests include investigations of the causes of conflict and peace as well as the study of race/ethnicity from an international perspective. Ongoing research explores interstate rivalry, classification systems of war, complexity in international politics, territorial disputes, the impact of migration patterns on conflict, and Latino foreign policy issues. Valeriano has been published in the *Journal of Politics, International Studies Quarterly, Policy Studies Journal,* and *International Interactions.*

INDEX

accountability: and international criminal law, 82; in law of armed conflict, 72, 81–83
act of aggression, defined, 82
Advanced Research Projects Agency (ARPA), 7
Afghanistan, US invasion (2001), 76
agency coordination, 50
Agreement on Government Procurement (WTO), 200
Ahmadinejad, Mahmoud, 150
Ahn, Luis von, 34–35n41
Air Force (US), 15, 19n35, 56n21, 163–64
Air Force Cyberspace Command (8th Air Force, US), 164
Air Force Doctrine Document 2-5, 56n21
Alexander, Keith, 4, 164
al-Qaeda, 62
Amazon, 8
ambiguity zone in law of armed conflict, 75
America's Army (computer game), 32
"Anda's Game" (Doctorow), 30
Andres, Richard B., 16, 89, 227
antiregulation approach, 31
AOL, 23
Apple II microcomputer, 23
application layer, 24
application problem in law of armed conflict, 71, 74–76
armed conflict, defined, 74–75. *See also* law of armed conflict (LOAC)
arms control approach, 75
ARPA (Advanced Research Projects Agency), 7
Arquilla, John, 13
The Art of War (Sun Tzu), 33n7
Ashiyane Security Group, 146
Assange, Julian, 216
assessment problem in law of armed conflict, 72, 78–80
AT&T, 23
attribution problem: and cyber power, 213–14; and deterrence, 106, 114; diffi-

culty of, 10; in law of armed conflict, 71–72, 76–78
"Aurora," 96
authenticity, loss of, 39, 44
automated target selection, 43
autopoiesis, 124
availability, loss of, 39, 42, 44
Azar, Edward, 144

bad actors, 28
barriers to entry, 126, 212–13
Battlestar Galactica (television series), 25
behavioral mitigation, 78
Belik, Pavel D., 179
Berners-Lee, Tim, 8
Blair, Dennis, 89
blowback, 47, 230
Borg, Scott, 188n60
botnets, 7, 65, 98, 165
Brazil, power grid infiltration in, 99
Brenner, Joel, 99
Britain. *See* United Kingdom (UK)
broad-spectrum attacks, 44
"broken windows" phenomenon, 119n7
Bucci, Steven, 16, 57, 226
Bucharest Summit (2008, NATO), 161
"Buckshot Yankee," 96–97, 162
Bumgarner, John, 188n60
Bush, George W., 5

Cadigan, Pat, 26, 34n31
Canada, cyber attacks against, 96
Carr, Jeffrey, 187n40
cascading effects, 46–47
CASS (Chinese Academy of Social Sciences), 192
causal chains, 49
CDMA (Cyber Defence Management Authority), 167–68
Center for Strategic and International Studies, 9

237

Central Intelligence Agency (CIA), 100, 186n22
chaos, value of, 144
Chechen War (1994–96), 176
China, 191–205; challenges to Western dominance of cyberspace, 198–200; cyber attacks by, 13, 74, 77, 96, 200–202; cyber capabilities of, 15, 145–46, 147, 202–3; and cybercrime, 98, 145; cyber militias in, 98; and cyberwar treaties, 153; Internet censorship in, 193–98; Internet trends in, 191–93
China Next Generation Internet (CNGI), 200
Chinese Academy of Social Sciences (CASS), 192
Chongqing Evening News on Google's departure from China, 196–97
CIA (Central Intelligence Agency), 100, 186n22
Clark, Wesley, 9, 15
Clarke, Richard A., 147
Clausewitzian understanding of purposes of conflict, 107, 176, 208
Clinton, Bill, 8, 193
"clockwork universe" model, 107, 108
close-access cyber exploitation, 52
cloud computing, 43, 67
CNGI (China Next Generation Internet), 200
Coates, Peter, 163
cognitive psychology, 119n12
Cold War, 60, 106, 131
collective action, 116, 118
collective security, 82
command and control systems, 22, 41, 53, 175, 217
The Command of the Air (Douhet), 229
commons, 107
communication networks, 22, 62, 66, 212
community networks, 109, 110
competition, deterrence role of, 110
CompuServe, 23
computer gaming, 31–32
Conficker worm, 24, 54n3
confidentiality of information, loss of, 39, 44, 51, 64
conflict, deterrence role of, 110
constraints on cyber attacks, 153
containment, 106
content layer, 24
Cooper, Jeffrey R., 16, 105, 227
cooperation and coordination: on cyber attacks, 50–51; on cybercrime, 165; on

cyber defense, 167–68; in decision making, 119n15; deterrence role of, 110, 118
Cooperative Cyber Defense Center of Excellence in Tallinn (NATO), 161, 168, 169
corporate espionage, 59, 64, 98
corporatism, 34n31
Council Guidelines for Cooperation on Cyber Defence with Partners and International Organisations (NATO), 168
counterproductivity (deterrence element), 113, 114, 115, 116
Crichton, Michael, 25
crime, LOAC definition of, 74–75. *See also* cybercrime
cryptography, 31, 63
cyber, defined, 21–22
cyber attacks: from China, 200–202; classification of, 10–11; complexity of, 48–49; coordination with other entities, 50–51; direct effects of, 37–40; effects prediction and damage assessment, 45–48; indirect effects of, 40–41; intelligence requirements for, 44–45, 48–49; and *jus ad bellum*, 79–80; and *jus in bello*, 80; by nation-states, 61–63; on NATO states, 160–63, 167–69; objectives for, 41–42; operational considerations in, 37–51; planning construct for, 60–61; preparation process for, 44–45; target identification for, 42–43; uncertainty in, 48–49
Cyber Consequences Unit report (US), 188n60
cybercrime: actors responsible for, 11–12; cyberterrorism linking with, 57–68; European police cooperation on, 165; incentives for, 91, 94; as medium-level threat, 59; and national security resilience strategies, 132; planning construct for, 60–61
Cyber Defence Management Authority (CDMA), 167–68
cyber defense: and antiregulation problem, 93–94; and attribution problem, 92–93; and code of silence problem, 93; and cyber militias, 98–100; dynamics of, 90–91; existing mechanism for, 91–92; and geography problem, 93; history of, 95–96; and offensive incentive problem, 94–95; and social norms problem, 95; and spy vs. treaty problem, 94; and state-on-state cyber attacks, 96–97
cyber deterrence, 105–20; and antiregulation problem, 93–94; and attribution problem,

92–93; and code of silence problem, 93; cooperation, competition, and conflict in, 110; and cyber militias, 98–100; dynamics of, 90–91; existing mechanism for, 91–92; financial services approach to, 112–18; framework for, 110–16; and geography problem, 93; history of, 95–96; intellectual foundations for, 106–7; networked deterrence concept for, 110–12; and offensive incentive problem, 94–95; and social norms problem, 95; and spy vs. treaty problem, 94; and state-on-state cyber attacks, 96–97

cybered conflict, 121–28; cyberwar distinguished from, 125; international relations impact of, 140–42, 143–44

cyber exploitation: approaches for, 52–53; by China, 200–202; intelligence requirements for, 56n21; operational considerations in, 51–52, 53

cyber gothic, 27

"Cyber Jihad," 150

cyber militias, 98–100, 101, 103n20, 130

cybernetics, 21–22

cyber power, 207–24; and cyberspace's characteristics, 211–15; defined, 128–29; indirect nature of, 214–15; and national security resilience strategies, 128–32; stealthy nature of, 215; strategic environment manipulation via, 215–18; and strategy, 208–10; theory of, 218–20

cyberpunk, 26, 34n17

cybersecurity: international differences in, 159–72; for NATO states, 160–63, 167–69; US vs. European visions of, 163–67. See also national security

cyberspace: cost of entry for, 126, 212–13; and cyber power, 211–15; defined, 5, 220–21n4; and electromagnetic spectrum, 211–12; and information infrastructure, 6; layers of, 24, 213–14; man-made objects required for, 212; and national security, 6–10; replication of, 212; threats in, 10–13; and war, 13–16. See also other headings starting with "cyber"

Cyberspace and National Security (Kramer, Starr, & Wentz, eds.), 218

cyberterrorism: cybercrime linking with, 57–68; and LOAC, 76; as medium-level threat, 59; planning construct for, 60–61

cyberwarfare: cybered conflict distinguished from, 125; history of, 89–90; incentives for, 91; Russia's cyberwarfare doctrines, 175–78

Daemon (Suarez), 26–30, 34n31

damage assessment, 45–48

Danchev, Dancho, 161

data alteration, 42

data destruction, 41–42

data-mining technologies, 194

Data Protection Directive (EU), 165

DDOS. See distributed denial-of-service attacks

deception objective, 42

decision frames, 110, 120n22

decision making, 109

deep operations, 219

defense. See cyber defense

Defense Cyber Operations Group (UK), 167

Defense Department (US): on China's cyber attacks against US, 201; command and control focus of, 22; culture on cybersecurity issues, 9; cyber attacks against, 81; cyberspace defined by, 5; hackers recruited by, 145; and international law, 80; strategic initiative for cyberspace operations, 4; and USCYBERCOM, 21, 164

Defense Strategy for Operating in Cyberspace (DSOC, US), 132

De Landa, Manuel, 33n7

Demchak, Chris, 16, 121, 227

Deng Xiaoping, 203

Deng Yujiao, 195

denial-of-service (DOS) attacks, 39, 42, 64, 141, 216

dependencies, 113, 114, 116

deterrence: assumptions for, 108–9; of cybercrime and cyberterrorism, 62; and cyber militias, 100; intellectual foundations of, 106–7; and state-on-state cyber attacks, 97; understanding of, 105–6. See also cyber deterrence

Deutsche Welle on cyber attacks against Estonia, 161

Diehl, Paul, 143, 148

digital literacy, 30

Digital Sky Technologies, 179

direct effects, 37–40

Directive 95/46/EC (EU), 165

director of national intelligence, 15

discrimination principle, 76

disinformation campaigns, 13

distributed denial-of-service (DDOS) attacks, 40, 64, 74, 98, 146, 161, 216

distributed networks, 28, 32
Doctorow, Cory, 26, 30–31
Doctrine of Information Security of the
  Russian Federation (2000), 177, 178
domain name system (DNS), 43
domestic security, 130, 142
Dong Niao, 199
DOS. *See* denial-of-service attacks
Douhet, Giulio, 229
Dozois, Gardner, 25
DSOC (Defense Strategy for Operating in
  Cyberspace, US), 132
dual-purpose military forces, 56*n*21

eBay, 8
economic theory, 107, 110, 119*n*13
Economist on cyberspace as warfare domain,
  163
education, 192, 210
effectiveness assessment, 54
effects prediction, 45–48
8th Air Force (Air Force Cyberspace
  Command, US), 164
863 Programme (China), 203
Eklund, Ken, 32
electromagnetic spectrum (EMS), 211–12
"Electronic Jihad," 150
e-mail, 62, 178
Emerging Security Challenges Division
  (NATO), 168
encryption technologies, 63, 200
Energy Department (US), 54*n*5, 96
ENISA (European Network and Information
  Security Agency), 164–65
ESP Game (computer game), 34*n*41
espionage: accountability problem with, 81;
  by cybercriminals, 64; incentives for, 91;
  and LOAC, 74–75, 84; as medium-level
  threat, 59; and rivalry relations, 139; and
  treaties, 94
Estonia: cyber attacks against, 59, 74, 77, 161,
  173; cyber militias in, 100
Europe: cybersecurity approach of, 159,
  163–67; and cyberwar treaties, 153. *See also*
  specific countries
European Network and Information Security
  Agency (ENISA), 164–65
execution monitoring, 49

Facebook, 5, 7, 8
fate interdependence, 120*n*26
fear as motivating mechanism, 142, 144
Federal Bureau of Investigation (FBI), 64, 142

Federal Security Service (FSB, Russia), 178
Fidler, David P., 16, 71, 226
financial services approach to deterrence,
  112–18
Financial Times on data-mining by Chinese
  government, 194
First Chechen War (1994–96), 176
Fleet Cyber Command (10th Fleet, US), 15,
  19*n*35
fog of war, 78
Framework for Cooperation on Cyber
  Defence between NATO and Partner
  Countries, 168
France: cyber capabilities of, 15; national
  security resilience strategies in, 132, 133
Frazer, Gordon, 165
FSB (Federal Security Service, Russia), 178
fund-raising by terrorist groups, 62–63
futility (deterrence element), 113, 116
Futureland (Mosley), 34*n*31

Gain Probability, 109
Gain Value, 109
Galloway, Alexander, 27
gambling, online, 193
game theory, 110, 119*n*11
gaming, 31–32
Gazprom, 179
generative networks, 23, 24, 28
Georgia: cyber attacks against, 3, 60, 75,
  148–50, 161–62, 173; cyber militias in,
  100
Germany: cyber attacks against, 201; cyber-
  security in, 165–66
Ghostnet, 96, 201
Gibson, William, 5, 24, 26, 27
Goertz, Gary, 143, 148
Goloskokov, Konstantin, 188*n*57
Goncharov, Sergei, 179
Google, 96, 196–97, 201
Google Earth, 7, 63
Gorbachev, Mikhail, 174
Gordievsky, Oleg, 181
gothic aesthetics, 27
Gray, Colin, 17
Great Chicago Fire (1871), 160
Great Fire of London (1666), 159–60
Greece, phone-tapping episode in, 53, 56*n*20
Greylogic, 162
Gulf War (1991), 13, 219
Gusev, Igor, 181, 187*n*51
Gvosdev, Nikolas K., 16–17, 42, 60, 146, 161,
  173, 228

hackers: and cybercrime, 64; as lowest threat level, 58; and networks, 24; private sector employment of, 145; in Russia, 96, 146, 180–82; US recruitment of, 145

hacktivism, 146, 173, 195

Hague, William, 162, 163, 167

Haig, Douglas, 216

Hamas, 146, 150, 152

Hamre, John, 96

Han Han, 203

hardware configurations, 44

Hersh, Seymour, 141, 155

Herzfeld, Charles, 7

He, She, and It (Piercy), 34n31

Hezbollah, 146, 150, 152

Highlands Forum, 120n21

Homeland Security Department (US), 97, 100, 145, 164

"homo socialis" vs. *"homo economicus"* perspective, 110, 119n13

Huang, Andrew, 31, 32

human intelligence, 45, 209

The Human Use of Human Beings (Wiener), 21

IADS (integrated air defense system), 209

IBM (International Business Machines), 23

ICC (International Criminal Court), 82

ICJ. *See* International Court of Justice

ICTY (International Criminal Tribunal for the Former Yugoslavia), 76

Idaho National Laboratories, 54n5

identity theft, 98

impact shifting, 120n28

India: cyber capabilities of, 15; cyber militias in, 98

indirect effects, 40–41, 49

industrial control systems, 4. *See also* supervisory control and data acquisition (SCADA) systems

The Influence of Sea Power upon History (Mahan), 229

information requirements. *See* intelligence

Information Safeguards Base (China), 201

Information Security Doctrine of the Russian Federation (2000), 177, 178

information warfare, 175. *See also* cyberwarfare

Information Warfare Monitor (Canada), 96, 201

infrastructure: cyber attacks against, 97, 141; cyber attacks supported by, 62; and cyber power, 213–14; and deterrence, 92; regula-

tions for, 93; Russian military doctrine on, 175; as strategic national asset, 163

Inkster, Nigel, 17, 145, 191, 228

insurgent groups, 78

integrated air defense system (IADS), 209

integrity, loss of, 39, 44

intellectual property rights, 199, 200

intelligence: and Chinese cyber attacks, 201; for cyber attacks, 44–45, 48–49; and cyber exploitation, 51, 56n21; for kinetic weapon attacks, 55n9; and LOAC, 84; and Stuxnet worm, 123; by terrorist groups, 63; and treaties, 94; on WMDs, 65. *See also* espionage

inter arma silent leges, 72, 83, 84

internal DNS zone tables, 43

International Business Machines (IBM), 23

International Committee of the Red Cross, 83

International Corporation for Domain Names and Numbers, 199

International Court of Justice (ICJ), 73, 76, 77, 83

International Criminal Court (ICC), 82

International Criminal Tribunal for the Former Yugoslavia (ICTY), 76

international law, 72, 73, 80, 82. *See also* law of armed conflict (LOAC)

international relations, 140–42, 153. *See also* rivalry relations

International Strategy for Cyberspace (ISC, US), 3, 133, 164

International Telecommunications Union, 10, 11, 174

Internet: architecture of, 24; censorship of, 193–98; in China, 191–98; creation of, 7; economic impact of, 91; infrastructure, 145, 191; layers of, 24; and national security, 6; networked nature of, 22; in Russia, 174–75; trends in, 5; Western dominance of, 198–200. *See also* cyberspace *and other headings starting with "cyber"*

Internet Protocol (IP), 24, 43, 44

Internet Protocol version 6 (IPv6), 200

Internet service providers (ISPs), 178

Internet Wars (Dong Niao), 199

interstate rivalry. *See* rivalry relations

Iran: cyber capabilities of, 146, 147; cyber militias in, 98; Israel's rivalry with, 150–52; state-on-state cyber attacks against, 97; and Stuxnet worm, 4, 122

ISC. *See* International Strategy for Cyberspace

ISPs (Internet service providers), 178

Israel: cyber attacks against, 66; cyber capabilities of, 15, 146–47; cyber militias in, 98, 146; Iran's rivalry with, 150–52
Israeli-Palestinian peace process, 150

Jagoda, Patrick, 16, 21, 37, 225
Jiang Zemin, 191–92, 197
Johnson, Larry, 5
joint interagency cyber task force, 15
Joyner, James, 16, 159, 228
Jun Bao on Internet dangers in China, 198
jurisdiction problems, 93
jus ad bellum, 72, 79–80
jus in bello, 72, 76, 77, 80

Kazakhstan, cyber militias in, 100
Keohane, Robert O., 120n22
Khan Academy, 8
kinetic weapons: cyber attacks in conjunction with, 42, 60; direct effects of, 37–38; effects prediction and damage assessments for, 45–46
Klein, James P., 148
Klein, Naomi, 29
Knake, Robert K., 15, 147
Korns, Stephen, 213
Korolev, Aleksandr, 177–78
Korten, David C., 29
Kramer, Franklin, 159, 160
Krikunov, Aleksandr, 177–78
Kuehl, Daniel T., 218, 220n4
Kuryanovich, Nikolai, 184
Kyrgyzstan, cyber militias in, 100

Latvia, cyber militias in, 100
law enforcement: communication systems for, 66; and cybercrime, 67, 180–81; deterrence role of, 91, 92
law of armed conflict (LOAC), 71–87; accountability problem for, 72, 81–83; application problem for, 71, 74–76; assessment problem for, 72, 78–80; attribution problem for, 71–72, 76–78; and behavioral mitigation, 78; cyber attacks in armed conflict, 75; cyber conflict's challenges for, 72–74; definitional issues, 74–75; and international criminal law, 82; and legal mitigation, 77; and permissible weapons rules, 78–79; and technological mitigation, 77; threshold for application of, 75–76; zone of ambiguity in, 75
League of Nations, 82
Lebanon, Israel's invasion of (2008), 152

legal analysis of armed conflict. *See* law of armed conflict (LOAC)
legal authority for cyber exploitation, 53, 56n16
Legality of the Threat or Use of Nuclear Weapons case (1996, ICJ), 73
legal mitigation, 77
Levin, Peter, 9, 15
Lewis, James A., 118
Li Gang, 194
Li Qifan, 194
Liang Qiao, 202
Liberation Army Daily on China's cyber capabilities, 202
Libicki, Martin C., 31
Libya: social media use by rebels in, 130; US attack on (1986), 76
Lin, Herbert, 16, 33, 37, 140–41, 212, 226
Lisbon Summit (2010, NATO), 161, 163
Lithuania, cyber militias in, 100
Little Brother (Doctorow), 30–31
Liu Zhengrong, 198
LiveJournal, 179
LOAC. *See* law of armed conflict
Lobban, Iain, 166
Loss Probability, 109
Loss Value, 109
Lovebug worm, 24
Lute, Jane Holl, 15
Lynn, William J., III: and Cooperative Cyber Defence Center of Excellence, 169; on cyber attacks against Defense Department, 96, 162; on cybersecurity evolution, 160; on Defense Department culture on cybersecurity, 9; on information infrastructure, 6; on infrastructure cyber attacks, 97, 141; on low barriers to entry for cyberspace, 11; on shared warning responsibilities, 163

MacKinnon, Rebecca, 196, 197
Mahan, Alfred Thayer, 229
Maizière, Thomas de, 165
Malmström, Cecilia, 165
malware, 64, 97, 141, 145, 152
Maness, Ryan, 16, 139, 228
Manning, Bradley, 216
Markov, Sergei, 188n57
The Matrix movie series, 25, 28
McConnell, Bruce, 15
McConnell, Mike, 99, 207
McGonigal, Jane, 32
Medvedev, Dmitry, 173, 174

metadata, 34n41
microbloggers, 191
Microsoft, 178
Microsoft Windows, 11, 54n3
military: in China, 193, 202; cybersecurity as domain of, 124, 159, 160; dual-purpose forces, 56n21; information technology-based vulnerabilities of, 15, 210; and national security resilience strategies, 132; Russian military doctrine, 175–76; US Air Force, 15, 19n35, 56n21, 163–64; US Navy, 15, 19n35. See also Defense Department (US)
military necessity principle, 77
Milner, Yuri, 179
Ministry of Communication and Press (Russia), 178
Ministry of Defense (Georgia), 3
Ministry of Public Security (China), 193
mixed-motive games, 110, 117
mobile computing, 67
mobile phones, 56n20
Mobile TeleSystems, 179
Moltke, Helmuth von, 216
money laundering, 63
monitoring of cyber attacks, 49
"Moonlight Maze" operation, 96
Morozov, Evgeny, 182
Morris, Robert, 24
Morris worm, 55n13
Mosley, Walter, 34n31
multiple parallel decision frames, 120n22
mutually assured destruction, 60

Nashi (youth movement), 181, 182, 188n57
National Defense Strategy (2005, US), 9
National Defense Strategy (2008, US), 9
Nationale Cyber-Sicherheitsstrategie (Germany), 165
National Intelligence Annual Threat Assessment (2010, US), 139
National Military Strategy (2011, US), 4, 9
national security: and cyberspace, 6–10; resilience strategies, 128–33. See also cyber defense; cyber deterrence; cybersecurity
National Security Agency (NSA), 164
National Security Strategy (UK), 167
nation-states: and attribution problem, 101; coordination of cyber attacks with allied nations, 50–51; cyber attacks by, 59, 61–62; cybercrime supported by, 98–99; and deterrence, 92

NATO. See North Atlantic Treaty Organization
Navy (US), 15, 19n35
netbooks, 67
Netizen community in China, 194, 195, 196
networked deterrence, 110–12
networks: defined, 21, 22–24; destruction of, 42; network effects, 113; safety in, 31–33
network warfare support (NS) operations, 56n21
Neuromancer (Gibson), 24, 27
New Media Consortium, 5
Newsweek on Russian hackers, 96
Newton's "clockwork universe" model, 107, 108
New York Times on Stuxnet worm, 155
New Zealand, cyber attacks against, 201
Nicaragua v. United States (1986, ICJ), 76, 77
911 systems, 66
no-first-strike policy, 10
noncooperative biometric identification, 120n30
nonlethal weapons, 73, 78, 83
nonproliferation approach, 75
norms: cybered conflict as, 126; and deterrence, 117; in international relations, 153
North Atlantic Treaty Organization (NATO): and Cold War deterrence strategy, 60; coordination and advising on cyber defense, 167–68; cyber attacks against member countries, 59, 160–63; cybersecurity approach of, 159; responses to cyber attacks, 167–69
Novosyolova, Yelena, 175
NSA (National Security Agency), 164
NS (network warfare support) operations, 56n21
nuclear deterrence, 106
Nuclear Facilities Virus, 152
Nye, Joseph, 111

OAF (Operation Allied Force), 98, 103n20
Obama, Barack: on cybercrime, 98, 100; cyber policy declaration (2009), 132; and cybersecurity awareness, 9; on cyber threats, 89; on digital infrastructure as strategic national asset, 163
online gambling, 193
open-source technology, 31
operating systems, vulnerability of, 11, 44
operational considerations: in cyber attacks, 37–51; in cyber exploitation, 51–52, 53
Operation Allied Force (OAF), 98, 103n20

"Operation Aurora," 96
"Operation Buckshot Yankee," 96–97, 162
opportunity costs, 113
organized crime, 59, 98. *See also* cybercrime
Ostrom, Elinor, 118, 119*n*15

Pace, Peter, 60
Pakistan, cyber militias in, 98
parallel decision frames, 120*n*22
Parikka, Jussi, 26
Patriot Act of 2001 (US), 165
Patriotic Education Programme (China), 195
payload, 51, 79
penalty (deterrence element), 113, 117
People's Daily editorial on Internet dangers in China, 198
People's Liberation Army (PLA, China), 193, 202
pharming, 52, 56*n*17
phishing, 13, 64, 122
phone-tapping episode in Greece, 53, 56*n*20
physical layer, 24, 141, 213–14
Piercy, Marge, 34*n*31
ping, 48, 55*n*15
pinyin, 192–93
piracy, 98
PLA (People's Liberation Army, China), 193, 202
PLA Daily on Internet dangers to China, 198
planning construct for cyber attacks, 44–45, 60–61
Plato, 31
plausible deniability, 78, 144, 153–54
"plus-sum" outcome, 115, 119*n*4
political incentives for conflict, 90–91
polymorphic operations, 120*n*31
pornography, 194
"positive-sum" outcome, 119*n*4
Potanin, Vladimir, 179
power. *See* cyber power
prediction of effects, 45–48
preparation process for cyber attacks, 44–45, 60–61
Presidential Decision Directive 63 (US), 8
Prey (Crichton), 25
private sector: coordination of cyber attacks with, 50; hackers employed by, 145; and regulation, 93–94
Prodigy, 23
Prokhorov, Mikhail, 179
propaganda by terrorist groups, 62–63
proportionality principle, 76, 77
Prosecutor v. Tadic (1999, ICTY), 76, 77

protocol layer, 24
proxy wars, 60
"pseudo-commons," 118
public goods, 108
punitive retaliation, 106
Putin, Vladimir, 174, 177

Quadrennial Defense Review (2010), 4
qualitative content analysis, 157*n*32

Rasmussen, Anders Fogh, 169, 182
rational behavior, 107, 108–9, 117
Rattray, Greg, 218
Realist model, 106–7, 110, 120*n*22
reciprocity expectations, 109
recruitment by terrorist groups, 63
Reding, Viviane, 161
Reed, Thomas, 55*n*6, 89, 186*n*22
regulation: and cybersecurity, 160; and deterrence, 117; in Europe, 165; and networks, 31; of networks, 23
remote-access cyber exploitation, 52
report-back capability, 53
resilience, 128–33
Reveron, Derek S., 3, 91, 208, 212–13
reversibility of effects, 39, 41
Ricardo, David, 107
Rid, Thomas, 166, 169–70
riots under LOAC, 74–75
risk modeling, 119*n*11
rivalry relations, 139–57; case examinations, 147–54; of China, 145–46, 147; and constraints on cyber attacks, 153; cyber conflict's impact on, 140–42, 143–44; future of, 155–56; importance of, 142–43; of Iran, 146, 147, 150–52; of Israel, 146–47, 150–52; and normal relations range, 153; and plausible deniability, 153–54; of Russia, 145, 146, 147, 148–50; and "shock value" of cyber attacks, 154; of US, 144–45, 147
Rodriguez, Alex, 180
role-playing games, 32
Ronfeldt, David, 13
root kits, 64
rules of engagement, 53, 56*n*21
Russia, 173–89; assessment of, 182–84; China's alliance on information security with, 198; cyber capabilities of, 15, 145, 146, 147; and cybercrime, 98, 145, 183; cyber militias in, 98, 99; cyber programs and initiatives in, 178–80; cyberwarfare doctrines in, 175–78; and cyberwar

treaties, 153; and Georgia conflict, 3, 60, 75, 148–50; and hacker community, 96, 146, 180–82; Internet vernacular in, 175; technological modernization in, 174–75; vulnerability to cyber attacks, 183–84. *See also* Soviet Union

Russian Business Network, 98, 181

Rustock (botnet), 165

Samsonov, Viktor, 176

Sapphire/Slammer worm, 46

Sasser worm, 24

Satellite imagery, 7

SCADA. *See* supervisory control and data acquisition systems

Schmidt, Howard, 163

Schneier, Bruce, 31, 230

science fiction, 5, 25, 26, 31

Second Life virtual world, 5, 25, 63

security. *See* cybersecurity; national security

self-defense, 9, 74, 76

self-initiating responses, 116

self-interest, 110

self-knowledge, 31

semantic layer, 213–14

Serbia, cyber militias in, 98, 130

Sheldon, John, 17, 207, 229

Sherstyuk, Vladislav P., 184

Shevchenko, Arkady N., 185n21

Shirley, John, 26

"shock value" of cyber attacks, 154

Simon, Herbert, 107

Singer, Peter, 11

Slammer worm, 55n7

Slaughter, Anne-Marie, 107, 111–12

smart-grid technology, 67

smartphones, 67, 164

smart power, 111

smart weapons, 73, 83

Smith, Adam, 107

Snow Crash (Stephenson), 25

social engineering attacks, 40

social layer, 24

social media, 130

social networks, 109, 112, 187n40

soft power, 111

sovereignty, 212

Soviet Union: and Cold War deterrence strategy, 60; listening devices planted in US embassy typewriters by, 53; technology stolen by, 55n6; US cyber attack on gas pipeline in, 89, 186n22. *See also* Russia

spam, 64

speculative security, 21–35; cyber defined for, 21–22; in *Daemon*, 26–30; in *Little Brother*, 30–31; networks in, 22–24, 31–33

spillover effects, 50

spoofing, 13

spyware, 165

Starr, Stuart H., 218

State Council Information Office (China), 192

State Intellectual Property Office (China), 199

steganography, 63

Stephens, Philip, 211

Stephenson, Neal, 25, 26

Sterling, Bruce, 26

Strategic Warfare in Cyberspace (Rattray), 218

Strategy for Operating in Cyberspace (US Defense Department), 9–10

Stuxnet worm: assessment problem with, 80; attribution problem with, 77, 154; and cybercrime, 66; as cybered conflict, 122; deployment of, 152; and deterrence, 227; as first to target industrial control systems, 4; and intelligence operations, 142; and international criminal law, 82; and LOAC, 79; Microsoft Windows vulnerabilities exploited by, 11; and rivalry relations, 155; as state-on-state attack, 97, 123; strategic value of, 216

Suarez, Daniel, 26–30

Sudan, US attack on (1998), 76

Sun Tzu, 31, 33n7

supervisory control and data acquisition (SCADA) systems, 13, 43, 55n7, 64, 66, 210, 227

Symantec, 17n3

Synners (Cadigan), 34n31

syntactic layer, 141, 213–14

tactical effects, 47, 142

Taiwan, cyber militias in, 98

Tamm, Ilmar, 169

target identification, 42–43

task interdependence, 116, 120n26

technical deconfliction, 50

technological mitigation, 77

Terminator movie series, 25, 28

terrorism: cyber capabilities of, 62–63; Iran's funding of, 150; and national security resilience strategies, 131, 132. *See also* cyberterrorism

theft of services, 39

theory of cyber power, 218–20

"theory of the mind," 119n12
Thomas, Timothy L., 176
Thompson, William, 143, 148
threats in cyberspace, 10–13
Time magazine on Chinese cyber attacks, 96
"Titan Rain" cyber attacks, 96, 201
Touré, Hamadoun, 10
traceroute, 48, 55–56n15
transnational criminal organizations, 131,
    132. *See also* cybercrime; organized crime
transparency, 7
transportation networks, 22, 38, 97
treaties, 153
trojans, 13
Tsymbal, V. I., 176
Tukhachevskii, Mikhail, 219

UAVs (unmanned aerial vehicles), 73, 83
Ultima Online, 25
unintended effects, 55n13
United Kingdom (UK): cyber attacks against,
    162–63, 201; cybersecurity approach of,
    159, 166–67; national security resilience
    strategies in, 132, 133
United Nations (UN), 9, 10, 11, 82
United States: cameras planted in Soviet
    embassy copiers by, 53; cyber attacks
    against, 74, 97, 162; cyber attacks by, 13,
    89, 186n22; cyber capabilities of, 144–45,
    147; cybersecurity approach of, 159; and
    cyberwar treaties, 153; deterrence doctrine
    in, 60, 105–6; intelligence operations by,
    94; national security resilience strategies
    in, 131, 133; separation of authority in,
    91–92; "spiking" of technology stolen by
    Soviet Union, 55n6. *See also*
    USCYBERCOM
unmanned aerial vehicles (UAVs), 73, 83
Unrestricted Warfare (Liang Qiao & Wang
    Xiangsui), 202
Uplink: Hacker Elite (computer game), 25
USA Patriot Act of 2001, 165
US–China Economic and Security Review
    Commission, 196
USCYBERCOM: creation of, 4, 90, 139,
    163–64; and LOAC, 78, 83; mission of, 21,
    71, 164
Usmanov, Alisher, 179

Valeriano, Brandon, 16, 139, 228
Van Creveld, Martin, 216, 217
Vasquez, John, 140, 143

viruses, 7, 24. *See also specific cyber attacks*
Vodafone Greece, 56n20

Wall Street Journal on Russian and Chinese
    infiltration of US electric grid, 97
Wang Chen, 194
Wang Xiangsui, 202
WAPI (WLAN Authentication and Privacy
    Infrastructure), 200
war: and cyberspace, 13–16; fog of war, 78;
    LOAC definition of, 74–75. *See also*
    cyberwarfare
Wargames (film), 25
War in the Age of Intelligent Machines (De
    Landa), 33n7
Warsaw Pact, 60
weapons of mass destruction (WMDs), 7, 65,
    73
web-based attacks, 11–12. *See also* Internet
website defacement, 98, 141, 146, 148, 152
"When Systemadmins Ruled the Earth"
    (Doctorow), 30
Whitehouse, Sheldon, 98
Wiener, Norbert, 21–22
Wikileaks, 7, 216, 222n41
Wikipedia, 8
Williamson, Oliver, 119n15
Winton, Harold, 218
wireless routers, 52, 67, 200
WLAN Authentication and Privacy Infra-
    structure (WAPI), 200
WMDs (weapons of mass destruction), 7, 65,
    73
Wolfers, Arnold, 107
women in cyberspace, 5
Woodcock, Bill, 161
word processing software, 192–93
World Trade Organization (WTO), 200
World Wide Web, 8, 22. *See also* Internet
World without Oil (computer game), 32
worms, 7, 13. *See also specific cyber attacks*
WTO (World Trade Organization), 200
Wylie, J. C., 218

Yakemenko, Vasily, 181

"zero-day" exploits, 115
zero-sum, 107
Zittrain, Jonathan, 23, 24, 29, 32
zombies, 7. *See also* botnets
zone of ambiguity in law of armed conflict,
    75